CAPTIVE IN THE CONGO

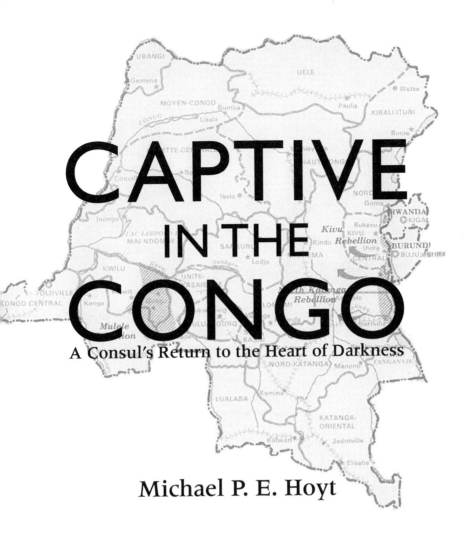

CAPTIVE
IN THE
CONGO

A Consul's Return to the Heart of Darkness

Michael P. E. Hoyt

NAVAL INSTITUTE PRESS
Annapolis, Maryland

An ADST-DACOR Diplomats and Diplomacy Book

Naval Institute Press
291 Wood Road
Annapolis, MD 21402

Library of Congress Cataloging-in-Publication Data
Hoyt, Michael P. E.
    Captive in the Congo : a consul's return to the heart of darkness / Michael P.E. Hoyt.
        p. cm.
    "An ADST-DACOR diplomats and diplomacy book."
    Includes bibliographical references (p.) and index.
    ISBN 1-55750-323-0 (acid-free paper)
    1. Hoyt, Michael P.E.—Captivity, 1964. 2. Congo (Democratic Republic)—History—Civil War, 1960–1965—Personal narratives, American. 3. Congo (Democratic Republic)—History—Civil War, 1960–1965—Atrocities. 4. Hostages—Congo (Democratic Republic)—Biography. 5. Diplomats—United States—Biography. I. Title.

    DT658.22 .H69 2000
    967.5103'1—dc21

                                                            00-056642

Printed in the United States of America on acid-free paper ∞
07 06 05 04 03 02 01 00   9 8 7 6 5 4 3 2
First printing

For Jo,
who passed away in November 1998,
and
Reed, Phelps, Scot, and Evans

Contents

The ADST-DACOR Diplomats and Diplomacy Series

For the past 225 years extraordinary men and women have represented the United States abroad under all kinds of circumstances. What they did and how and why they did it remain little known to their compatriots. In 1995 the Association for Diplomatic Studies and Training (ADST) and Diplomatic and Consular Officers, Retired (DACOR) created a book series to increase public knowledge and appreciation of the involvement of American diplomats in world history. The series seeks to demystify diplomacy by telling the story of those who have conducted our foreign relations, as they saw them and lived them.

Today's diplomats still face challenges and risks demanding the mettle of pioneer times. The story told here of Consul Michael P. E. Hoyt and his staff, held hostage by rebels in the midst of violent insurgency in the Congo, is a vivid case in point. Hoyt's first-person narrative traces his attempts as the diplomat in charge to deal rationally with an irrational situation. Along with the political, diplomatic, and military elements, the book presents the psychological side of a daunting episode. In the foreword, former ambassador Monteagle Stearns, then political counselor at the embassy in Léopoldville, sets forth the story's historical context and significance.

A precursor to subsequent assaults and hostage crises, the 1964 captivity of the U.S. consulate staff in Stanleyville (now Kisangani) was the first such incident since the eighteenth-century Barbary Coast days. The personal ordeal of these hostages, whose numbers grew to include other Americans and Belgians, lasted from 5 August 1964 until their dramatic rescue 111 days later on 24 November by Belgian paratroops flown in by U.S. Air Force C-130s. In the end, after repeatedly being led to what they thought was their imminent execution, Hoyt and his staff survived the rebels' last desperate attempt to gun them down, as told in the book's unforgettable climactic moments. In 1965, Hoyt and his colleagues received the State Department's highest honor—the Secretary's Award. Hoyt went on to head consulates in Nigeria and Cameroon and was chargé d'affaires in Burundi during the 1972 massacres.

Not all such dramatic episodes end so happily for our diplomats. Just inside the diplomatic entrance to the U.S. Department of State, two large stone plaques list the names of 186 Americans who lost their lives abroad under heroic, tragic, or inspirational circumstances while advancing our country's interests. Sadly, almost every year, the list grows longer. Those who died and all the other dedicated Foreign Service people, like Michael Hoyt, who have endured perilous ordeals truly deserve recognition and grateful thanks from the nation they served.

Edward M. Rowell, President, ADST
Kenneth N. Rogers Jr., President, DACOR

Foreword

Soldiers speak of the confusion of the battlefield. Michael Hoyt's account of his 112-day ordeal as a hostage of antigovernment, anti-American rebels in the heart of Africa shows that the diplomatic battlefield can be just as chaotic and equally deadly.

In August 1964 Hoyt was serving as U.S. consul in the city of Stanleyville (today Kisangani) in the Republic of the Congo. He had arrived at his post less than a month before, having been transferred there from the capital, Léopoldville (today Kinshasa), where he had served in the embassy as commercial officer for almost two years. Hoyt's assignment to Stanleyville was expected to last only two months, until a new consul arrived from Washington. The actual period was twice that, but to Hoyt and his four colleagues in the besieged consulate it came to seem a lifetime. For less fortunate hostages, like American missionary Dr. Paul Carlson, it was.

Consul Hoyt's story is especially interesting today for several reasons. First, it is an account of a remarkable and terrifying adventure. We have in the intervening years learned much about hostage-taking as an instrument of foreign policy. It is a form of terrorism used by extremist states or desperate minorities to influence the policies of stronger powers that oppose them. Although rarely successful in achieving this, it has frequently proved fatal to the hostages. Perhaps this sense of punishing a stronger power through its defenseless representatives is what really appeals to hostage-takers and makes it so hard to deter them. Certainly, Hoyt and his colleagues took their places in a long and melancholy line of American hostages, which started in Algiers in 1785, proceeded through Tripoli, Rio, Khartoum, and Bogotá to Tehran in 1979, and will surely stretch into the future. Whether to negotiate with hostage-takers and, if so, how are still open questions in diplomacy.

A second aspect of Hoyt's story that makes it relevant to an understanding of U.S. foreign policy today is the light that it casts on the diplomatic perspectives of the cold war, especially the way American administrations viewed developing states trying to remain on the sidelines of the superpower confrontation. For the Kennedy administration, the Congo was the first battlefield in the struggle for the hearts and minds of the Third World. John Kennedy himself had a special interest in Africa. As a senator, his most dramatic foreign policy pronouncement had been to call for Algerian independence in 1957. After winning the presidency in 1960, he announced the selection of his assistant secretary of state for African affairs, the former governor of Michigan, G. Mennen Williams, before he had selected his secretary of state. U.S. policy toward the Congo at the time of Hoyt's captivity is only explicable in this cold war context, as is the decision to leave Hoyt and his colleagues in their perilous position in Stanleyville in the first place.

A third reason for paying attention to the Stanleyville episode is that it was a result of the first genuine peacemaking operation undertaken by the United Nations. The defense of South Korea in 1950 had nominally been conducted under the UN flag, but it was essentially an American military operation. The UN mission to the Congo, unlike Korea, was created in a rare moment in 1960 when U.S. and Soviet foreign policies appeared to converge. Soon enough the moment passed and the two superpowers were again on a collision course, leaving the United Nations isolated and under attack from all sides.

The Congo rebellion, of which Hoyt was one innocent victim, in the end victimized and nearly destroyed the United Nations. The organization was confronted with its first serious financial crisis and with Nikita Khrushchev's proposal to abolish the office of the secretary general and replace it with a *troika* representing the Western and Soviet spheres of influence and the nonaligned. The final wound inflicted on the United Nations by events in the Congo was to deprive the organization of its most gifted and courageous secretary general, Dag Hammarskjöld, who died in a plane crash in 1961 while on a Congo peace mission. Today, when the situation in ex-Yugoslavia makes the African concerns of the Kennedy and Johnson administrations look relatively uncomplicated, the Congo crisis of 1960–65 reminds us that the United Nations has been undertaking thankless jobs handed it by its members for a long time. Then, as now, the United Nations proved no stronger than the shared purpose and united will of its members enabled it to be. As the United Nations in the new millennium considers another peacemaking initiative in the Congo, we must hope that the organization and its members will profit from the disasters of the 1960s.

Finally, Michael Hoyt's narrative shows once again that foreign policy decisions have human consequences, not only for the objects of foreign policy but for those who implement it. His story is a reminder that the American Foreign Service is staffed by courageous and disciplined men and women and a timely rebuke to those who think that diplomacy, in the words of one U.S. senator, is about "marble palaces and renting long coats and high hats."

To understand how Hoyt got into the lethal plight in which he and his companions found themselves, we need to examine the events that led up to the Congo crisis and the ways in which U.S. policy makers responded to it.

The rebellion that engulfed Stanleyville in August 1964 had begun in the eastern Congo that spring but was linked to the violent events that followed the proclamation of Congolese independence from Belgium in July 1960. The Republic of the Congo, as the new state was baptized, was ill-prepared to manage its own affairs in 1960, and Belgium was ill-prepared to assist the Congolese in making the transition successfully. Belgian administration of the Congo had been oblivious to the winds of anticolonial change that began to sweep the African continent after World War II. Charles de Gaulle had offered the states of French Equatorial Africa self-governing status within the French Community in 1958 when he paid his first presidential visit to Brazzaville, across Stanley Pool from Léopoldville. After that visit, pictures of de Gaulle became more popular in the western Congo than pictures of the Belgian king.

Historically, Belgian leaders were less interested in the political future of the Congo than in its vast economic potential. This, and the dream of enlarging Belgium's horizons by creating a colonial empire, had first attracted King Léopold II to the Congo in the 1870s. Copper, cobalt, uranium, industrial diamonds, palm oil, and rubber were among the colony's most lucrative natural resources; their efficient and cost-effective exploitation had been the chief preoccupation of Belgian colonial administrators since the king had relinquished his Congolese fiefdom in 1908 and the Belgian state had assumed responsibility for it.

As a consequence, when the Congo became politically independent, its newly appointed leaders had no experience in conducting affairs of state, and there were no more than a handful of university graduates (most of them preparing for the priesthood) to supply professional cadres. There were no Congolese doctors, no engineers, no senior managers, and—most critical of all in the short term—no ranking military or police officers able to maintain order while the transfer of authority was taking place. When Congolese security forces mutinied a few days after independence, the result was virtual anarchy in key population centers.

Violence directed against the remaining Belgians created panic and confusion that the new Congolese government, headed by an inexperienced prime minister, Patrice Lumumba, was unable to control. Lumumba was a member of the Batetela tribe from the Maniema, an area south of Stanleyville particularly exploited under Belgian rule. It was Stanleyville that Joseph Conrad reached in 1890 as a riverboat captain and where his experiences led him to write the attack on Léopold's brutal exploitation of the Congo in *Heart of Darkness.*

Within days after the Republic of the Congo became independent, the richest of the Congolese provinces, Katanga, declared its secession from the rest of the country. It was here, in the eastern Congo, that Belgian investment, principally in copper, was most profitable and Belgian influence, principally over the self-proclaimed president of Katanga, Moïse Tshombé, most conspicuous. Soon the Congolese government itself was split between radical nationalists grouped around Lumumba and moderate nationalists grouped around the republic's president, Joseph Kasavubu. The bitter fruits of Congolese independence seemed to be civil collapse, savage internal strife, and external dismemberment.

xiv

In these unhappy circumstances the Congo crisis was internationalized. The opinion of independent African states, except for South Africa, was unanimous in interpreting the Katanga secession as a political maneuver by the West Europeans, principally Belgian business interests, to preserve their mining concessions in the most economically desirable part of the Congo. The United States and the Soviet Union, although they agreed about little else in the Congo, also opposed Katanga's secession. In doing so, however, they were pursuing diametrically different objectives. The Kennedy administration was determined to show the newly independent African states, and the wider nonaligned world, that the United States was prepared to take the lead against neocolonialism. The Soviet Union, whose anticolonial credentials required no burnishing in Africa, saw the suppression of Katanga separatism as the surest way to expel Western capitalists from the Congo. It was with these differing expectations that in mid-July 1960 the United States and the Soviet Union together voted in favor of a Security Council resolution authorizing the secretary general to organize a force to restore order in the Congo. The resolution passed with no votes against and only Britain and France abstaining.

What brought the cold war back to the Congo within a matter of days was the widening chasm between Congolese political leaders in Léopoldville. While both the Americans and the Soviets opposed Tshombé in Katanga, in Léopoldville the United States favored the moderate leadership of Kasavubu and the Soviet Union the radical nationalism of Lumumba. After months of bitter internal dissension, the arrest and eventual murder of Lumumba by security forces loyal to the conservatives ended all hope of reuniting the leadership of the central government no matter what happened in Katanga. Lumumba's cause was taken up by Congolese nationalists outside Léopoldville, especially in his native province of Maniema, in Kivu on the eastern borders of the Congo, and in the thickly forested northern province of Orientale, the capital of which was Stanleyville. These leaders declared themselves the heirs of Lumumba and Stanleyville the true capital of the Congo. By the end of 1960, the central government was faced by a right-wing secession in Katanga and a left-wing secession in Orientale.

A combination of UN force and Congolese palavering, brokered mainly by the United Nations and the United States, brought an end to the northern and eastern secessionist movements in early 1963. By mid-1964, when the UN forces withdrew, Tshombé had made his peace with Léopoldville and had accepted an invitation to lead the central government as prime minister. Radical nationalist leaders who had not been co-opted by the central government were in exile or in hiding. They were, however, by no means reconciled to the assumption of power by Tshombé and the conservatives. In the departure of UN security forces they saw the opportunity for a new bid for power. This was the origin of the rebellion that began in the eastern Congo in the spring of 1964 and was gathering strength to move on Stanleyville as Michael Hoyt and his family arrived there in mid-July.

The rebel leaders were a motley assortment of second-tier Lumumbists, mainly from the east and north: Gaston Soumialot, "General" Nicholas Olenga, and Christophe Gbenye, who had been minister of the interior under Lumumba. To the extent that their movement had an ideology, it was a mixture of nationalism, village Marxism, and magic, the latter particularly powerful in the ranks of the "Simbas," the Batetela foot soldiers whom Olenga led into battle. Although Washington worried that these forces would open the way to a Soviet or Chinese takeover of the Congo, the likelihood of this actually happening seems distinctly small in the retrospect of over three decades.

The extent of Gbenye's political indoctrination can be judged from a visit he paid to the U.S. embassy in the summer of 1963. Explaining that he was seeking American financial support for a new party, Gbenye reached into his briefcase and produced a letter to the Soviet ambassador. When the mistake was called to his attention, he apologized and exchanged it for an identical letter to the American ambassador. It was Gbenye who, in June 1961, had held Frank Carlucci (later to become secretary of defense in the Reagan administration) a prisoner in his hotel room. Carlucci, then a young Foreign Service officer, had been attempting to negotiate an end to the Stanleyville secession.

If the political convictions of the rebel leaders were superficial, however, their capacity for destruction and their willingness to terrorize, to kill, and to eviscerate were not. They were determined to threaten and humiliate those they considered neocolonialists, especially the Belgians and Americans. There is ample evidence of this in Michael Hoyt's account of his captivity.

Why did the embassy and the State Department decide to leave Hoyt and two colleagues in Stanleyville? (In the event, five American officials remained, because two of the consular staff who had been ordered out missed the last plane.) In situations of this kind, the risk of

xvi

failing to evacuate diplomatic and consular personnel from a threatened post varies with the circumstances, but the factors to be weighed in making the decision are broadly the same. The risk to the personnel if they remain must be balanced against the effect on the host government of removing them and against the number of private American citizens who will be left behind if the officials depart. The same factors were considered when Saigon was taken over by the communists in 1975 and Tehran by the ayatollahs in 1979.

In the case of the Congo, the situation was complicated by the disinclination of some twenty-five American missionaries in the Stanleyville consular district to leave their stations. Believing themselves to be outside the political struggle, devoted to humanitarian and spiritual ends, the missionaries could not imagine that they would be considered hostile by the rebels. It was a belief that several died defending.

Washington and Léopoldville were also concerned about the strength of the newly installed and extremely controversial Tshombé government. The United States wanted to keep the American flag flying in Stanleyville to demonstrate its support for the central government. This had been the overriding purpose of American policy since the beginning of the Congo troubles. Hoyt himself took this responsibility very seriously and at great risk to his own safety. The flag was aloft at the consulate when the rebels entered Stanleyville and remained aloft until the halyard was cut by gunfire. It is fitting that before being called off, the first plan to rescue Hoyt and his colleagues was code-named "Operation Flagpole."

Another factor that affects the decision to evacuate or stand fast is the quality of intelligence available on the extent and gravity of the threat. This was always a problem in the Congo, where great distances, difficult terrain, unreliable communications, and the ubiquitous rumors pouring out of the "jungle telegraph" tended to make almost anything seem possible. Hoyt describes the variety of unconfirmed and often contradictory reports reaching the Stanleyville consulate on the position of the rebels and the capability of the Congolese government forces to repel them. When the city fell there had been almost no resistance. The first rebels that Hoyt saw through the consulate window as they entered Stanleyville were a file of unarmed men, dressed in white and waving palm fronds, led by a witch doctor.

It was the sinister, and to Westerners incomprehensible, influence of witchcraft on the Simbas and some of their leaders that made captivity such an appalling experience and gave it such a disorienting atmosphere of unreality. This was particularly true when the effects of magic were intensified, as they frequently were, by hemp and alcohol. Not only were Hoyt's captors undisciplined and divided among themselves, their behavior was wildly unpredictable. The hostages would be moved without warning from the consulate to the Sabena Guest House cottages at the airport and from there to the Stanleyville prison. At one point they were lodged briefly and without explanation in luxurious accommodations in Stanleyville's best hotel. It was never clear what was to become of them. They knew that there were frequent executions at the Lumumba monument. The rebels were said to be disemboweling some of their victims, and there were even reports of cannibalism.

It is surely a tribute to Hoyt and his staff that in conditions like these their principal concern was to defend the honor of the United States and the integrity of its African policy. At the end of their first day of captivity, having survived a violent assault on the consulate vault, where they had barricaded themselves, the Americans ascertained that the attackers had withdrawn. They emerged cautiously from the vault, sent a reporting cable to the embassy, and set about cleaning up the mess left behind by the rebels. Hoyt's comment to the embassy was, "USG [U.S. government] cannot retreat into a shell while events unfold." In the same spirit, he later successfully resisted rebel attempts to force him to denounce American intervention in the internal affairs of the Congo.

Washington, meanwhile, was groping for any thread that might lead to the release of the hostages. Negotiations were conducted with intermediaries in Bujumbura and Nairobi. These efforts came to nothing. It was unclear who, if anyone, was actually in charge of the rebels or could speak for their leaders. In Léopoldville, Tshombé had decided that only force could accomplish the release of the captives and the return of Stanleyville to the control of the central government. Having little faith in the reliability of the Congolese security forces, he began clandestinely to recruit white mercenaries under the command of the South African soldier of fortune, Mike Hoare.

These actions touched off a furious debate among Washington policy makers. One group believed that the hopes of the United States to present itself as anticolonialist would be doomed forever by any sign of cooperation with Tshombé and the white mercenaries. The newly independent African states would turn against Washington and Moscow and would score a crucial victory in the struggle for preeminence in the Third World. Another group of policy makers was willing to take this risk. Like Tshombé, they had become convinced that nothing short of the effective application of force would defeat the rebels and free the hostages. Fortunately for Hoyt and his companions it was the latter group that prevailed.

The rescue plan worked out by Washington and Brussels called for a battalion of Belgian paracommandos to be transported in U.S. Air Force C-130 aircraft to a staging area in southeastern Congo at Kamina, a former Belgian military base with hangars and a paved airstrip. The paracommandos were to drop on Stanleyville airport and secure it as Tshombé's mercenary-led columns entered the city on the ground. Air cover would be provided by the "Congolese Air Force," composed of American T-28 propeller-driven aircraft flown by Cuban-exile pilots recruited by the Central Intelligence Agency. It was hoped that if preparations for the operation could be kept secret, and if the air and ground assaults were properly synchronized, the rebels would be taken by surprise and the captives liberated before harm could be done to them. The operation was code-named Dragon Rouge, and it almost came off as planned.

The drop occurred on 24 November 1964, just before first light. It had been delayed twenty-four hours to give the ground forces more time to reach their objective. The air operation was smoothly executed, although there were anxious moments when the C-130s prepared to rendezvous with the T-28s at a point upriver from Stanleyville. The U.S. Air Force pilots could not understand the Cubans flying the T-28s and in the tropical darkness before dawn they feared a midair collision. It was only when an English-speaking Cuban got on the air that they located each other.

The Belgian paracommandos secured the airport without meeting serious rebel resistance. Tshombé's ground forces, however, had experienced further delays and only arrived on the outskirts of Stanleyville after the paradrop had taken place. Instead of facing an attack on two fronts, the rebels were able to concentrate their attention on the Belgian paracommandos. The Simbas hurriedly mustered the hostages in the street and marched them toward the airport with the apparent intention of using them as human shields. For whatever reason—panic or confusion—this did not happen.

Before they reached the airport, the rebels opened fire on the hostages. Of a total of about 250, most of them Belgians but including Hoyt and other Americans, eighteen were killed in the onslaught and forty seriously wounded. Among the dead were two Americans: the missionary doctor, Paul Carlson, and the missionary nurse, Phyllis Rine. Michael Hoyt and his four colleagues miraculously lived to tell the tale that Hoyt has written in this book.

What can be said today of the meaning of the Congo crisis and Operation Dragon Rouge? Certainly they were invested with greater cosmic significance by the cold war than they deserved. It is ironic that a U.S. policy that originated in the Kennedy administration's desire to prove itself anticolonial ended in support of the Congolese leader most identified with neocolonialism. But the hearts and minds of the Third World were not really at stake in the Congo. The developing states of Africa and Asia tended to define their relations with the United States and the Soviet Union in terms of self-interest rather than ideology. Dragon Rouge brought down on the Americans and Belgians furious denunciations in the United Nations, but the fundamental problems of Africa could not be measured on an East-West axis. They were North-South problems, and they have yet to be solved.

Of the major Congolese characters in the Stanleyville drama, Gen. Joseph Désiré Mobutu, as he was known when commander of Congolese armed forces, became president of Zaire in 1965—exactly a year after the rebellion was crushed by the Dragon Rouge rescue operation. Mobutu's ruthlessness and self-aggrandizement obliterated from the world's collective memory the sins of Moïse Tshombé, who died in captivity in Algiers in circumstances as mysterious as those surrounding the death of Lumumba. (Mobutu himself was toppled in 1997 in the rebellion led by Laurent Kabila and died in exile later the same year.) Nicholas Olenga's military career ended in Stanleyville, as did the political career of Gaston Soumialot. Olenga vanished after being imprisoned first in Khartoum and then in Kinshasa; Soumialot was reported to have been killed by some of his own followers, probably in eastern Zaire.

As for Christophe Gbenye, I ran into him in Abidjan, the capital of Côte d'Ivoire, in 1978. It was on the dance floor of the Hotel Ivoire where a gala ball was being given by the conservative president of the Ivory Coast, Félix Houphoüet-Boigny, to celebrate the marriage of his daughter to Gbenye's son. The young couple had met in Geneva, where both were attending private school. Houphoüet-Boigny had persuaded Mobutu to release Gbenye from house arrest in Kinshasa to attend the wedding. When I was reintroduced to Gbenye, the former rebel leader presented me with his Kinshasa calling card. Under the street address it bore the notation, *"Résidence Surveillée."*

Monteagle Stearns

Preface

Stanleyville is the visual center of the African continent. It is in the middle of the white space that the narrator of *Heart of Darkness* (written by Joseph Conrad in 1902) said he pointed to as a child and to which he vowed to go. Conrad had gone there in 1890 and wrote his story of the ascent up the river into the darkness to find the horror that was the brutal exploitation of the Congo. After its "discovery" by Henry Morton Stanley in 1877, Stanley Falls Station became the center for the devastation and development of the northeastern third of the Congo, first by Tippu Tib (Hamed bin Muhammed el Murjebi) and then by the Belgians. In the aftermath of Congo Independence in 1960, Stanleyville became the center of the Lumumbist "leftist" secession.

This book is an account of the period from July to November 1964, when I headed the American consulate in Stanleyville. During most of this time, the consulate staff was held hostage by forces rebelling against the central government to which we were accredited. This book records this unique chapter in diplomatic history.

My account is based on documents sent through official channels, obtained through the Freedom of Information Act and from those available at the Lyndon Baines Johnson Library in Austin, Texas; documents and memos I wrote and retained; a journal David Grinwis, the vice consul, and I kept at the time and wrote up later; newspaper accounts of the time; and my best recollection of people and events. This is my own story, portraying events as they occurred. It is an adventure story, including its emotional moments. While we all maintained or contained our emotions, we felt keenly the mortal danger that existed.

I wrote this book to make a contribution to the historical record, while trying to arrive at an understanding of what I went through during my time in Stanleyville. V. S. Naipaul stated it better when he said that the written word "offers protection, protection from chaos, from oblivion, from darkness and humiliation." Like Salim in Naipaul's book *A Bend in the River* (1980), I too came to Stanleyville "to make good, to get a lift above the ordinary, to meet the challenges and be a doer. I succeeded and I failed, but I met the challenge."

Surviving was the main battle to be won, but there should also be some lesson for the future. Perhaps it is this: For diplomacy to endure, all those participating in the international community must respect the internationally accepted rules. As it happened, those who failed to respect these norms in Stanleyville did not survive to participate.

Personnel of the Central Intelligence Agency who worked in the consulate are identified. An official U.S. government document (Odom, *Dragon Operations*, 10) names David Grinwis as "the CIA's representative under cover of vice-consul." He holds a special place in my heart that only those who have shared an intense emotional experience can understand.

The narrative is confined to the contemporary scene. I try not to anticipate events or reveal facts and events that I learned about only afterwards. The notes document much of what happened and contain information and comments revealed to me later. An effort was made to fully identify all individuals, organization and business names, and acronyms mentioned in cables; however, this proved impossible. Any errors or other misrepresentations of fact are mine alone.

I want to express my gratitude to the Naval Institute Press for pursuing this project, and for the fine work done by Eric Mills, Barbara Johnson, and Kristin Wye. My thanks go to Margery Thompson of the Association for Diplomatic Studies and Training for the persistence and skills she has devoted to this book over the past years.

CAPTIVE IN THE CONGO

Prologue

STANLEYVILLE WAS NOT MY FIRST POSTING IN THE CONGO. I HAD first come to this troubled country in the fall of 1962 at the age of thirty-two. A Foreign Service officer for six years, I was posted as second secretary and commercial officer in the American embassy in Léopoldville, capital of the Congo, which had gained its independence from Belgium two years earlier. (The Congo became Zaire under Joseph Désiré Mobutu in 1965; Léopoldville became Kinshasa and Stanleyville became Kisangani. After the takeover by Laurent Désiré Kabila in 1997, the country was renamed the Democratic Republic of the Congo.)

My wife, Jo, and our four children, Reed, Phelps, Scot, and Evans, ages 12, 8, 7, and 2, respectively, accompanied me to my posting in Léopoldville. I had spent the previous year at Northwestern University for graduate studies in economics and African affairs and had looked for a posting in Africa. The commercial slot in Léopoldville was open, and I persuaded the State Department to give it to me in place of an initial assignment to Tel Aviv. My previous postings had been as vice consul in our consulate general in Casablanca, Morocco, and third secretary in our embassy in Karachi, then capital of Pakistan.

I knew the Congo would be a challenging assignment. The Congolese army had mutinied a few days after Belgium granted independence in June 1960. The country fell into chaos. I had read accounts of how Europeans were brutalized by army troops and in Casablanca I had met one of our embassy officers fleeing the violence. He said there was little hope the country could recover.

The United States led the effort to bring in the United Nations to restore order and to end the secessionist movements that threatened the country with disintegration. U.S. policy was guided by the view that the Soviet Union and communist China would take advantage of the chaos to gain influence in the new nation. Several hundred white foreigners were killed, mostly by rampaging Congolese soldiers. Many hundreds of thousands of Congolese lost their lives in tribal conflicts that broke out when order collapsed. With substantial U.S. political and financial backing, the United Nations ended the secessions and restored a semblance of order and stability.

Nearly two years after my initial arrival in the Congo, at the end of June 1964, the UN Security Council decided the Congo was secure enough to justify withdrawing all UN security forces. The last of these was the contingent of Nigerian Police based in Stanleyville, the final area considered pacified. UN civilian technicians remained in the Congo to carry on economic and political programs. The Russians and Chinese had been thwarted, and the United States had built up a large stake in maintaining the stability and integrity of the Congo.

Security was now the responsibility of the Congolese army, *l'Armée Nationale Congolaise* (ANC), as the army was renamed after its transformation at independence from the Belgian-officered colonial *Force Publique*. It was the ANC that had posed the greatest problems for the United Nations. Its chief of staff, Col. Joseph Mobutu, as he was then known, maintained a tenuous control over the ANC after the UN forces left.

Since independence, the American embassy in Léopoldville had been the driving force behind U.S. efforts to restore order in the Congo and to reconstruct the shattered economy. In the embassy's economic section, my nominal task was to promote American commercial and investment opportunities, but I engaged in other activities to promote our overall aims. Until the arrival of U.S. Agency for International Development (USAID) personnel, I ran a $40 million U.S. import support fund to provide goods as part of an effort to control rampant inflation. I was also given the responsibility to wind down a U.S. government–financed contract to provide air transport capability to the ANC. An air support program, run from the embassy under the U.S. military mission to the Congo (called COMISH), now supported the ANC. I organized the distribution of relief supplies, established our first police assistance program, and worked closely with UN civilian personnel on several projects. I traveled to every province in the Congo, by air, road, and river, and became familiar with the many political and economic problems facing the troubled and chaotic country.

In June 1964, a replacement arrived in Léopoldville to take over my commercial functions, and I expected a change in duties to fill the time until my two-year tour was up in October. I received a call to come to the office of the deputy chief of mission, Robert Blake, at the embassy.

"Mike, how would you like to go to Stan?" Bob said. "Clingerman needs to leave earlier than his replacement, sometime in the fall. The ambassador and I think you would do a good job for us there. It's a tight spot, and we know it will be tough. How about it?"

Bob was asking me to replace John Clingerman as head of our post in Stanleyville, which was one of three U.S. consulates in the interior of the Congo. The others were in Bukavu on the eastern border and in Elisabethville in Katanga Province to the south. The one in Stanleyville covered the northeastern third of the Congo, the former Orientale Province. As principal officer, I would be responsible for all American interests and programs in the region.

I knew Stanleyville and its sinister atmosphere from several stays on trips to the interior. It had been the center of the most anti-white, anti-West, and anti-American of the secession movements. It was the political base of the Congo's first prime minister, Patrice Lumumba,

3

whose erratic behavior and appeal to the Soviet Union for assistance had prompted U.S. policy makers to turn to the United Nations to restore order. Lumumba was dismissed and then assassinated near Elisabethville in early 1961, under circumstances that led many to believe the United States was involved.

The harsh repression of the Stanleyville secession that followed Lumumba's fall left bitter memories. The reinstatement of central authority had not improved discipline of army personnel stationed there, and the lack of organization and control in central and provincial administrations led to anarchy. The central authorities were presently struggling to contain several insurgencies developing in neighboring areas. In spite of the ominous prospects, I was tempted by the challenges presented and was eager to take charge of a post for the first time.

"Yes, I'd like that," I told Bob. When the first consul sent to Stanleyville in 1962 pulled out, shortly after I first arrived in the Congo, I had volunteered to go. Because there was no schooling for my children, Clingerman was chosen instead. I now had my chance.

"I can send the three oldest kids to Arizona for the summer," I said. "Jo and Evans can come with me to Stan. Should work out well."

"That's great. Mac wants to see you," Bob said, referring to the ambassador, McMurtrie Godley, and we went into his office.

Godley was a bear of a man who welcomed the problems of the Congo as a challenge for his considerable talents. He focused the energies of all parts of the embassy on meeting the recurring crises. Before becoming ambassador, he had been the Africa Bureau's lead official behind U.S. efforts to keep the Soviets out of the Congo. Only a few months earlier, he had replaced Edmund Gullion, who, as newly inaugurated President Kennedy's appointee, had ended the secessions.

"I have an important assignment for you before you go to Stan," Mac told me. "Organize the Fourth of July celebrations here. You can leave after that."

The independence celebration was a bash. All activities were poolside at the ambassador's residence. Fireworks were ruled out for fear they would spook the ANC, but everyone enjoyed the daylong activities. At midnight, the about-to-be appointed new prime minis-

4

ter, Moïse Tshombé, former head of the Katanga secession the embassy had fought so long to put down, flew in for a visit. Mac introduced me as the newly appointed consul in Stanleyville to this dynamo of a man, and I shook his hand before he sped off into the night.

At the end of the following week, after getting the older children off to Arizona, packing our household effects for an as yet unknown post-Congo assignment, and saying good-bye to friends in Léopoldville, my wife and I and our youngest son were ready for our summer interlude in Stanleyville.

At the Bend in the River

Tuesday, 14 July, through Tuesday, 4 August 1964

THE FLIGHT FROM LÉOPOLDVILLE TO STANLEYVILLE ON TUESDAY,
14 July 1964, crossed the thousand miles of dense green forest that
filled the huge sweeping arch of the Congo River. It was "a mighty
big river," Joseph Conrad said, "resembling a big snake uncoiled,
with its head in the sea, its body at rest curving afar over a vast country."[1] The trip was short and pleasant in the air attaché's luxurious
Convair. The shining river appeared only moments before we landed
at the runway carved from the thick forest. The hot equatorial air,
laden with the moisture of the forest, hit our faces as we came down
the ramp. Consul John Clingerman and his wife Polly greeted me,
my wife Jo, and our son Evans.

We climbed into the official black Ford Fairlane sedan parked at
the ramp with the American flag fluttering at its stanchion on the
right fender. The driver drove past the peeling pale pink buildings
that housed the terminal and control tower and continued on to the

6

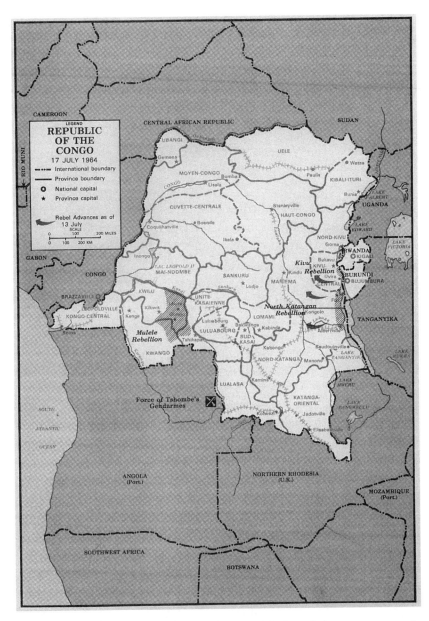

Republic of the Congo, detailing intelligence data for rebel movement as of 17 July 1964.
Combat Studies Institute, Leavenworth, Kansas.

mile-long road east into town. Several multistory buildings in the center of town rose out of the surrounding low dwellings that housed some three hundred thousand souls.

Stanleyville sits at the beginning of the navigable portion of the Congo River after it emerges from the last of a series of seven cataracts, Stanley Falls. The Congo River then heads downriver to Léopoldville. It was here that Henry Morton Stanley first discovered, on his voyage down the Lualaba River in 1877, that the river bends sharply eastward from its northward course and becomes the Congo River, which spills out into the Atlantic Ocean. Joseph Conrad visited the area in 1890 and wrote his scathing indictment of the exploitation of the Congo, *Heart of Darkness,* first published in 1902. A combined rail and water transportation system now links Stanleyville to the Katanga mining region a thousand miles to the south.

Driving past the city center, following the river past the wharves, we soon swung through a gateway in the low stucco wall enclosing the large green front lawn of the consulate. The offices and residence were in a side-by-side stucco duplex and overlooked the river. Jo and Evans went with Polly to the residence side while John took me to the consulate.

"You know our receptionist, Antoine Lingili, don't you?" John asked. "He looks after everything for us. Anything you need, just call on him."

John took me to his office and we reviewed recent developments. "On June 22," he said, "I reported on an attack by unidentified rebels on the *gendarmerie* camp here. You must have seen my cable on it at the embassy.[2]

"A lot of arms were stolen which still have not been recovered," he continued. "I requested armed guards for the consulate at the time, but they haven't turned up. The guards you see in front are unarmed and supplied by the civil authorities.

"Another concern I have is that a large group of army troops who deserted from the fighting with rebels in northern Katanga is due to arrive soon from Kindu. My worry is that the deserters will outnumber the troops here and could cause all sorts of trouble. I doubt the authorities here can control them. They need to be dispersed to their

home villages. And, I hear Kindu itself is now threatened by rebels."
Kindu is about two hundred fifty miles south of Stanleyville.

John took me around the offices to introduce other members of
the staff. I knew most of them from previous visits. Vivian Lambert,
a Belgian, was the consul's secretary for unclassified work. There were
five Congolese clerks, messengers, and drivers. David Grinwis, the
vice consul, was not in his office. His secretary, Joan Allen, greeted
me warmly. Jim Stauffer, a former navy radio operator who ran the
communications equipment, came out from the vault leading from
David's office. "I'm waiting for my replacement to arrive any day," he
said. "After nearly two years here, I'll be glad to get out."

Ernie Houle, a retired navy chief, the consulate file clerk and
administrative assistant, greeted me from his cubbyhole, a narrow
vault-room behind a heavy steel safe door. A short, slight man in his
fifties, originally a French-Canadian, he mumbled a welcome as he
attended to his papers. "He does his work quietly, without complaint,"
John said later.

On the other side of the duplex, rented from a doctor who had
built it for his offices and living quarters, Polly showed Jo and Evans
the consul's residence and introduced her to the servants. "Tata Paul
is the best part of being the consul's wife," Polly said of the ancient
wizened Congolese cook. "He's the finest cook this side of Brussels."
She sold Jo their entire inventory of food and liquor, a common
Foreign Service practice.

After a quick lunch, Jo, Evans, and I rode back to the airport with
John and Polly. They ran up the ramp to the Convair and waved back
at us, obviously glad to be leaving. I knew it must have been a difficult
year and a half for them. They had established a new post in a hostile
environment that was now faced with new threats from unknown
forces.

On the drive back to the consulate, we could see the town was
bustling with activity in the afternoon sun. The American flag flapped
at the fender pole, symbolizing my first posting as U.S. consul. At the
consulate, I sent my first cable: "Clingerman departed 1500 local.
Assumed charge. Signed, HOYT."[3] I was now officially responsible for
American interests in this vast, remote, and troubled region of Africa.

9

The consulate in Stanleyville had been established in early 1963. The first consul was soon replaced when he proved unsuitable, leading to John Clingerman's sudden transfer there. Prior to that time, Frank Carlucci and others from the embassy in Léopoldville had covered the Stanleyville area during the turbulent Lumumbist secessionist period. For a brief period, Carlucci was held hostage in his hotel room by Christophe Gbenye, a secessionist government minister at the time.[4]

WHEN I ARRIVED in Stanleyville, seven Americans worked in Stanleyville as part of the official U.S. Foreign Service family. Five of us worked at the consulate: Ernie, administrative clerk; David, vice consul, and his secretary, Joan; Jim, communicator; and myself as consul and principal officer. Jo would be my secretary, to type classified messages, when her temporary security clearance came through. At the Cultural Center and Library of the U.S. Information Service (USIS), located in the center of town, were Max Kraus, the director, and his assistant, Phil Mayhew; they had both recently arrived. About a dozen people were hired locally, Congolese and Europeans, to assist with the myriad tasks necessary to keep operations going. A half-dozen servants staffed the residence.

The key member of the staff was David Grinwis. He worked for the Central Intelligence Agency (CIA), under cover as vice consul in charge of consular affairs. I assumed he carried on the usual CIA operations of running informants and agents in the area. What I valued most was the knowledge of people and politics that he had gained over his more than two years at post. I especially hoped he had contacts in rebel groups.

In David's domain was the consulate's communications facility, a wireless teletype run by Jim. Only "Agency" people—as those in the Foreign Service refer to CIA personnel—were allowed access to the vault adjoining David's office. It contained the radio equipment and David's files. The radio connected us to a worldwide secure network linking all American embassies and consulates, the State Department, the White House, the Department of Defense, the CIA, and other U.S. government agencies. It was our umbilical cord, our living link to the outside world.

Under my control was another radio, a single side band radio (SSB), with a voice transceiver located in a locked wood cabinet in a back room. It tied us into the local radio network centered on the embassy in Léopoldville. The Stanleyville consulate's call sign was River Rat, appropriate to our riverine location.

After sending my take-charge cable, I went to see David in his office. I knew him from my trips to Stanleyville and anticipated working closely with him. He was about my age, tall and thin, with dark hair and angular features. Precise in manner and action, his deeply set, penetrating eyes revealed a quiet intensity. He enjoyed classical music, good food, and fine cognac, all tastes I shared.

"David, I've been looking forward to working with you," I said. "John told me pressure is building up from the rebels."

"Yes, it is," he replied. "I'm glad you're here. Frankly, John had reached the point where he had difficulty coping. Burned out, lost his nerve, or something. I was looking forward to your coming. Stan is not the easiest place for us to work. If we do it together, we should be able to handle it. However, the situation is precarious and dangerous."

"I'd like to share all the information we get, particularly on insurgent activities," I said. "We should consult closely to try to figure out what is going on."

"I'm writing a report now from one of my people," he said. "I'll show it to you when it comes back for distribution."

THE NEXT MORNING, I began scheduling meetings. The highest local official in Stanleyville was the newly appointed president of the province of Haut-Congo, François Aradjabu. I asked Vivian, my Belgian secretary, to request appointments for me to meet Aradjabu and for Jo to make a courtesy call on his wife. The top officials responsible for security in the city were the heads of the army, officially called the *Armée Nationale Congolaise* (ANC), and the city police. Vivian made appointments for later that day.

Antoine, our receptionist, came into my office to tell me Gleb Makaroff had come to see me. The manager of Chemin du Fer et du Lac (CFL), the company responsible for the rail and water transportation system south of Stanleyville, he was a large, older man with a full

11

black beard who gave me a strong handshake. An engineer, he had spent many years in the Congo and had survived the postindependence violence with apparent equanimity. I liked him immediately.

"Those Kongolo ANC deserters arrived at Ponthierville yesterday and are now headed for Stan," he said. "I will let you know when any other messages arrive." Ponthierville is the railroad seventy-five miles south, at the beginning of the Stanley Falls cataracts, where river navigation recommences southward.

I telephoned Major Banza, chief of staff at army headquarters. I asked if he had heard Makaroff's news and if preparations were under way to handle the deserters. "Yes, I know," he told me. "I'm not sending troops to meet them. We will take them under our control when they arrive in Stan." I told him I would see him later that morning.

Tearing off a sheet of yellow legal paper from the pad, I put it in the typewriter on my desk and drafted my first reporting cable. I typed: "ACTION: Secstate, Amembassy Leopoldville, INFO: Brussels, Bukavu, Elisabethville, USUN [our UN mission office in New York]." These were the addressees that closely followed Congo events. I marked it "LIMITED OFFICIAL USE," the category above UNCLASSIFIED. My draft read:

Congolese ANC Deserters
CFL had word from Ponthierville that one boat load ANC deserters had arrived there July 14. ANC Stanleyville gave assurances all preparations made for their reception but none sent to Ponthierville.

HOYT [5]

I then left to see Commandant Banza, sometimes referred to by his courtesy title of major. He was chief of staff of the Third Army, headquartered in Stanleyville, and supervised the commanders of individual units. Lt. Col. Leonard Mulamba, a highly regarded officer now in Bukavu directing the forces fighting rebels in the eastern region, commanded the Third Army. The Stanleyville headquarters was situated in a small building in the middle of a large fenced yard at Camp Ketele, just east of the city, not far from the consulate. Banza was a small, intense man, who wasted no time getting down to business.

"Very pleased to make your acquaintance," he told me, trying to put me at ease. We spoke in French, which he used easily. "We have always had good relations with the consulate. We must remain in close touch."

I was sure he was eager to maintain contacts with the consulate because he knew our embassy had easy access to the chief of staff of the ANC, Col. Joseph Désiré Mobutu, and his headquarters staff in Léopoldville. It was widely known that Mobutu and the army had close ties to the American embassy, military attachés, the ambassador, and especially CIA officers. The previous CIA station chief, Larry Devlin, was known to have been Mobutu's closest contact in the embassy. Banza must have realized the consulate represented a link to the logistical support the United States was providing the ANC, which often had a chaotic chain of command.

I returned Banza's pleasantries and asked about the deserters and the latest on the rebel threat to Kindu.

"We don't expect any particular problem with the deserters," he said. "We have no news on rebel activity around Kindu." We promised to keep each other informed of any news we received, and I left.

I next visited police headquarters and met Paul Decelle, Belgian police adviser and acting chief of police. He had been an adviser to Moïse Tshombé during the Katanga secession in 1960 and had just been assigned to Stanleyville, undoubtedly to keep an eye on developments in the most difficult part of the new prime minister's country. He showed me stacks of boxes of tear gas canisters and launchers, supplied under the USAID police support program I had initiated.

"These are the closest things to weapons the police have," he said. "We need real arms to be effective."

"Have they been trained to use arms?" I asked. "Would they be reliable if given weapons?"

"I must admit they need more discipline and training," Decelle said. "But if we are attacked by rebels, or if they infiltrate, without arms the police will simply run away."

"I'll see what I can do," I told him. I was not convinced it would be appropriate for the police to have arms and delayed making a recommendation to the embassy until I could make a better assess-

13

ment. In a cable sent the next week, I reported on what Decelle had said and recommended that "consideration be given to arming the police."[6]

The only other professional diplomats in Stanleyville, besides the Americans, were those in the Belgian and Sudanese consulates general. Consuls from other countries were appointed from the civilian community and had honorary titles. The consuls and the business community were important sources of information. I knew some of the people from prior visits and had worked with their company head offices in Léopoldville.

The Belgian consulate general was located in the largest building in town, the almost-completed double-towered complex named the Immoquateur. It had a dozen stories. Offices were on the first few floors and above were apartments where the American staff members lived. In charge was Vandenbrande, a large, middle-aged man, who welcomed me warmly in his office.

"You have come at a critical time," he told me in a tired voice. As with most Belgians, he spoke easily in English. "The rebels appear to be advancing from the south of Kindu without opposition from the ANC."

It was evident he was knowledgeable about the rebel situation, and we discussed it for over an hour. "The common thread to the insurgencies in two nearby areas," he said, "is the involvement of former supporters and self-claimed successors of Lumumba," referring to assassinated former Prime Minister Patrice Lumumba. I had followed the rebellions from Léopoldville. In Kwilu, a province many hundreds of miles to the southeast of Stanleyville, a well-organized rural Maoist-style insurgency had sprung up earlier in the year, led by Pierre Mulélé, a minister under Lumumba. The rebellion had been contained by the ANC after fierce fighting early in the spring, but remnants of *Mulélists* remained threatening in isolated pockets in the Kwilu.

I was less familiar with the uprisings he was referring to in the eastern and southern regions. They were closer and of more immediate concern to us in Stanleyville because they threatened to spill over into our jurisdictions. I knew that on 15 May rebellious Bafulero tribal forces, with leaders connected with the former Stanleyville secession, had driven the ANC and the central government administration out of Uvira. Located at the head of Lake Tanganyika, Uvira was just across the border from Bujumbura, the capital of newly independent Burundi, giving the rebels access to the outside world. It was widely reported in the press that the Chinese communists provided financial assistance, primarily funneled through rebel leader Gaston Soumialot. These rebels now threatened Bukavu to the north. They had been repelled once from Bukavu, thanks to Mulamba's effective leadership, local tribal opposition, and U.S. aircraft bringing in troops and supplies. American-supplied T-28 fighter aircraft piloted by Cuban exiles flew highly visible and effective sorties against the rebels. Mulamba had remained in Bukavu because the rebels threatened to attack again.

"Soumialot is well known in Stan," Vandenbrande continued. "He worked as a salesman for SEDEC [a large Belgian wholesale/retail distributor], beer mainly. We heard that he was sent to Bujumbura by Gbenye to be the Eastern representative of the CNL." The *Comité Nationale de Libèration* (CNL) was formed by Christophe Gbenye, minister of interior in the first Congolese government under Lumumba. Gbenye had been principal deputy to Antoine Gizenga, leader of the secessionist government in Stanleyville, after Lumumba's dismissal. He was interior minister again in the first Adoula government as part of the deal to end the Stanleyville secession. After Gbenye was dismissed by Cyrille Adoula in 1963, he formed and made himself president of the CNL as successor to Lumumba's party, the *Mouvement Nationale Congolaise–Lumumba* (MNC-L). Gbenye resided in Brazzaville, in the former French Congo, across the river from Léopoldville.

"Rebel forces moved west to Kasongo, in the heartland of the Batetela, Lumumba's tribe," Vandenbrande continued. "ANC troops fled. These rebels are now probably headed for Kindu. It's in my consular district, and I'm going there later this week and will report to you what I see."

"Kindu's in our Bukavu consulate's jurisdiction," I said, "but it's close enough for me to want to know what's happening."

15

I thanked him for his information and said as I was leaving, "As I see it, the biggest problem is getting the ANC to fight. I wish Mulamba would get back soon."

I had an appointment in the afternoon to see the manager of SEDEC. I talked to him about an awkward problem that had arisen with our USAID-financed import support program. Some enterprising American exporter concocted a highly spiced canned chicken called *Poulet Pili-Pili,* named after the favorite Congolese spice. Unfortunately, after many tons of the stuff had been shipped, some cans swelled and burst open. Although botulism was not found, the USAID mission and the Congolese authorities had decided to withdraw the product as discreetly as possible from the retail market.

"We need to get rid of the stuff you have on hand," I told the manager. "It can either be dumped in the river where it is deep enough not to be retrieved, or buried on land with bulldozers. We don't want them stolen and consumed."

"I'll let you know when we come up with a disposal plan," he told me.

I passed an open warehouse door when I left SEDEC and saw rows of small ivory tusks strewn on the floor. I thought times had not changed much since Arab and Belgian colonial times—ivory was still collected as an important trade item.

At the British-American Tobacco Company (BAT) cigarette plant I met Peter Rombaut, the manager, who also served as honorary British vice consul. Young, bright, and energetic, he showed me cigarettes being manufactured with American tobacco financed under the USAID import support program. I later visited the Stanor brewery, which made beer from American hops and malt supplied under the same USAID program.

On Friday I accompanied Jo and our three-year-old son Evans on a courtesy call on President Aradjabu's wife. Aradjabu was the first of the *Arabisé*—followers of Tippu Tib—community to head the provincial government in Stanleyville since Tippu Tib was appointed to that post in 1887 by Stanley for King Léopold II of the Belgians. A Zanzibari trader and slaver, Tippu Tip had helped Stanley in his 1874–77 expedition down the Lualaba River. Tippu Tip had subsequently followed Stanley's trail to Stanley Falls and established a slave and ivory collection operation that devastated the entire region. Tippu Tib was appointed governor of the Stanley Falls region because Stanley needed him to provide support for his Emin Pasha Relief Expedition. When Joseph Conrad came to Stanley Falls in 1890, he wrote that "in Reshid's [Tippu Tib's son] camp just above the Falls, the yet unbroken power of the Congo Arabs slumbered uneasily."[7] After the Belgians defeated Tippu Tib's forces in the Arab Wars of the early 1890s, many of his people, mixed Swahili-speaking Arab-Africans and detribalized Africans, remained in the area and prospered as a distinct community called the *Arabisé*.

When we arrived at the "Palace," as the building housing the president's residence and offices was called, we were shown into the reception area, a large room looking out onto a luxurious rolling lawn. Mrs. Aradjabu, a young woman of ample proportions, greeted us warmly in Swahili. Swahili is the language of the *Arabisé* and most Africans to the east and south of Stanleyville, as opposed to Lingala, which is the language of the ANC that is used downriver. Conversation was awkward, as she spoke less French than I spoke Swahili. François Aradjabu came to the rescue. He was short and portly, probably in his early forties, and as black as his predecessor Tippu Tip. His round face broke into a smile as he good-naturedly shooed Evans off his chair, the one with the large elaborately embroidered "P."

"I hope you are settling in well," he said in excellent French. "We're just moving in ourselves." Tea was served. Because this was a social visit, there was no opportunity for a substantive discussion. "We will have a longer talk later," he told me as we prepared to depart. "Perhaps we can have lunch next week."

That evening Max Kraus, Phil Mayhew, and David came to the residence for dinner. It was early, and Evans was playing in the living room while we socialized. Max, an older USIS officer, was born in Germany and loved to tell stories about his varied life in his still noticeable accent. Phil was a new Foreign Service officer on assignment to USIS. Both had arrived just a few days before I had. They had an active program of promoting American culture from their library located downtown. During cocktails, David talked about when Lumumba

17

was sent by President Joseph Kasavubu and ANC commander Mobutu to the Katanga in 1961, where he was killed by Tshombé's men.

"He was almost dead when the plane arrived in E'ville," David said. "Lumumba and his two companions were thrown off the plane with their hands tied behind them. They were loaded on a truck, and that was the last seen of them."

I WENT TO SEE Belgian consul general Vandenbrande again Saturday morning. He had spent the day before in Kindu with a Belgian embassy officer. "The town is about to be taken over by *Mulélists*," Vandenbrande told me. "Mulamba was in Kindu the day before with an officer from the American consulate in Bukavu, trying to organize a defense. I am sending an Air Congo DC-3 tomorrow to evacuate women and children to Bujumbura. I expect the city will fall to the rebels within a few days."

When I returned to the office, I wrote a cable relating what Vandenbrande had told me. I reported that he "states that Kindu all but in hands of Mulelists and expects formal takeover in few days."[8]

Later in the day, Guy Humphries, a former American missionary turned planter, dropped by the consulate. A short, thin, self-confident man, Guy told me the Lever plantation manager at Elisabetha, a huge palm oil plantation near his own to the east, had told him rebels around there were training as many as six hundred *jeunesse*. He showed me the spots on the map over the wide areas where the rebels were active. The *jeunesse* were young, radical hoodlums who had a history of causing trouble all over the Congo, especially during the disruptions of the past four years.

Several activities served to draw me into the local community. The Catholic mission invited me to make a ceremonial distribution of U.S.-donated surplus food to indigent families. I posed for pictures: nuns by my side, Congolese women with their babies strapped to their backs, taking packs of flour marked USAID from this burly white man with a crew cut and dressed in a tie and dark suit. There were cocktail parties both at noon and in the evening, and the tennis club had film showings. When we went out at night, we hired sitters for Evans from the American missionary community. Two young Mennonite men, serving as conscientious objectors in a program called PAX, and Phyllis Rine, a teacher, seemed to enjoy coming to our residence.

On Sunday my family and I visited the local zoo. I had heard that many animals had been eaten during the troubles. The buildings were dilapidated and the scruffy animals that had survived lounged sleepily in dirty cages. Monkeys and apes stared out, oblivious to people gawking at them. Evans enjoyed it, but Jo and I found it depressing. Returning home, we passed over the Bailey bridge installed by UN forces after the "troubles" immediately following independence in 1960. We looked down far below to the white waters of the Tshopo River spilling into the Congo over spectacular falls.

Jo and I had dinner at the Pourquoi Pas, a fine Italian restaurant in the Hôtel des Chutes, overlooking the Congo River. Katherine Hepburn, Humphrey Bogart, Lauren Bacall, and the crew making the film *African Queen* had stayed in this hotel when the filming was done near Ponthierville. Even at night, the boat traffic with the other bank was heavy. We enjoyed our meal, overlooking silvery reflections on the soothing ripples of the wide river.

"I think I'm beginning to get a handle on things here," I told Jo. "Some developments are worrisome, but I don't believe we are in any imminent danger in the city. We should enjoy it here. Maybe we can play golf at the airport course during the week."

I RECEIVED A CALL from the SEDEC manager on Monday. "Our people in Kindu reported this morning that they heard shooting during the night," he said. "They found that all their trucks had disappeared, presumably requisitioned by rebels."

I called Banza at army headquarters and asked what he knew about the situation in Kindu. "All contact with our forces in Kindu has been broken," he said. He sounded more excited than I had heard him before. "If the rebels come here, we will evacuate to the north in trucks. I have asked Léopoldville to send aircraft to be here on standby."

I thought his reaction was out of proportion to the sketchy news we had. Conditions did not appear to warrant calling in aircraft, presumably to evacuate officers and their families.

I consulted with David. He said he had similar reports on the agitated state of the ANC. "They don't know whether the rebels are headed for Stan or Bukavu," he said. "It depends on which way they head after reaching Punia. The new road from Punia and Lubutu to Stan is complete, and it would take only four hours to reach us."

On Tuesday, 21 July, I wrote a cable describing what we had learned. "Only really hard news from Kindu is that rebels in city and probably have trucks." Concerned over the lack of information on rebel movements, I asked about the possibility of air reconnaissance of the area.[9]

David came into my office later in the afternoon. "Here is that report I told you about last week," he said. "I just got it back, sanitized for distribution. It has some interesting details on the rebels and their intentions."

The CIA report, dated 14 July, said one of David's sources, a paid informant I assumed, told him Soumialot, as head of the eastern section of the CNL, had sent a message to Stanleyville to say that a CNL "delegation" would arrive in Stanleyville the end of July or the first week in August. "The arrival of this delegation," his informant said, "will be the signal for a general attack by the Popular Army against local ANC troops." The attack was expected to rout the ANC, drive out the current administration, and establish a "popular" government. He said President Aradjabu had expressed support for the CNL, but he suspected him of being "two-faced" and intended to have him "killed" when the rebels took over.[10]

Additionally, David said he had an earlier report describing a meeting of dissidents where plans were discussed to assassinate or capture one of the American consulate staff.

I was accustomed to seeing CIA field reports. Some contained bizarre tales of what agents told their handlers. These were often heavily discounted, particularly when they dealt with intentions rather than actual events. I boiled down David's reports to their essential elements, that is, that certain rebels were making plans to attack

20

Stanleyville and some had hostile intentions toward the Americans in the consulate. It did not occur to me that David's source might be describing a scenario that would develop almost exactly along the lines he described.

SEVERAL OF my commercial and military sources confirmed that Kindu was in the hands of rebels on Wednesday, 22 July.[11]

On Thursday, Jo and I had a chance to relax for a few hours. We played golf on the nine-hole course carved out of the jungle surrounding the airport, losing many balls in the dense dark foliage encroaching on the fairways. That evening, Jo and I accompanied David to Lucy and Alex Barlovatz's home for dinner. They were David's closest friends in Stanleyville. Alex was a Belgian doctor of Serbian origin who had come to Stanleyville many years before and established a popular clinic where he treated Europeans and Africans. The Barlovatzes had known Lumumba well before he became the Congo's first prime minister and were godparents to his children.

"Lumumba spent some time in the Stanleyville Central Prison," Alex said. "I visited him there, using as a pretext to look after his health. He didn't like it much there. He is still a very popular figure here."

It was a most pleasant evening, with good food and wine, topped off with cognac. Lucy played the piano, and we listened to classical music on the phonograph. The Barlovatzes were people who had survived the Congo's troubled times with dignity and compassion.

I CALLED ON Hassam El Amin Elbéshir, the Sudanese consul general, the next day. He appeared withdrawn and almost frightened, and I had little success in drawing him into any meaningful conversation. We parted with the usual exchange of promises to keep in close touch on developments. I could only speculate on why Sudan maintained an important consular presence in Stanleyville. Sudan's involvement with this area dated from the time Stanley blazed the trail in 1887 from here through the Ituri forests to rescue the besieged Emin Pasha on the lower Nile. During the Stanleyville Lumumbist secession in 1961, air access to Stanleyville came primarily from southern Sudanese airports. Exiled followers of Lumumba gravitated to the Sudanese capital of Khartoum.

Back at the consulate, I received a call from Commandant Banza. He said he was sending a company of troops to Wanie Rukula, forty miles southeast of Stanleyville on the road to Lubutu, to defend the bridge there. Another company was being sent to Ponthierville to defend the beaches. I went to the OTRACO wharf area and observed troops being loaded on a barge for ferrying across the river to the railhead on the Left Bank. It looked like a professional operation. I returned to the consulate to report on this and other bits of information. I labeled the report "Kindu SITREP," indicating that I would be reporting on this situation on a continuing basis. I reported that the positions being taken up by the ANC were "stated to be easily defensible and control road, rail, and river access to Stanleyville. 400 troops remain Stanleyville."[12]

On Saturday Makaroff, the manager of CFL, brought me an intercepted message sent by CFL Kindu to the CFL station in Bujumbura. He said it was obviously sent under the control of the Popular Army. It read: "Situation Kindu calm. CFL installations under military guard. Magazines not pillaged. Two grave incidents. Pere Cordier (a colon) and his two boys killed by bandits. Frere Lucien killed by bandits. Bandits have been captured and will be executed." It went on to specify that the areas around Kindu were "captured by *Mulélist* troops under command General Olenga, Louis. . . . Popular Army 15 kilometers from Stanleyville," it claimed. "General appeals to all foreigners not to flee. Their security is assured."

I immediately showed the message to David.

"I have definite word that Punia is in control of rebels, and I have reported that," he said. "Aradjabu, Banza, and Ducelles have been informed."

"The reference in the intercept to '*Mulélist*' troops is interesting" I said. "Vandenbrande also referred to the rebels in this area as *Mulélists*. This is the first time I know of that they have called themselves that. But I doubt they have any connection with the rebellion in Kwilu. It's over a thousand miles to the west."

"I don't think they're part of the Kwilu rebellion, either," David said. "This 'General Olenga' is new to me."

"His asking the European population to remain must mean he realizes they must remain to keep the economy rolling," I noted. Independence had brought many Congolese into important roles in the military and the administration, but very few had significant roles in commerce and industry.

I next called Banza. He said he was in contact with his troops in Ponthierville and Wanie Rukula. "They report all quiet there."

I wrote a cable summarizing the contents of the intercept and relayed other information I had received. In the evaluation, I suggested steps to be taken to improve security. I concluded with a gingerly worded alert to the embassy on the possible need for a limited evacuation. It read in part:

> Steps that can be taken improve security situation include reinforcement ANC and police in Stanleyville. Whatever can be done in Leopoldville by embassy to encourage ANC to take vigorous and expeditious action should be done. . . .
>
> Evaluation: Known facts at this time are that rebel groups of undetermined size and with unknown arms potential but probably equipped with good transport are 300 kilometers or less away from Stanleyville. Roads between rebel location and Stanleyville are good. Can assume rebels have intention move on Stanleyville. Defensive forces between rebels and Stanleyville are two ANC companies, at two separate locations which offer excellent defensive positions. These troops, however, considered unreliable by Belgian advisers here. Troops in city considered more reliable and could put up stand. Police could also take some action against rebels. If rebels come to Stanleyville there is danger to European lives as evidenced their admitted failure control bandits in Kindu.
>
> My recommendation for moment is that embassy should envisage possibility of supplying for an aircraft on urgent basis to evacuate essential documents, dependents, and possibly unessential personnel.[13]

I reread this cable when I went to the office on Sunday to organize my work for the week ahead. Moïse Tshombé, the new prime minister, was visiting Stanleyville, and I knew it would be a busy

23

period ahead. I realized that by raising the possibility of evacuation I might have implied conditions were more critical than they actually were. I wrote another cable, seeking to downplay the imminence of the rebel threat. "The previous telegram," I wrote, "should not be interpreted mean Stanleyville under immediate threat rebel takeover." I cited a report David had just sent via his channels saying "rebel force very small and tactics followed are to infiltrate a town before actual takeover." I continued: "Stanleyville should be much harder nut to crack than Punia or Kindu. We must insist on bolstering military and police defenses and taking appropriate measures against infiltrators."[14]

THE U.S. EMBASSY in Léopoldville had previously asked me how Tshombé, to be accompanied by Antoine Gizenga, the former leader of the Stanleyville secession, would be received in Stanleyville, the political base of Tshombé's now eliminated arch rival, Lumumba. In a cable sent the previous week, I had concluded that, in spite of his anti-Lumumbist history, most people I contacted thought Tshombé would "be given an enthusiastic if not wild reception." He was regarded as a "winner . . . and, perhaps most important, a prospect for peace and security."[15]

On Tuesday, 28 July, Tshombé met with the Stanleyville consular corps for what he described as "an exchange of views." Tshombé told us he was heartened by his reception in the area and expressed his support for President Aradjabu. He promised to address the area's most pressing economic problems. Vandenbrande asked him about the problem of the rebel takeovers in Maniema. His only response was that he saw "the need for a psychological program to counteract the feeling of defeatism in Stanleyville."

"There needs to be tight security control in the city," I chimed in. "Have offensive measures been taken against the rebels? Is Punia going to be retaken?"

"That is completely under control," Tshombé replied, but he was not specific about what measures had been taken. "You need not worry. Be sure the European population is not the first to panic."

A press conference followed in which Tshombé said the rebellions were "completely isolated movements" and promised to effect reconciliation with each. After Tshombé left, Aradjabu told the press that the warmth of Tshombé's reception justified his own support for the central government.

Vandenbrande spoke to me after the meetings. "A Belgian reporter in Tshombé's entourage said he had seen Soumialot in Bujumbura. Soumialot had bragged he would be taking Stan within a few days. I warned Aradjabu a couple of days ago about the danger of infiltrators working for the rebels coming into the city, but he didn't seem to believe me."

"I don't believe Tshombé is as concerned about the rebel advance as he should be," I said. "Nothing concrete is being done to shore up security."

New York Times correspondent Tony Lukas was in the entourage accompanying Tshombé. He came to see me at the consulate. "Have you found out anything about the rebellion on the trip?" I asked him.

"Not much," he said. "I think Tshombé has been successful on his tour. He doesn't appear particularly worried about the rebels. I've followed him for a long time. I am amazed at his ability to survive in Congo politics."

"Tshombé was appointed partly because he promised to negotiate with the rebels to end the violence," I said. "Have you seen any movement in this regard?"

"I don't see Tshombé getting talks going with the rebels," Tony said. "There's nobody to negotiate with."

"The rebels have not been stopped in the field," I said. "The ANC has not changed its habits and won't fight. It lacks leadership. Unfortunately, Mulamba is in Bukavu, facing a serious threat there. I don't see Stan falling anytime soon, but the threat is there. I hope you can tell the American embassy in Leo how serious the rebellion is becoming." He promised he would. I knew he was in close touch with Political Counselor Monteagle Stearns and others in the embassy. The embassy was not giving me any feedback on my reports, so I did not know how seriously they were taking the progress of the rebellions.

My report on the visit covered the meeting with the consuls, the press conference, and the comments I received. I concluded: "Tshombé had established base in Stanleyville and he has done something bolster

25

Aradjabu's government. Disheartening see that Tshombé has not really tackled problem of insurgency in the vast area Eastern Congo."[16]

ON MONDAY, 27 July, Jim Stauffer's replacement had arrived. Don Parkes, also a former navy radio man, was shorter and heavier than Jim. I saw him briefly. "Welcome to Stan," I said. "I'll see you later when you get squared away." He had little to say, stroking his short chin beard as he disappeared into the vault. He appeared nervous and abrupt in his movements, almost morose. I thought he might still be confused after his flight into the heart of Africa.

Makaroff brought more messages the CFL had intercepted from General Olenga in Kindu. He was now signing himself Nicholas instead of Louis. One was addressed for relay to Stanleyville and read: "Europeans of Stan cannot flee. They must stay in place. They must continue their activities. All guarantees are really assured." Another message protested "against declaration made yesterday in Stan by M. Tshombé in favor of national reconciliation. No reconciliation between sheep and wolves, that is, no reconciliation between nationalists and assassins Lumumba." I summarized the messages and sent it by cable without comment.[17]

A cable from our embassy in Brussels arrived on Wednesday informing us that the Belgian foreign office had decided to replace their consul general in Stanleyville with an officer from the Léopoldville embassy. The reason, I surmised, was that Vandenbrande was thought to be overly pessimistic about the security situation. He had told me that if Kindu fell to the rebels, Stanleyville would surely follow. His replacement would be Baron Patrick Nothomb, a young officer I had met briefly in Léopoldville. His title came from his descent from a national hero who led Belgium to independence from Holland in 1832. I thought Vandenbrande had done an excellent job and had objectively and knowledgeably assessed the danger posed by the rebels. I took advantage of the Brussels cable to press the need for action in the face of rebel advances. "Hope projected removal Belgian CONGEN Vandenbrande," I wrote in a cable to Léopoldville, copied to Brussels and Washington, "not reflection Belgian Embassy Leopoldville thinking rebel threat [Lake] Tanganyika not to be dealt with in serious fashion. Suggest Embassy determine Belgian Embassy view situation Stanleyville and coordinate efforts deal with it."[18]

EARLY THURSDAY MORNING, I drafted and sent out a reply to a 28 July cable from the embassy in Léopoldville asking the three Congo consulates to evaluate the danger posed to Americans citizens in our districts if T-28 aircraft or mercenaries were used against the rebels. The embassy cited reports stating that "rebels will retaliate by killing whites."[19]

I had been too busy to reply earlier. I thought there was ample evidence that American-supplied aircraft already being used against the rebels posed a threat to Americans. A June article in *Time* magazine, readily available in the Congo, reported that rebels in Uvira had denounced America for attacks on them by T-28 aircraft.[20] I had seen several press reports that Soumialot had said he could not guarantee the safety of Americans in rebel-occupied territory if U.S. aircraft were used against them. We also had the intercepted cables, which detailed the threats made by Olenga. After updating our list of American citizens, I wrote:

EMBTEL 84
Reply to reftel as follows:
1. List Americans: No American citizens in Consular District in area under rebel control. In immediate region Stanleyville which I believe only area my district actually under threat rebel takeover, Americans currently number 43, composed 7 USG [U.S. government] employees and 2 dependents, 34 missionaries (9 men and 25 women and children).
2. Danger to above listed American citizens exists if T-28's used but not effectively enough to prevent takeover Stanleyville. Danger exists to less degree if non-American missionaries [mercenaries] used.
3. Protection for American citizens and property if T-28s actually used and if Stanleyville under imminent threat takeover only possible if all citizens evacuated. Property left would be lost.
4. Summary: No Americans in district under rebel control. If Stanleyville taken by rebels after use T-28 and mercenaries, Americans would be in danger their lives if had not been previously evacuated.[21]

ON FRIDAY PRESIDENT Aradjabu invited me for lunch. He had been
an organizer in Lumumba's MNC-L party and was a professional public
health worker. He had a reputation for honesty. Many people believed
he had a sincere interest in promoting the welfare of the population.
He greeted me warmly, his white teeth sparkling in his round face. We
ate lunch on the veranda overlooking the vast lawn. The food was
lavish, and the champagne kept coming.

"Having just taken up these duties, I am looking for help from all
sides," he said. "I know the United States is a staunch supporter of
peace and stability in the Congo. I look forward to the cooperation of
the consulate. If there is anything or any information you may need,
please feel free to call on me.

"There are subversive elements in the city who will take advantage of anything to cause trouble," Aradjabu continued. "We have
taken a variety of measures to counter them. The authorities in the
communes have money and instructions to gather intelligence on
agitator activities. We plan to arm the police when the army releases
weapons. We also expect reinforcement of army units here.

"I must tell you, I am disturbed over the attitude of the expatriate community," he continued. "After the killing of several whites in
Kindu, some of the big firms have decided to send dependents away,
or at least to move up their normal summer plans."

"I will do what I can to calm nerves," I promised. I left our meeting thinking that we were at the beginning of a constructive relationship.

On returning to the consulate, the cable I wrote reflected much
of what Aradjabu had said. My lead line was: "Situation Stanleyville
stable but threatened by planned evacuation European dependents."
I went over what Aradjabu had told me at lunch, saying that he was
confident he was taking measures to prevent the city from being
taken by rebels. "Stanleyville," I concluded, "not under the active
threat takeover by rebel troops. Certain agitators known to be in city
and will probably attempt soon to create disturbances. . . . Authorities taking active measures counteract them. Evacuation European
dependents could cause chain reaction leading to fall of city." I pointed
out the danger of permitting the city to fall under the control of rebels

supported and recognized by the Chinese communists (ChiComs) and others opposed to the central government. I recalled that the last time this happened, under the Gizenga secession, material support was funneled from the outside through the Stanleyville airport. I said I would try to persuade the European community to put off the evacuation of dependents and urged the embassy to do likewise with their parent organizations in Léopoldville.[22]

Thus I ended the workweek and the month of July in an upbeat mood. I had completed two full weeks in charge. I felt I had covered all aspects of my work and had given the best advice I could on actions required. Jo and I had cocktails that evening by the back lawn. Monkeys in the neighbor's yard chirped and flittered among the branches of the palm trees.

"I haven't had much of a chance to talk to you," I told Jo. "It has been a hectic time. How have you been doing?"

"I've visited with the American missionaries. They don't appear worried about the rebels. Evans and I have stayed pretty much at the house. Shopping is better than I thought. There are lots of fresh goods available. The large native market is a joy of food and color."

The brown Congo River, visible in the background, seemed scarcely moving from this distance. It became obscured in the soft equatorial evening rain. Stanleyville was peaceful. Violence was far away.

ANGRY SHOUTS OUTSIDE my window woke me early Saturday morning, 1 August. I dressed hurriedly and went outside. Several ANC paracommando soldiers were beating one of our consulate guards with their rifle butts.

"What's going on?" I yelled, trying to get them to desist.

"They stole arms from *gendarmerie*," growled the leader of the paras in rudimentary French, "working for rebels."

"Who stole arms?" I asked.

"Yes, that one, Yetu," he said, pointing to the standing guard. The one they were brutally smashing on the head and arms was writhing on the ground.

"Let me call headquarters," I said. "We can sort this out."

29

"No! We have orders," he said and motioned for his troops to gather their prisoners and leave. They cartwheeled the two guards down the driveway using their rifles as clubs. They pushed them onto a truck and drove off.

With nearly two years in the Congo, I knew the ANC's propensity for violence. I had been threatened on occasion but had not witnessed such a methodical, ferocious beating. I called Major Banza at headquarters for an explanation.

"I know nothing about it," he said. "I will investigate and meanwhile replace the guards immediately with some of our soldiers."

David Grinwis arrived at the consulate and told me Aradjabu had made a radio speech last night in which he railed against the rebels and called on the population not to assist them. He had also opposed forming a European armed standby reserve that Police Commissioner Decelle had suggested a few days ago.

"Aradjabu seems to be firming things up," I said. "It is hard to believe that report of yours that he has been in contact with the rebels. Maybe he thought better of it after Tshombé's visit and decided to back the central government."

The UN regional office in Stanleyville called and told me they were pulling their people into Stanleyville from outlying regions and were sending dependents to Léopoldville. I knew that most commercial firms were due to send dependents out early on summer vacations, starting next week. The men would remain. Makaroff called to say they had a report that ANC troops had cut off river traffic far down on the Congo River at Bololo. This was disturbing news because we would then be isolated except by air.

David said his informants now told him the rebels no longer intended to take the city directly but planned to go first for Ikela to the north. He said his army contacts told him the ANC was preparing to move against agitators in the city but could tell him nothing about the guards seized by the paras.

30

I drafted a cable reporting on Aradjabu's speech, UN plans to regroup and evacuate, business company plans for early vacations, and what David had learned. The report ended, "Summary: Situation calm with seemingly effective measures being taken against rebel threat. Short-term stability seems assured. Longer-term solution needs serious attention. News of possibility Congo River traffic being cut off below Bololo disquieting."[23]

Late Sunday evening, David came to see me. "I've picked up news that rebels are in Wanie Rukula. That's only forty miles from Stan, on a good paved road. My source told me the fall of Wanie Rukula would mean the 'automatic fall of Stanleyville.'"

"I'll call the army and see if they know anything," I said.

The only person available at headquarters was a Belgian military assistance officer. "Yes, we heard a rumor to that effect," he said. "Some drunken ANC fired on fishermen in pirogues on the river. There is no evidence the Popular Army is in the vicinity. We have sent a Belgian subaltern to investigate."

Several people called to report hearing about rebel activity close to Stanleyville. "I'll leave a message with my contact for Banza to call us," David said. "I'll be in my office."

At two in the morning, the lights of a car came up the driveway. I went outside and saw it was Major Banza. We went over to the consulate's offices.

"We know the attack at Wanie Rukula was by Popular Army forces," Banza told us. "It was beaten off by our troops, but they ran out of ammunition. The driver of the truck carrying spare ammunition fled before delivering it. We are sending reinforcements to the area immediately." He promised to keep us advised and left.

"Jo and Evans should go to the Immoquateur apartments," I said to David. "I don't feel they're safe here."

"That's a good idea," David said. "I'll call Phil to tell him I'm bringing them."

I went to wake Jo. "There is fighting not far from here," I told Jo. "There's no imminent danger, but I think you should stay downtown in our staff apartments while we sort things out. You can stay with Phil Mayhew."

Jo and Evans were too sleepy to object, and they dressed hurriedly. They rode off with David while I stayed to make my report.

31

That afternoon I had sent a cable relaying what I had learned about the Wanie Rukula attack and now wrote another detailing what Banza had said, adding that I was sending my family to safer ground. Jim Stauffer was at the office, and he put it on the wire immediately.[24]

After David returned, he and Jim decided to spend the rest of the night in their offices. I spent the night alone in the residence.

VIVIAN LAMBERT, my Belgian secretary, came into my office Monday morning, 3 August. "As you may have heard, SEDEC and the other companies have decided to send women and children away early. We have decided to leave also. That won't be happening until about the sixth. I don't really want to go. We survived before, but perhaps this time it's different," she said.

I sent a cable to the embassy suggesting they send a junior vice consul to replace her, to help with administrative chores and help me "keep abreast [of the] ever-changing situation."[25]

I heard a car in the driveway. A Land Rover screeched to a stop in front of the door and out popped a stocky young man with a full shock of brown hair. He bounced up the stairs to the front door. It was Baron Patrick Nothomb, whom I had met only briefly in Léopoldville. He was the replacement for the abruptly withdrawn Belgian consul general Vandenbrande.

"Good to see you, Patrick," I said.

"Great to be here, Mike," he replied. "Just making my rounds to see what's going on."

We talked about Wanie Rukula. "The young officer sent there to investigate has vanished," he told me. "If you learn anything, please ask your embassy in Léopoldville to keep our embassy informed. Our telex is not operating." The Belgian consulate did not have the independent communications capability we had. They sent their messages through the commercial post, telegraph, and telephone (PTT) service. Patrick then left, his Land Rover careening around the curved driveway, off to his next stop.

Later in the afternoon, he telephoned me. "A Belgian trader who just came from Wanie Rukula has confirmed that the army post there was attacked Sunday by local villagers. They were said to be supported by rebels from Maniema or Kivu who spoke Swahili. The ANC simply dropped their arms and fled," Patrick concluded.

I broke off work and went next door for lunch. Jo and Evans had come back to the residence, and we had a pleasant meal. I returned to the consulate and completed writing up the morning's events. Before I could finish, Antoine Lingili, the consulate receptionist, said Radio Stanleyville had just announced a curfew beginning at 3:30 that afternoon. Everyone had to be off the streets. The telephone rang almost immediately, summoning me to a meeting at army staff headquarters.

Arriving at Camp Ketele, I joined the others called by the military to discuss the curfew. Included in the meeting were President Aradjabu; other consuls, including Belgian vice consul Paul Duqué in Patrick's absence; Belgian community leaders Michel Faeles and Petrofina director and chamber of commerce president José Romnée; and ranking Congolese and Belgian military officers.

"Imposing a curfew would spread panic," Aradjabu argued, addressing the assembled ANC officers. "It would imply the authorities were not in control."

The expatriate civilians supported him. The military reluctantly agreed to rescind the curfew. None of the consuls had spoken up during the discussion, but before leaving I wanted to find out more about the rebel advance. "Do you have any precise information on the military situation?" I asked the ranking military officer, Lieutenant Colonel Kimpipi.

"I know nothing about it," he said simply.

On the way back to the consulate, through deserted streets, Kimpipi's astonishing words, "*je n'en sais rien,*" rang repeatedly in my ears. With Third Army commander Mulamba in Bukavu, Kimpipi was in charge of the troops in the field, and Banza was staff director at headquarters. I was disheartened by their lack of knowledge of the military situation or by their unwillingness to discuss it with us.

First, I dashed off a cable with the information I had to date. In reporting on the attack at Wanie Rukula, I said the ANC had "dropped arms and fled." The curfew was rescinded "after President supported by European representatives protested," the 4 P.M. report said.[26]

33

Reflecting further on the implications of Kimpipi's words, and after learning from David that the rebels at Wanie Rukula had appeared to be "well organized," I wrote another cable. It read:

1. Further reports received indicate action Wani[e] Rukula against ANC supported by organized rebel groups. Reliability ANC is essential question. Immediate threat Stanleyville can be considered exist. If ANC gives way, there would be fighting in or around Stanleyville and security city could not be assured. View this possibility, request aircraft be on standby basis Leopoldville or elsewhere to evacuate dependents and women employees from Stanleyville. Will advise further on SSB contact 0800 August 4 but will give SITREPS by cable.

2. Further request Embassy make sure ANC headquarters fully aware gravity situation.

3. Please pass SITREPS to Belgian Embassy as TELEX not functioning this afternoon. Also pass Belgian Embassy (a) ADJ Raucroy missing at Wanie Rukula. (b) Curfew lifted and population holding steady.

I gave the report to Jim, and he sent it out at 6 P.M.[27]

This was the third time I had raised the possibility of evacuation. On 25 July, after the fall of Kindu, I had said the embassy should "envisage possibility" of evacuation aircraft. I had resurrected the subject in my cable of 30 July, recommending the evacuation of Americans from areas threatened by rebels if T-28s were used against them. We had received no response from the embassy to these messages.

I spoke to Monty Stearns at the embassy in Léopoldville on the SSB later in the afternoon and made my request more explicit. "Situation here is very serious," I said. "When can aircraft come?"

"Aircraft will be there tomorrow to evacuate American citizens and nonessential U.S. personnel," he said. The swift response surprised me. Somehow, I had expected them to take more time to come to a decision and to organize it.

I telephoned Jo at the residence. "Call all the missionaries you can," I told her. "Tell them aircraft will be at the airport tomorrow to evacuate all who wish to go. Oh yes, you and Evans should be prepared to go, too."

After a quiet supper, my driver took Jo and Evans to the Immo-

34

quateur apartment. David and I talked over coffee and cognac before settling in for the night.

"David, do you remember when Bukavu was threatened by rebels in May? I saw the cable to the consul, Dick Matheron, instructing him to stay 'behind the lines' and report on what was going on if the rebels took the town."

"I didn't see it. But I'm not surprised Mac would do that," he said, referring to U.S. Ambassador McMurtrie Godley.

"Do you think we should stay if it appears the rebels will take over?"

"It would be stupid," David replied. "These guys are virulently anti-American. I doubt we would be allowed to do anything useful. But I don't believe Mac would pull us out, and my boss is not one to stand up against him."

"Maybe we should try to leave, anyway," I suggested. "If it got sticky enough, we could pull out on our own."

He made no comment. In the short time we had worked together, he tended to leave management decisions to me as head of the consulate. However, after two years here, I felt he knew even more than I did the mortal danger we would be in if these rebels took over. The local military, unreliable as they might be, at least knew the U.S. government was firmly committed to them. Our diplomatic and consular immunity would count little with the rebels because they would know nothing of international codes and practices. UN, diplomatic, and other civilian personnel had suffered along with the Congolese during the various troubles over the past four years. During the Stanleyville secession in 1961, eleven Italian airmen working for the United Nations were brutally murdered, mutilated, and probably eaten near Kindu by dissident ANC troops of the Third Army. What more could we expect of rebels probably reincarnated from these same forces? I was convinced we would be in grave danger if we stayed, but I could not make a decision now. At some point, it would have to be made. I put it from my mind as I went to sleep.

"MICHAEL, WAKE UP." It was David, shaking me. "Someone from the ANC is here to talk to us. Come over to my office." It was two A.M. I

35

threw on clothes and hurried over to the consulate. David introduced me to Capt. Henri Tshamala from the army group's intelligence unit. He had come to brief David on the military situation.

"Our troops have fallen back from Wanie Rukula," he said. "They are fighting at a point only sixteen kilometers from Stan. I don't think they will hold. Rebels will probably enter the city. There will be murder and pillage in the communes. Please contact our headquarters in Leo immediately to send reinforcements. We need aircraft to frighten the villagers and rebels." We told him we would do what we could, and he left.

"David, do you have any confirmation of this from other sources?" I asked.

"No, but I think we must take his warnings seriously. He's quite reliable."

"OK. Tell Jim to fire up his equipment. I'll draft a cable."

I typed out what Tshamala had said. I assumed he was David's covert liaison to the ANC. I therefore said ANC headquarters had supplied the information and made the request for reinforcements. I concluded that although we had no independent confirmation of what he had told us, we should accept their analysis. After consulting with David, I could say that the "consulate" advises:

1. Immediate dispatch evacuation aircraft.
2. Request Embassy pass above information to GOC and other appropriate persons.
3. Continuous monitor SSB network.
Consulate proceeding with destruction plan.

The message went out FLASH precedence, the highest category, at 3 A.M.[28]

We began to prepare for evacuation. Under established procedures, we were to destroy or ship out all sensitive or classified material if we thought hostile or unauthorized persons might have access to the premises. On the lawn by the swimming pool, at the back of the duplex, Jim and David set up seven steel fifty-five-gallon destruction barrels lined with incendiary material.

While they began carrying out material to burn, I drove to army staff headquarters at Camp Ketele. Belgian and Congolese officers were milling around, without apparent purpose. "What is the situation?" I asked. "What is being done?"

"We're trying to shore up the defenses of the camp," Banza told me. "We fell back last night to a position fourteen kilometers from here." This confirmed what Tshamala had told David and me earlier. "We have had no contact with the rebels since yesterday when we fought them at kilometer fifty-three," he added.

Tshamala had told us fighting had taken place much closer to the city. I had no tactical military training—I was an air traffic controller in the Air Force during the Korean War—but nothing I saw convinced me effective action was being organized to fight the rebels.

Returning to the consulate, I drafted a cable outlining what Banza had said, pointing out the inconsistency in reports:

> demonstrates fragility situation Stanleyville due primarily to lack reliable information and interpreters. ANC quite capable panic and collapse. Situation Wani[e] Rukula and consequences for Stanleyville still far from clear. Need for evacuation dependents and sensitive material still exists and would appreciate receiving information re availability aircraft. Also, still deem it imperative GOC bolster ANC Stanleyville both in effectives and in leadership. HOYT

The message went out at 8 A.M.[29]

By now staff members Don Parkes, Ernie Houle, and Joan Allen had arrived at the consulate and had filled the barrels with piles of papers taken from their various safes. They put matches to the linings, and, one by one, the barrels lit with a swoosh of flame. Soon all seven were burning brightly. Flames shot up, blowing about the thick tree branches overhead, chasing away the chattering monkeys. When the flames subsided, they carried out more papers. Ernie's small safe was soon emptied, but Don and Jim, with Joan and David's help, kept bringing out more material from their vault. The code machines would be destroyed at the last moment. After that, encoding and decoding would be by a laborious handwritten one-time pad system.

"Here's a message from the ambassador," David said, handing me a piece of paper with the teletype tape still wet. "THE GRINWIS AND

COMMUNICATOR TO STAY IN CASE REBEL FORCES ENTER CITY." It was signed "Godley" but was a "back-channel" message without a number.

I was stunned. As head of the consulate, I would normally be the last to leave in such a situation. I thought Mac must have completely lost confidence in me. "I can't believe that's right," I told David. "Just you and Jim to stay? Must be a garble. Send a service right back."

A few minutes later, David handed me a new text. "HOYT, GRINWIS, AND COMMUNICATOR" were those named to stay.[30]

"That's better," I said to David. "But damn Mac, he doesn't give us any choice. As we said, this is stupid. Do you suppose your boss [the CIA station chief] knows about it?"

"Since the message came back-channel, directly between our two stations, he must know. At the very least, he would've had the opportunity to object."

"I know this is Mac's idea," I said. "I just wonder if the Department and your people know about it."[31] We had expected it, but we had no time to dwell on it now. Without discussion, it was assumed Jim would be the communicator to stay.

Jo had arrived back from The Immoquateur and was packing bags for when she and Evans would leave. "Jo, take my driver and go see those missionaries you talked to last night," I said. "Try to persuade them to evacuate at least the women and children."

When she returned, she said, "Everyone is refusing to leave. They told me they had invested too much spiritually and materially in the Congo to abandon it now. In the past, when they left in times of trouble, they had returned to find their property destroyed. And besides, they said, they had never had any trouble with the local Congolese. 'It's God's will we stay,' they told me."

Earlier that morning, I had called Al Larson, the senior member of the local American missionary community, and asked him to come see me at the consulate. He arrived from his station located at Kilometer Eight north of town. "We know the rebels are within a few miles of Stan," I told him. "We are evacuating this afternoon. There is real danger. You should get your people out."

"Are you leaving yourself?" he asked me.

"I'm staying with essential personnel. All others are leaving. At least you should send your families out."

"I don't think there is that much danger," he said. "But I will see if some of the families want to leave and get back to you later."[32]

I did not pursue it further. He had been in the Congo much longer than I had. "The aircraft will be coming in this afternoon," I said. "Anybody that wants to leave can use them. In any case, keep in close touch with us."

Jo came to my office after finishing her packing. "Do we have to leave?" she asked. "Is there really that much danger?"

"I've been ordered to stay with David and Jim. Everyone else is to go. Ask Tata Paul to prepare lunch for everyone. We expect the airplanes this afternoon."

I decided to go to the airport because that was where the action was. I told the driver to fly both flags on the car, the American flag on the right fender and the blue flag with the consular "C" on the left. I wanted to impress any jittery ANC troops with my official status.

As we drove through the city, the streets were nearly deserted. Inside the terminal with the peeling pink paint, the Belgian military advisers in civilian clothes were pacing nervously. "The ANC officers are not following our advice," they told me. "The military situation is critical. We're waiting for an aircraft to take us out." They acted as if the planes couldn't arrive soon enough. I recalled the young Belgian adjutant missing at Wanie Rukula and understood their concern. White military personnel would be prime targets of rebel forces.

A DC-4 ANC aircraft landed, and a company of paratroopers ran down the ramp and formed into a column. Perhaps these were the reinforcements I had requested. Shirtless, black skin shining brightly under the hot tropical sun, and their heavy weapons and ammunition belts slung over their shoulders, they moved off at a brisk trot toward town. Seeing well-armed, disciplined troops coming to our assistance was reassuring. The feeling was soon dispelled as I spoke to Captain Tshamala from army intelligence. He was there with his wife and children.

"Why isn't your family here?" he asked. "Aren't you sending them out?"

"Yes, of course. They are at the consulate, waiting for aircraft due this afternoon."

"Don't wait that long. Things have deteriorated since I talked to

39

you this morning. I am trying to find space for my family to take them out right away."

I went to a telephone and talked to Jo at the consulate. "The driver is coming to get you now. You, Evans, and Joan should come out right away."

At that moment, a twin-engine Beechcraft with U.S. military markings taxied up to the terminal. It was *Bugsmasher,* Army Attaché Col. Knut Raudstein's plane. Knut and his wife Shirley had been our close friends in Léopoldville. I went out to greet the pilot, Maj. Harold D. Asbury, and a crew member while the tanker was refueling the plane.

"Knut sends his regards," Asbury said. "He said to tell you not to let them get you down. Is there anything we can do to help? We are prepared to fly out anyone who needs to go."

I looked into the cockpit and saw the floor littered with automatic weapons and ammunition. "You came prepared," I said. "The situation is deteriorating rapidly. I have three people for you to take. They're on their way. When you fly out, see if you can spot any rebel activity."

When Jo, Evans, and Joan arrived in my car, Evans appeared hesitant to get into the airplane. "Will they throw me out of the airplane when we land?" he wailed. He must have overheard us talking one night a few weeks ago about Lumumba's treatment after his flight to Elisabethville. We tried to reassure him and boosted him into the back seat with Joan. Jo squeezed in beside them.

"Don't try to be a hero," Jo told me. "Stay alive and come back to me."

"Don't you worry," I said. I just wanted them to leave so that I could get back to work. I leaned in to kiss her good-bye. "I'll talk to you after you take off," I said. They pulled the door shut, and the plane taxied to the runway.

40

I climbed the stairs to the control tower. I was familiar with the operations there from my Air Force days in air traffic control. After the plane was airborne for a few minutes, I picked up the mike. "Bugsmasher, Bugsmasher, can you see anything? Over."

"Negative, nothing. Over," was Asbury's reply.

"Bye, bye, baby doll," I said into the mike twice and closed off the transmission, "Out, here." The tiny plane disappeared over the solid wall of tall trees of the thick jungle that extends all the way to Léopoldville.

I RODE BACK to the consulate, flags still fluttering, relieved that Jo and Evans were now safe, and I did not have to worry about them. The center of town was unusually quiet for that time of day. We followed the riverside road to the consulate. The Congo River was brown and wide at this point, with the Left Bank buildings just visible. The usually busy OTRACO wharves were deserted, and no boats were on the river.

Max Kraus was at the consulate, having closed the Cultural Center and Library. He and Phil Mayhew were helping bring the seemingly endless supply of documents to the burning barrels. Phil had brought two young women, American tourists hitchhiking through central Africa, who were now stranded in Stanleyville. They sat calmly waiting on the front steps, with no idea of what was happening.

"Enough of that," I told them. "You need to leave right away. Phil, take the girls in the van and go directly to the airport. Max, be sure to pick Ernie up at the Immoquateur on your way."

The bewildered girls waved gaily from the van as they drove out. Max's car disappeared around the curved driveway. Don took off in Jim's car to pick up his suitcase at Jim's apartment before going to the airport. David had left earlier in his car, saying he had to see some people and to pick up something important at his house.

In about half an hour, Max called from the airport. "Ernie didn't make it with me," he said in his slow, accented tones. "Something about not being dressed. He didn't have his shirt on. He said Don would pick him up. Airplanes are coming in out here, and we're helping people get on. I'll leave the keys to the vehicles with Paul Duqué, the Belgian vice consul. He's staying here with Baron Nothomb."

"You and Phil leave on the next plane," I said. I was disturbed because Ernie had not been picked up, but I assumed Don would check to see if Ernie was still there. Their four apartments were close together. I called Ernie and told him to look for Don and to get out.

A few minutes later, David called from Ernie's apartment. "Don

41

is gone, and Ernie is still here," he said. "Someone told me they saw Don driving off. Peter Rombaut of BAT just came in. He said he would stay and see to it Ernie got to the airport. I'm coming right away."

At that moment, Don drove up. "What are you doing here?" I asked.

"I guess I took the wrong turn. Anyway, I thought I was to pick up that pouch Ernie prepared."

David drove in next. "On my way from the Immoquateur by the Ketele road, I passed a group of seven people, presumably rebels, in a single silent file, without weapons. They took no notice of me. An ANC truck with a recoilless rifle drove up and began firing down the street." He opened his briefcase to show me what he had picked up at his house, a large amount of bundled Congolese currency. "I thought this would come in handy."

"I guess we can't risk sending Don out now," I said.

Before I had a chance to ask about Ernie, we turned to watch the ANC truck with the recoilless rifle. The soldiers manned the gun and began firing it and a bazooka down the road; their shots disappeared into the green and black vastness of the Ituri forest, extending east for a thousand miles to the swamps of the White Nile.

It was now about 5:30 in the afternoon. I had not made a telegraphic report since my early morning cables and turned to my typewriter. "Since consulate and grounds obvious battle ground on road leading into the city," I wrote, "propose abandon consulate for apartments in city if fighting advances enough to make it possible."[33]

We burned Ernie's diplomatic pouch in the dying embers of the last destruction barrel. Jim said he had put the hammer to his coding machine. The scorched lawn gave off a heavy odor of burnt grass. On the SSB radio with the embassy, I said we had completed the destruction.

42

The ANC troops climbed back into their truck and drove off toward the wharf area. A few minutes later, a single file of thirty or forty men appeared, led by a tall, imposing figure, walking sedately from the forest. Dressed all in white and apparently unarmed, they waved palm branches. They moved with grace in an eerie ethereal silence.

They paused in front of the consulate, pointed toward us, then continued toward the wharves and disappeared from view.

"Must be a rebel group with a *fêticheur*," whispered David, using the French term for witch doctor. "That's not the same group I saw before."

Heavy firing was heard from the direction of the OTRACO wharves and the Protestant church. A few minutes later, the white-clad column returned. "I think they lost a few," David said. They had, however, lost none of their poise.

The ANC troops and truck reappeared. Spreading out on each side of the road, the men used the consulate garden walls for protection. The front lawn was wide and grassy. A tall pole in front of the consulate carried a large American flag. The troops laid down rapid fire after the retreating column.

"ANC advancing rapidly and in numbers beyond consulate on road to Wanie Rukula," I wrote, describing what I thought was a lively military action for my next cable. "If advance maintained may not abandon consulate due to psychological effect."[34]

I called ANC headquarters and described what their troops were doing in front of the consulate. I asked what their plans were. "All troops are being withdrawn to headquarters for the night," Banza told me. The troops before the consulate gathered their equipment and left.

The firing around us had cut the ropes holding the American flag, leaving it at half-staff position. We could not pull it up or bring it down. I made a mental note to have it fixed and sent another cable. "Pole shot and rope cut by gunfire but consulate flag still flying 1800 local."[35]

Events had happened so quickly that I had not thought further on getting Don and Ernie to the airport. I called Ernie's apartment again. Rombaut said he had not been able to get Ernie off. "It's too risky to put anyone on the road to the airport now," I said. "Just stay put. Maybe we can do something in the morning."

The telephone rang shortly after dark, and I answered. The caller identified himself as the air attaché from our embassy in Brazzaville.

43

He said he had flown to Stanleyville for the evacuation. "I'm here to take you out. Come, and we'll leave."

"But we have orders to stay," I told him.

"Leave, you idiots. This place has gone crazy."

His plea made me pause and think. Although we had orders to remain, my instincts told me to leave. I knew there was grave danger in staying, but doing so now presented other risks. I feared running the gauntlet of frantic ANC troops to get to the airport more than stray rebels. There was no time to discuss the possibilities with David. I had to make the decision myself and right away. "We're not coming," I told the attaché.

"You're mad to stay," he said.

"Get off soon as possible," I said.

He muttered something about "fools" and hung up.

I called ANC headquarters and got Lieutenant Colonel Kimpipi. "We plan a massive attack in the morning to drive out the rebels," he said. "Remain at the consulate."

"Can you send some troops to protect us?" I asked.

"No, can't do that, but we patrol during the night. Tell us anything happening there." He sounded confident. Perhaps he thought his troops had defeated and driven back the unarmed white-clad column.

"We're turning on all our lights. Be sure your troops know we are here."

I wrapped up the day's events in an unclassified cable:

Stan SITREP 1700Z [7 PM local] Aug 4 Silence reigns around consulate after sharp 3 hour firefight almost all of which took place on and about consulate property. Reports received and events viewed by con offs indicate attack up Wanie Rukula road by 30–40 slow marching rebels armed with religious wands. About half that number observed retreating in same fashion after reported slaughter behind Protestant church 200 yards towards town from consulate. ANC counter-attacked slowly after initial retreat to center town. Attack gained momentum aided by heavy machine guns recoilless rifles, bazookas on trucks. Attack died out at dusk and all ANC have gathered at downtown hqs. Only very sporadic firing continues at distance. Have lighted buildings and grounds and have so advised cmd col. He advises ANC will continue attack tomorrow and will patrol during night. He asks we advise him any incident during night. He sounded victorious and happy. At start fire fight Mayhew made successful courageous dash skirting firing to gain airport carrying two American girl tourists. Preliminary inspection reveals only damage 2 bullet holes residence windows and holed flag pole. City lights and water supply normal. HOYT[36]

Over the SSB, Monty told me Jo and all the other evacuees had arrived safely in Léopoldville.

David and the others stayed in the offices. I went to the empty residence and slumped into a chair in the living room with a drink. Tata Paul had left, and I was too exhausted to fix myself something to eat. A heavy downpour beat on the roof and swept through the trees. It created a cool stillness. Occasional scattered firing continued in the distance. Otherwise, the night was quiet. When the rain stopped, I saw the moonlight shimmering on the relentless quiet flow of the Congo River. Sleep came from exhaustion and innocence.

The curtain had closed.

Vengeance

Day 1: Wednesday, 5 August 1964

SLEEP ENDED EARLY WEDNESDAY MORNING, 5 AUGUST, AS thoughts of the events of the past few days broke through to my consciousness. On Monday I had asked for evacuation aircraft after I realized army command was not organizing its troops to fight rebels threatening Stanleyville. Missed connections and the missionaries' refusal of my offer to take them out had marred Tuesday's evacuation. Ernie Houle and Don Parkes, two of my staff members scheduled to leave, had not made it to the airport as planned. Thus, they and the missionaries remained my responsibility in a potentially life-threatening situation. In the afternoon, a rebel band had crossed and recrossed in front of the consulate, bracketed by futile firing from ANC troops. David Grinwis, Jim Stauffer, and I had been ordered to stay, so I had reluctantly let the last evacuation flight leave without us. We had been ordered to stay, and stay we did.

I knew the rebels would come again. The *Armée Nationale Congo-*

laise (ANC) leadership would not lead; the troops would not fight. The American consulate was directly on the path the rebels must take to reach the city. We were isolated and vulnerable. I thought we would be safer in our apartments at the Immoquateur downtown, out of the firing zone and among the many residents there. Such a move would require notifying my superiors in Léopoldville and Washington and would need coordination with the army. I dressed and left the residence for the consulate next door to draft a cable. On a yellow legal sheet I typed:

TO: Secstate Wash DC
        Amembassy Leopoldville
FLASH   Unclassified

Considering retiring from consulate to apartments downtown. Consulate too exposed and tactics ANC is not to hold positions. Therefore very well be overrun again. I consider this unnecessary risk to personnel. Will advise when leaving. HOYT

I made my report unclassified to avoid encoding and to get it on the wire immediately. We had destroyed our crypto machine and coding was slow on the one-time pad. I showed the draft to David Grinwis, the vice consul. He had spent the night in his office with Jim and Don, the two communicators. "David, I have decided it's just too dangerous to stay here," I said. "We should move to The Immoquateur where we'll have safety in numbers."

"I agree we're in great danger here, but this is where our communications are," he said. "We can only leave if we can make arrangements with the army."

Jim and Don came out of the vault and my message was on the teletype by 6:50 A.M.[1]

I called Banza, the chief of staff at ANC headquarters. "I think we should move out of the consulate," I said. "We don't feel safe here with the fighting taking place around us."

"Yes, but our forces are about to begin operations," he said. "Stay there until I can send troops to escort you out."

I wrote a short cable:

47

ANC plan begin operations any minute. They advise wait in consulate until advance of troops and will escort us to apartments. Reliability ANC execute this plan doubtful but reluctant move while ANC operation underway. Will wait for ANC advance. HOYT

It went out at 6:58 A.M.[2]

ANC troops arrived in trucks and deployed on both sides of the road in front of the consulate, much as they had done the day before. They crouched behind the low brick wall enclosing our large front lawn. The Congo River protected their right flank, the consulate their left. They manned the recoilless rifle mounted on the back of the truck and fired into the empty and silent forest. The rat-a-tat of a heavy machine gun mixed with the boom of the canon. There was no visible or audible response from the vastness of the jungle that was absorbing the ordnance. After an hour of this, the troops gathered their equipment and withdrew without a glance at us.

David stood watching at the window. "I think I see what looks like rebel troops lurking out there in the bush," he said.

The phone rang. It was the control tower operator at the airport. "The ANC is fighting out here," he said.

Another call came from the Air Congo office. "All is quiet around the terminal."

I thought we might still get people to the airport for evacuation if aircraft came in and we could get safe passage. Another cable updating the action was sent at 9:15 A.M.:

ANC troop movements before consulate both going and coming. Scattered firing. Still plan retire to apts. Attempting contact other Americans and tell them intent gather at apts. those wishing evacuate. Rebels seen before consulate. Report from control tower says "ANC fighting" at airport. Air Congo at airport reports all quiet. HOYT[3]

I called ANC headquarters again. "We have forbidden all traffic in the city," Banza said. "Stay in the consulate. We have told our soldiers about the consulate. I will advise you when to move out."

I was typing up this new information when Professor Loewen called from the university in Stanleyville. He asked me to pass on to

48

the Canadian embassy that he and his family were safe. He said all other expatriates were fine. I finished my report and put my name on it. Jim sent it out at 9:55 A.M.[4]

Calls came in from Americans and others with similar information. I told them we were tentatively planning for further evacuation if more aircraft came and we could reach the airport safely. No one would give me a definite answer about when we might be able to leave. I sent another message to Washington and the Léopoldville embassy:

Status Americans Stan
1. Consulate personnel four Americans in consulate. One American in apt.
2. Missionaries: [Clifford] Schaub family of four and Miss [Phyllis] Rine on northern edge of town. Loewen dependents wife and believe five children at university. All above well.
Larson family of three at mission eight kms north of town not in contact with consulate since 1500 local yesterday but presumed well.
3. None of missionaries have yet decided evacuate but anticipate evacuation Houle and Parkes plus possibly 12 missionary dependents this afternoon on aircraft referred to embtel 114. HOYT[5]

The embassy telegram cited was from Léopoldville. It had informed us that a U.S. military assistance aircraft would be arriving during the day, bringing Lt. Col. Leonard Mulamba from Bukavu to take command of the defense of the city, and said the aircraft could be used for evacuation purposes.[6]

"With Mulamba, Stanleyville could hold," David said.

The control tower operator called again. "An American airplane has flown over the city. They radioed to say the pilot was hit in the foot by a bullet. They went away without landing."

I looked at David. "There goes the last hope of getting the ANC to fight. We're stuck with Banza and Kimpipi." It had been Lieutenant Colonel Kimpipi's remark that he knew nothing of the military situation that had prompted me to call for the evacuation. I sent another cable that went out at 11:14 A.M.: "Control tower reports COMISH [the

49

U.S. Military Mission to the Congo] plane pilot shot while flying over fighting and aircraft returning without landing. Airport still appears safe for landing. HOYT."[7]

We continued calling army headquarters for someone to lead us out, but no one came.

IN THE LULL that ensued, I felt secure enough to think of lunch. "Jim, you can come with me to the residence for lunch," I said. "David and Don can keep watch and then come eat when we've finished." We had discussed earlier what to do in case of an attack or other danger that would require us to hide. The four Congolese employees who had stayed the night would go into Ernie's small vault leading from the reception room. The Americans would go into the larger communications vault next to it, accessible from David's office.

Jim and I went to the other side of the duplex through the back door. It was normally closed off, but we had opened it yesterday to facilitate carrying out the papers to be burned. Tata Paul had prepared a huge *capitaine* (lake fish) that was to have been lunch yesterday, but our meal was postponed when the evacuees left earlier than planned. It looked delicious, especially since I had not had time for breakfast. Jim and I were about to dig in when the phone rang. It was David. "Come back to the consulate," he said and hung up. I put the phone down, hesitated a moment, reluctant to leave the appetizing meal. The phone rang again. "Hurry! Hurry!" David screamed this time. "Come, they're attacking!"

I ran out the back door and across the enclosed lawn by the swimming pool. The odor of grass burnt by the heat of the destruction barrels still lingered. I ran through the door into the consulate. Although I had neglected to tell my lunch partner what was happening, he was close behind. Jim dashed past me to David's office. As I came by the reception desk facing the glass front doors, the staccato sound of automatic firing and breaking glass made me drop to the floor. I started crawling.

"Come, quickly!" David pleaded from the door of his office.

I saw one of our Congolese employees huddled in a corner across the room. I crawled over and pulled and pushed him hurriedly to the doorway of the small vault where the other three were already ensconced. "Shut the door, quickly," I said. They pulled the steel door closed as I lunged through David's office door and ran into the large vault.

Jim and Don shut the flimsy outer wood door that served as soundproofing and swung the heavy steel door closed behind me. They threw the handle down on the locking mechanism and spun the dial of the combination lock. David and I helped them shove a heavy safe against the door.

I looked about, seeing the room for the first time. It was the CIA communications facility and classified storage unit under David's jurisdiction and not normally accessible to non-Agency personnel. A dozen gray steel filing cabinets were pushed together in the center. The drawers were open, empty of the files burned yesterday. Two tall racks filled with radio equipment lined one wall. Two teletype machines were next to them. An old air conditioner rattled in the sole window. Several scuffed steel desks and a few chairs completed the furnishing of the fifteen-foot square room.

David whispered to me what had happened. "From my office window I saw about ten heavily armed men walking down the road past the consulate, rebels, I assumed, draped with tree branches. They shook their fists at us. That was when I called you the first time. Then they started running up our driveway. I called again. As you came in from the rear, they started firing into the front of the building."

As he spoke, we could hear through the walls muffled sounds of firing outside. Glass shattered, as the front doors were presumably forced open. There was the crunch of boots on broken glass as they entered the consulate. Strange, harsh, and excited voices shouted unintelligible commands. The vault filled with the sounds of shots fired inside the building, of feet stomping on the terrazzo floors, and of furniture breaking.

"I'll send a message," Jim whispered. He punched out a tape with the words "CONSULATE UNDER ATTACK," connected it into a loop, and clicked it on the teletype machine. The message ran continuously. The clack of the keys seemed terribly loud in the vault's confined space.

"Probably won't get out," Jim said. "A message was just coming in. Blocks our outgoing."

He and Don unpacked a portable, manually operated, emergency

51

radio from a canvas bag. "With another transmitter, we might get through," Jim said in a low voice. "It can be backup if the power goes off." It was powered by a hand generator and operated by two cranks rotating on opposite sides, like a sailboat pepper grinder.

"Shit, there's only one handle," Don said. "Damn thing's useless." Jim threw the offending pieces into a corner.

I called ANC headquarters on the telephone Jim had just installed. Normally there was no telephone line in the vault because it could pick up transmissions from the now-destroyed coding machine. No one answered. I dialed the Sudanese consulate general's office in the hope that they might have contact with the rebels. Again, no one answered. David took the phone and called his Belgian friends, the Barlovatzes. "Lucy, we're under attack by rebels," he whispered. "Try calling army headquarters. Call the Belgian consulate. Call anybody you can think of to get us some help." He told me she said she would do what she could.

I called Ernie at his apartment. Peter Rombaut, the British honorary consul who had stayed to try to get Ernie out, came on. "We're under attack at the consulate," I said softly. "We're in the vault, and they're firing all around. Please call somebody."

"I'll try to get you help," he said. "Hang in there. I'll be in touch."

"*Fungua, fungua,*" was shouted from inside the consulate.

"That's Swahili for open," whispered David. He was by the light-proof message slot to the vault where our four local employees had taken refuge. "I think they've been scared into opening their door," he said. "They're gone. My driver just came to the slot and whispered for us not to move."

We heard wood splinter as the outer door to our vault was wrenched off. The sound of steel striking steel began on the inner door. Then our world went black. Power must have been cut off at the panel outside. The air conditioner stopped. The click of the teletype ceased. I thought of the emergency radio lying discarded in the corner. Darkness enveloped us and isolated each into himself. After a momentary pause, the pounding on the door resumed.

Our small space filled with sounds of the pounding. Interspersed was the muffled noise of shots fired in the confines of David's office and the sharp ping of bullets hitting the steel door. A much louder crash, like a thunderclap, shook the room. I jumped in my chair. My eardrums popped. I thought a cannon had been fired at the door. The boom came several more times and then ceased. The metallic pounding on the door began again. It sounded like a sledgehammer or an axe. The pounding alternated with small-arms fire.

As I became accustomed to the dark and less distracted by the attack on the door, I noticed a bit of light coming in through tiny cracks around the air conditioner. I knew enough air would come through for us to breathe.

I was in a chair behind the filing cabinets bunched in the center of the room, directly opposite the door. Jim was hunched next to me. "Got a cigarette?" I asked in a low whisper. I had quit smoking; now it did not matter. He handed me one and closely shielded a lit match. I inhaled deeply and gasped as the unaccustomed smoke hit my lungs and throat. It felt good.

WITH THE SOUNDS of the pounding and shooting in my ears, I thought of what would happen if the attackers succeeded in breaking down the door. Help was certainly not on the way, and the door could not hold indefinitely. The attackers must be part of the Popular Army and were probably being led by Gen. Nicholas Olenga, the man who had railed against the countries supporting the central authorities in the intercepted messages we had received. The attackers must know this was the American consulate from the flag flying outside, still at half-staff. Why else were we targeted for attack? When these men finally burst into the room, after so much effort, would they have enough control to stop their firing? Surely they would spray the room and everyone in it with their bullets.

For the first time in my life, I felt death near and certain. What would I do when it came? I thought of my wife Jo but quickly put her from my mind. It was too painful to think how my death would affect her. A sharp aching pain was developing in my stomach. It was fear pressing on my gut.

As the pounding continued, tiny strips of light began to appear before me in the darkness. The faint outline of the door appeared as

53

the jamb loosened from the wall. The pounding was having results. I could think of no reason for the men to slacken their efforts before the door or the frame gave way. I tensed in anticipation. The four of us—David, Jim, Don, and I—remained still and silent.

The pace of the pounding slackened. Soon it stopped completely. Had they grown weary of their task? Were they not certain someone was in here? We surely had made enough noise earlier for them to hear us. I heard the shuffle of feet and the low murmur of voices, contrasting with the previous stomp of boots and high-pitched, excited shouts. Glass clinked on glass. They must have found the bottles of wine in the office. David's driver hissed through the message slot again, *"Ne bougez pas!"* ("Don't move!"). We kept even more still, almost afraid to breathe.

There was complete silence now from within the consulate. Had they gone away? Were they waiting for us to come out? We made no noise and waited, frozen by fear.

I forced myself to break the silence and whispered to David, "Do you think they're gone?"

"I've no idea," he replied as he edged closer to speak more softly. His shape was barely visible in the darkness.

"I think we'd better stay put," I said. "At least until we're sure they're not around."

"Yeah," David said.

We were silent, each of us with our own thoughts. I tried not to think about what or who might be lying in wait out there and concentrated on the passage of time.

Nightfall came at its equatorial six o'clock. Light no longer came through the cracks around the air conditioner. Heavy firing boomed softly in the distance. Could it be the ANC was counterattacking? A tropical evening rain beat heavily on the roof, and my tensed nerves slackened. I smoked more cigarettes, inhaling deeply to get the harshest effect. The sharp pain of fear continued to grip my stomach.

SILENCE REIGNED in the consulate. About nine, I broke free from the fear-imposed inertia. "Time we get out of here," I whispered. "We're not accomplishing anything here. Let's get the safe away from the door."

Jim and Don pushed it back silently. With some difficulty they unlocked the heavy steel vault door and slowly pushed it open. I peered around it, cautiously looking into the darkened room. I saw no one and heard nothing. The air was fresher than in the vault. The smell of cordite hung about the office. Had they gone away or were they waiting until we revealed ourselves?

No matter, I could stay still no longer. I moved slowly around the dark rooms, feeling what must be spent bullets and broken glass crunching under my feet.

"I'll see if I can get the power back on," Jim volunteered. He went outside and threw the main lever. No lights came on because it had been daylight when the power was cut.

"Turn on every light we have," I said. The brightness that resulted was welcomed after the dark we had experienced during the past hours. Light shining out from the consulate revealed the surrounding blackness. I waited for a reaction. Nothing happened. No one appeared.

Papers were strewn about the offices, and windows were broken. An incredible number of empty cartridges and spent bullets lay on the floor, sprinkled among the broken glass. Empty wine bottles and glasses were on the coffee table. A short-handled shovel was propped up next to the twisted wood outer door to the vault.

"All that pounding with only a shovel?" I asked.

There was little other damage. The flags remained on their poles behind the reception desk. The other offices were not disturbed. A dispatch I was writing on the region's economy was still in my pending basket. My *Economist* calendar lay open on my desk. I wrote on the space marked Wednesday, August 5, "1:30 Consulate Attacked." The flags behind my desk were undisturbed. Scattered firing sounded in the distance, but we heard no other noise. We neither saw nor heard anyone outside.

I unlocked the cabinet holding the SSB radio and called the embassy in Léopoldville, hoping someone was monitoring. "Cedar, Cedar, this is River Rat, River Rat," I whispered into the mike.

"River Rat, River Rat, this is Cedar," came the immediate response. It was Monty Stearns, the political counselor. He had evidently been waiting for us to call.

In a hushed voice, I described briefly and discreetly what had happened: the consulate had been attacked by rebels, and we had locked ourselves in a room. I said the rebels had tried to break down the door but had left after finding our alcohol. Firing was heard from the airport. I asked if they could tell me what had happened in the city.

"All contact was cut off by early afternoon," Monty said. "The city has probably fallen."

"Four of us are safe and well in the consulate," I said. "Admin clerk is downtown in his apartment. Please inform Jo I am okay." I was nervous about using the radio, thinking it was possible the rebels could be monitoring it. Besides, anyone could come into the consulate at any time. I broke off contact abruptly, hung up the mike, and locked the radio in its cabinet.[8]

I went to my desk, ripped off a sheet from the yellow pad, cranked it into the typewriter, and began typing my reporting cable. Concentrating on writing helped steady my shaking hands. I wrote quickly:

SECRET FLASH

Consulate attacked 0113Z [should have been 1132] Aug 5 by Popular Army and firing light automatic weapons. We four retired to commo vault. They cut power off for one hour attempted break down vault door. Band remained until 0200Z [should have been 1400]. Heavy firing heard until that time. We emerged 1900Z to reestablish power. Property not heavily damaged or looted. Still desultory firing in city and no evidence circulation [traffic]. Have returned to vault after SSB contact Leo without knowledge local authorities who seem unaware our presence or commo capability. Awaiting instructions. Will send further info ASAP. HOYT

I handed it to Jim without review. He and Don had already fired up their equipment. They coded it by hand and sent it out back-channel directly to CIA communications in Léopoldville.[9]

"I am not certain how, or if, we should contact the rebel authorities," I said to David. "With our strong commitment to the central authorities, I don't want to take any action that would imply recognition of rebellious forces. I can only assume these guys are part of Olenga's Popular Army."

"I'm sure of that," David said. "From what I saw, they wore former ANC uniforms, with lots of palm leaves."

I dialed Ernie's apartment. Peter answered immediately, apparently waiting for our call. "Are you all right?" he asked. "Lucy and I have been calling everyone in town to ask for help, even the archbishop. No one could do anything."

"We are fine now," I said. "How about you?"

"We're okay," Peter said. "No one has bothered us. From what we can see from up here, the streets are controlled by the rebels. We hear the airport and army headquarters have been taken."

I dashed off another cable to relay what he had said about conditions in the city. "Due attack on consulate will await further developments," I concluded. "But we must reveal ourselves soonest."[10]

We went out the front door to see what had happened to the residence. The light rainfall was refreshing. The door to the residence was locked and undisturbed. We went in. Two or three bullets had gone through the front windowpanes. A few pieces of broken glass lay on the living room sofa. Otherwise it was as we had left it at lunchtime. Tata Paul must have cleaned up the uneaten lunch and departed.

I opened the refrigerator. There was the *capitaine*. "Come boys," I said, still speaking in a whisper. "Let's get something to eat." It tasted great, even cold. A few beers brightened our outlook.

WE SLOWLY TOOK control of our shaken nerves. We were relieved to be alive, smiling, treating our close encounter with death more lightly than we had a few moments before. We began to talk above a whisper.

"That was sure a close one," said Jim.

Don appeared too stunned to say anything even this inane, but relief showed on his face.

"At least we're alive," said David.

"Yeah," was all I could come up with.

We went back to the offices where I drafted a message: "Emerged from refuge beginning tonite by turning on lights and sleeping in residence. USG cannot retreat into shell while events unfold. Tomorrow will open consulate but do not propose seek out authorities. When am approached will protest attack and await developments. HOYT."[11] Anticipating I would not receive the instructions I had requested, I had formulated my own.

After sending the cable, Jim came to me. "Look what's happened to the lock on the vault." He showed me where the rebels had sheared off the outside combination dial. "Without the dial, we can't open the door from the outside. Someone has to stay in the vault if we want to lock it." We decided Jim and Don would lock themselves in the vault. They spread blankets on the floor.

David said he had tried to use the telephone in the residence, but the line had apparently been cut in the firing. We decided we would stay in the offices for the night. We needed to keep in close touch in case something happened. I also did not want to be alone in the residence.

As we prepared to sleep in chairs in David's office, we heard faint pops of firing in the distance and some closer by. The rain stopped.

I looked out the window and saw moonlight revealing the gentle waves of the Congo River. I could almost imagine the faint roar from the distant Stanley Falls. The stillness and calm were welcome after what we had just been through. My exhausted mind and body eased into troubled sleep.

> Going up that river was like traveling back to the earliest beginning of the world, where vegetation rioted on the earth and the big trees were kings. An empty stream, a great silence, an impenetrable forest. And this stillness of life did not in the least resemble a peace. It was the stillness of an implacable force brooding over an inscrutable intention. It looked at you with a vengeful aspect. (Conrad, *Heart of Darkness*)

Simba! Simba!

Days 2 through 5: Thursday, 6 August,

through Sunday, 9 August 1964

A FEW HOURS OF FITFUL SLEEP IN A CHAIR IN DAVID'S OFFICE HAD blotted from my mind the previous day's events. But the rebel attack on the consulate, the pounding on the door, the cowering in the vault, came back to me in a rush as I awoke Thursday morning, 6 August. The dull ache of fear returned to the pit of my stomach.

The servants and consulate local staff did not come to work. David Grinwis, Jim Stauffer, Don Parkes, and I fixed ourselves a light breakfast. We swept up the broken glass and spent bullets and casings. I put a few of them in my pocket and took pictures to record the damage.

Don brought David and me a cable he had decoded on the one-time pad system. "It's good news for a change," he said.

It was a cable sent from the embassy at Léopoldville to Washington outlining their plan to rescue us. "Planning armed helicopter landing consular lawn Stanleyville," the operative portion read, "to rescue

59

four personnel now at consulate. Plan also include T-28 cover. . . .
Devlin has coordinated with Mobutu and . . . [he] concurs and has
put his plane, helicopter and two T-28s at our disposition." They recognized that Ernie Houle was in his apartment downtown and that
this was a problem yet to be resolved.[1]

After reading the message hurriedly, I handed it to David. "The
attack on the consulate must have been as great a shock to them as it
was to us," I said. "They're responding quickly, just like they did on my
request for evacuation Tuesday." Referring to Ambassador McMurtrie
Godley, I continued, "Mac sure changed his mind in a hurry. Tuesday
the ambassador ordered us to stay behind. Now he wants us out. The
attack was a wake-up call."

"It would be great to get out," David said. Jim and Don indicated
they were even more pleased with the prospect of leaving this nightmare. "I notice Devlin is back," David continued. Larry Devlin had
been the previous CIA station chief in Léopoldville. He had cultivated
Col. Joseph Désiré Mobutu, chief of staff of the ANC, as one of the
embassy's closest contacts. "That means they realize this is really
serious."

The message was burned as soon as we read it because we did not
want it around in case rebels burst into the consulate again. I was
delighted over the prospect of rescue. The attack on the consulate yesterday had brought the reality of the danger posed by the rebels to us
personally. David and I had discussed this just recently. However, I
had doubts the rescue plan could succeed. I believed the landing would
be normal and peaceful. Yet I knew we would be exposed to rebel
fire. In addition, I was concerned with Ernie being downtown. We had
to devise some way of getting him here before the rescue took place.

I unlocked the SSB radio and raised the embassy in Léopoldville.
Monty Stearns, the political counselor, was on the line. "River Rat,
this is Cedar," he said. "Have you received our message on our planned
operation? It is set for Friday. Do you agree?"

"Yes," I said. We could not be specific on details of the rescue
operation on a radio network that could be heard worldwide. "I agree
in principle. Operation sounds risky to me. Situation fluid. I wish

retain option of calling it off. Concerned we are not all here. Will have to get him here by that time."

"We understand," Monty replied. "We take responsibility for that. We still wish to go ahead with operation. Try to get all together by that time."

"OK," I said. "Signal that operation advisable will be green jeep parked in front of offices."

"Operation can be called back anytime before noon local tomorrow," Monty added.

"City is calm," I said. "Electricity and telephones are working normally. We heard army has been driven beyond airport. We hear some firing from that direction. Little or no movement of people or vehicles can be seen from here. No boats on river. Radio Stan went on the air this morning with announcement by [Gaston] Soumialot that 'true liberation had come to Stan.' It said revolutionary authorities were in control of the situation and urged citizens to remain calm and carry on normal activities. We are waiting for new authorities to contact us."

Monty broke off, advising us to remain in the consulate.[2] We thought the announcements on Radio Stan had been tapes of Soumialot's voice, in which he had proclaimed himself the "new Lumumba." David said he doubted that Soumialot could have arrived in Stanleyville so soon.

From the window I saw a couple of trucks drive by on the road in front of the consulate, filled with men dressed in khaki ANC uniforms decorated with palm branches. They shouted "Amèrikani, Amèrikani" as they sped off. The American flag, still dangling halfway up the pole, must have revealed our identity.

We kept the telephone busy. We learned the airport was quiet, inactive, and probably under rebel control. Firing could still be heard from that direction. Army headquarters did not respond. Someone called to say there were ANC soldiers holding out at Camp Léopold to the northeast of town and that they were attempting to fight their way westward. The remainder of the ANC troops was said to be retreating downriver. The troops from headquarters, we heard, had made it to the OTRACO wharves and crossed the river to the Left Bank. Peter

61

Rombaut, the honorary British vice consul, told us by phone he could see from the window of Ernie's apartment in the Immoquateur that bands of rebels were beginning to loot.

"The police are completely under the control of the rebels," Patrick Nothomb told me in a call from the Belgian consulate general. "Rebel leaders don't seem to be able to control their forces. We think the *jeunesse* might be turned loose. I plan to appeal to the authorities to bring them under control. Please tell your embassy to relay to ours that we are still alive."

I wrote several brief messages on the events of the morning and gave them to Jim and Don to code and send out.[3]

Early in the afternoon, several more trucks, filled with armed men dressed in ANC uniforms and palm branches, drove up the driveway. Horns honked a few times. We did nothing. After a short pause, they drove off. I looked out the window and saw they had taken two of the vehicles parked outside, my flagged sedan and David's car. They must have jump-started them because we had not left the keys in the ignition.

"We need to plan in case these roving rebels come to the consulate," I said to David.

"We have to maintain access to the vault," David said. "Jim and Don can stay inside with the door locked."

"You and I will stay in the offices to deal with anyone who comes," I said. David and I manned the telephones and waited for someone to come.

At six P.M., I raised the embassy by SSB again. I told them what we had learned during the day. I had almost finished when I heard loud banging on the front doors. "Closing station," I said and locked the radio in its cabinet.[4]

Six rebel soldiers were at the front door, brandishing their weapons, beating on the door, shouting, and otherwise indicating we should open up and let them in. David opened the doors, and they streamed into the consulate, shouting "SEEEEEEM'BA, SEEEEEEM'BA," then "MAI, MAI, MULELE MAI." By now these shouts were having their intended effect, getting our attention and instilling fear. They shook their weapons at us. I could not make out what they were saying, which was presumably in Swahili. They did not respond to my attempts in French to explain that our diplomatic and consular privileges and immunities protected us against their incursion. My words were unheeded and useless. They moved about the offices, opening doors, looking everywhere, shouting, and shoving us about.

When the leader came to the closed steel door of the vault, he shouted at David, *"Fungua, fungua,"* and threatened to hit him. We pointed at the bullet holes and the shorn knob, trying to convince him the door had been damaged and could not be opened. He appeared befuddled and vague, perhaps under the influence of beer or drugs. He did not pursue the matter. Inside the vault, Jim and Don kept quiet.

The leader took me outside and pointed to our remaining vehicles, shouting *"Fungua."* He swung his rifle back as if to hit me. I offered him the keys I had. He refused to take them, snarling and pointing angrily to the ground instead. I understood he wanted me to drop the keys at his feet. When I did so, he picked them up and matched them with the cars. He discovered there were two cars for which he had no keys, the green jeep and Jim's Ford. Jim and Don had them in the vault. Getting them would involve revealing they were hidden there. I stood by the cars, helpless, while the leader aimed his gun directly at my head, saying *"Fungua, fungua."*

"I don't have the keys," I said. "Would I be so foolish as to risk my life over a mere vehicle?" I doubted he understood me. I could do nothing. After a few moments' hesitation, he shrugged his shoulders and motioned his followers into the other cars.

They piled in. As they started each car, they stomped hard on the accelerators, racing the engines furiously. They roared off, grinding gears, and repeating their shouts of "Simba" and "Mulélé Mai." Several minutes later, a rebel came back in Joan Allen's white Volkswagen. With disgust he pointed to a flat tire and ran off, leaving the car.

"What's this 'Simba' bit?" I asked David.

"Simba is Swahili for lion," he said. "They're calling themselves Simbas. It's also some sort of war cry. Mulélé Mai is water of Mulélé, I suppose after the leader of the Kwilu rebellion. Water plays a part in their rituals. From what I understood, they have been taught to think that enemy bullets will turn to water if they follow strict rules. These

63

include looking straight ahead, not having sex before battle, and such like. *Fungua* means key or open."

Whatever the words meant, they soon became familiar to us as several more groups came by during the evening, shouting the same things. These groups did little more than look around. They acted as if they were either drunk or on drugs.

I called Hassam El Amin Elbéshir, the Sudanese consul general. "Have you any news of the extent of rebel control of the city?" I asked.

"We know very little," he responded. "I'm trying to get through to General [Nicholas] Olenga but haven't had any luck."

"Would you be interested in taking on responsibility for the consulate?" I asked. "We've been attacked and our vehicles stolen. We may very well be unable to carry on our consular functions. I may need someone to act for us."

"I don't believe we can do that," replied Elbéshir. "We are in a difficult situation ourselves." I suspected his reluctance stemmed from the presumed anti-American stance of the rebels and that he was in the same state of shock as we were over the rebel takeover.

"You should consider becoming doyen of the consular corps," I said.

He said he'd think about it and hung up. The Belgian consul was doyen by custom, but I thought the rebels would prefer an African.

I rang up Peter at Ernie's apartment. I asked him, as honorary British vice consul, if he would take over responsibility for administrative functions of the consulate, such as paying our employees, if we were unable to carry on.

"Sure," he said. "I'll do anything you want."

"That's great," I said, grateful for his support. "What can you see of the rebel activity from there? Do you see any way of getting Ernie down here?"

"There are rebels beginning to gather around, close to the buildings. They don't look too friendly. We can't risk going outside. I'll call you back later."

WHILE DAVID WATCHED for Simbas, I unlocked the radio cabinet to make final arrangements with Stearns for the helicopter rescue, now

64

dubbed Operation Flagpole. Monty asked about the position of the flagpole. I assured him it was in front of the consulate building, not in the center of the lawn, and well out of the way of the landing. I told him we would have to cut our main radio antenna, which stretched across the middle of the front lawn. We would wait until the last moment because we would then lose our only secure means of communication. The SSB, however, would still be operable because it used a different antenna. Monty told me the operation would take place about six in the evening of the next day, Friday, reiterating it could be called off anytime before noon. I told him again that the go-ahead signal, meaning the rebels were not near the consulate, would be the green jeep parked in front.

Monty continued, as if wishing to prolong the conversation. "How are you spending your time?"

"We've been playing bridge, but our kibitzer is not here," I said, to confirm that the four of us were there and Ernie was still at his apartment.

"Please do something for me," I continued. "VOA is broadcasting information about Stan. They cite reports from the consulate saying the city was calm. They should stop making reference to us." I knew the rebels could hear Voice of America (VOA) broadcasts in French, English, or Swahili and would realize that the American consulate was sending out messages. I noticed that VOA thereafter stopped commenting on the situation in Stanleyville.

The prospect of leaving Stanleyville seemed to me like an impossible dream. I tried to avoid thinking about the next day even as I wished and hoped it would end our nightmare. We had a quiet, simple supper and prepared for sleep.

The night did not pass quietly. Loud explosions went off around us, like bombs exploding. I could not imagine what they were.

"It must be ANC on the Left Bank," David said. "It sounds like mortars."

Across the river, opposite us, we saw bursts of lights and heard mortars, rifles, and automatic weapons being fired into the city. We crawled under our steel desks. I felt helpless, huddled under a desk, seeing and feeling the shells landing, sometimes far, sometimes near.

65

I smoked more of Jim's cigarettes; they were nasty, a brand called Albert in blue packs. They must have been made from leftover sweepings, not from good American tobacco.

The bombardment continued for several hours. I feared the immediate threat from armed, angry rebels more than I did the abstract idea of being hit in this random shelling. A heavy rain fell. The rain and the bombardment appeared to be keeping the rebels from roving.

As the firing from across the river subsided and the rain slackened, we began to hear another noise. It was the sound of firing from the center of the city. It developed into a continuous roar. Numerous types of weapons were being fired. Mixed in were loud flat pops that I guessed were tear gas canisters being fired from launchers, the ones I had inspected the week before. "The Simbas must be celebrating their victory," I said. "They don't seem to mind shooting off the supplies they found."

Peter called. "The Simbas have broken into the other side of the building and are terrorizing people there," he said. "They're looting and beating, looking for ANC troops. They haven't bothered us yet on this side. I don't know why." There could be no question of getting Ernie down to the consulate that night for tomorrow's Operation Flagpole.

With the Simbas on the prowl, we decided we did not want Jim and Don shut in the vault. We also did not want it open and accessible to the rebels. We swung the vault shut and locked it. Now we no longer had wireless communications. David and I stayed in the offices while Jim and Don slept in the residence.

The firing continued and some of it was close. I was amazed at the waste of ammunition. Maybe the rebel leadership could not control the celebrations. I slept fitfully with the noise of the shooting in my ears.

I WOKE EARLY Friday morning, 7 August, and was still sitting in my chair. The firing had ceased. David was asleep on the other side of the desk. It all came back to me in a rush: the attack on the consulate, our time huddled in the vault, the isolated feeling when no one came, the Simbas coming and threatening us, and the theft of our vehicles.

The sounds of the hours of gunfire celebration still rang in my head. I focused on the planned rescue that could take us away from it all. I could think of no way we could get Ernie to the consulate. A successful rescue operation, in my mind, would provoke the rebels into retaliatory action against him and other Americans, and probably against all Europeans as well. I thought the helicopter would be an easy target for the Simbas. They had demonstrated during the night that they had an ample supply of arms and ammunition.[5]

"We just can't risk that rescue operation," I said to David, who was now awake. "I had doubts on the feasibility of the operation from the beginning. A helicopter coming in would be a sitting duck to these guys with all their weapons and ammunition. They would certainly take terrible retribution on those left behind. It's too easy a way out. There must be a safer and better way. I've got to call it off."

David did not object. In the past, he had made it clear that he considered it the consul's role to make such decisions. I turned on the SSB radio. I assumed they were monitoring the frequency full-time and transmitted immediately. "Cedar, Cedar, this is River Rat, River Rat. Advise against Operation Flagpole. Our friends are all around us, armed and numerous."

"River Rat, this is Cedar. Your message received," was the simple reply.

"River Rat, clear," I said and locked up the radio. Giving up on the rescue was a disappointment, but it was something to put behind us. We now had to concentrate on diplomacy to extricate ourselves.

We telephoned The Immoquateur and learned more about the harrowing events of the previous night. Some of the bombardment by the ANC from the Left Bank had struck the twin buildings, clearly visible on Stanleyville's skyline. After the ANC firing from the Left Bank ceased, the Simbas took over. Probably frustrated by their inability to do anything about the bombardment, they broke into rooms, beat those they found, and raped at least one woman. They killed one Belgian man known to be active in Congolese politics and drove off with a truckload of Belgian men.

Patrick Nothomb, the acting Belgian consul general, had called Camp Ketele and reached General Olenga. He persuaded the general

67

to withdraw the riotous Simbas and to release the civilians. At daybreak, Olenga sent a vehicle to bring Nothomb and Peter Rombaut to a meeting at Camp Ketele. Peter said Ernie planned to go with them, but someone had suggested he should stay behind because his tattoo was visible through his T-shirt. The Simbas might identify him as military. At the camp, Patrick asked Olenga for and received Simba guards as escorts for himself and Peter. The general gave them permission to drive freely around the city. Peter said Patrick had protested the attack on the American consulate. Olenga claimed not to have ordered it and promised to call the consulate. However, he had not contacted us.

During the morning, several groups of Simbas, with their usual shouts and chants, came to the consulate. One left with the green jeep.

"I hadn't really thought through our signal for an all-clear on the rescue operation," I told David. "What would we have done if the Simbas had taken the jeep, and we still wanted the operation to proceed? Although I haven't heard anything yet from the embassy, I assume they canceled it."[6] The sole vehicle left was Joan's white vw Bug with a flat tire.

David told me he had a call from the servant at his house. No one had disturbed it. The consulate employees and residence servants still had not shown up for work, but several of them called to ask how we were.

Elbéshir, the Sudanese consul general, called. "Do you know what is going on?" he asked me. His voice was verging on the hysterical.

"Not much more than I knew when I talked to you yesterday," I said. "Have you been able to contact General Olenga?"

"Not yet. I'm trying."

Elbéshir called back in the afternoon. "I've seen the general. We have permission to leave for the Sudan immediately."

"Did you say anything about us?" I asked.

"No, sorry, I've got to go now," and he hung up. We heard nothing further from them and assumed they had left the city for the Sudan.[7]

I called staff headquarters at Camp Ketele several times and asked for General Olenga but could not persuade anyone to put me through to him. I called Franken, the Red Cross representative and honorary

Dutch consul, and asked him to try to reach Olenga to tell him about what I called the "precarious position" of the American consulate. "Tell him it was attacked and pillaged of vehicles," I said. "Ask him to provide us with guards." I was concerned that without such protection, rogue Simbas might attack us. Franken said he had already sent a message on our behalf but had received no reply.

I called the Congolese Catholic archbishop of Stanleyville to try a similar approach. I could only reach a subordinate who acted confused and frightened. The subject of the harassment of American consular personnel was a risky subject for anyone to bring up with the rebels, and I was grateful that at least Nothomb, Rombaut, and Franken had spoken up for us.

A SHORT TIME after dusk on Friday, I was delighted to see Patrick, with his Simba escort, arrive in his Land Rover. He jumped out, and we embraced.

"God, it's good to see you," I said. He seemed like a lifelong friend. I had just seen him on Monday at Camp Ketele to discuss the curfew, but it seemed so long ago. At the consulate, we had seen only Simbas since then.

"With these Simba guards," said Patrick, "I can go anywhere."

His show of mobility and his ebullient mood contrasted sharply with my feeling of isolation and gloom. I did not mention the aborted Operation Flagpole. There had been no intention to pick up anybody but the American staff at the consulate. Patrick would have been one of the ones to bear the brunt of the reprisals if the rescue operation had been undertaken or launched.[8]

"General Olenga sent word he would meet with the European community tonight at our consulate. I'm here to take you."

Patrick did not say Olenga had said to include us in the meeting, and I suspected he had come to get us on his own initiative. I was delighted at the opportunity to join my colleagues and be active again. David and I drove with him back to his offices.

69

Consuls and other community leaders were gathered there. I greeted Paul Duqué, the Belgian vice consul, but he had little to say. Everyone was concerned with various aspects of the rebel takeover.

Doctors worried about the number of unburied dead bodies that threatened to spread disease. Businessmen said most trade had come to a halt. Food distribution was limited, and they thought this could lead to unrest among the Congolese. All were disturbed by the cut-off in communications. The only casualties mentioned among Europeans were the death of one man and the rape of one woman at The Immo-quateur the night before. A UN European employee was beaten badly by Simbas during the day. We learned that, besides Nothomb and Rombaut, businessmen Michel Faeles and José Romnée had Simba escorts and permission to circulate freely around the city. Romnée, a short, completely bald, former paratrooper, was head of the Petrofina oil operations for the region. An obvious man of action, he was the head of the local Belgian chamber of commerce, the *Fèdèration des Enterprises Congolaise* (FEC). Faeles was his right-hand person.

I was warned about the anti-American complexion of the rebellion. "You Americans should avoid contact with the Simbas," someone said. "The Simbas at Ketele continually shout anti-American slogans. They say they had fought American soldiers on their way to Stan." I dismissed this information as ridiculous at first, but then I remembered what Soumialot had said in Albertville and the warning I had previously sent to the embassy about the use of mercenaries. Soumialot had said he could not guarantee the safety of American and UN personnel while giving assurances that Europeans would be treated well and protected.

"Can someone approach Olenga and ask him to place guards at the consulates?" I asked. Several said they would try.

When it became clear Olenga was not coming, Patrick took us back to our consulate. I established contact with the embassy by SSB and relayed discreetly the day's events. Monty told me I should continue to try to contact local authorities. That cleared up any doubt I had in my mind whether I should risk some sort of recognition of the rebellion by dealing with the rebel authorities.[9]

When Monty finished, my wife's voice came on the air. Jo said she was monitoring the radio with Maj. Harold Asbury's son at his house.

"Evans and I are just fine," she said. "Do you know when you will be getting out?"

"No idea," I said. "We'll just have to wait for the situation to normalize. Love you. This is River Rat, out."

The sound of her voice made me glow inside, but it pained me to think of her knowing the danger I was in. I knew it was causing her as much pain as it was me.

David and I sat at my desk. It was the first time we had the opportunity to discuss the events of the past days and we had much to sort out.

"I've begun to keep a record of what's happening," David said.

"Good. Begin with the taking of our guards on August 1st," I said. "Each night, or whenever we have the chance, we can go over the day's events."

David began making notes on a yellow legal pad in a tiny scrawl that was indecipherable by anyone but him.[10] We discussed all that had taken place since the first of August. We reviewed what we knew to date about the rebels, where they came from, and who they were and tried to determine the character of their movement.

"Although we don't know it for certain," I said, "we can assume those who attacked us Wednesday came from Kindu, under General Olenga's command. From the intercepted messages and Radio Stan broadcasts, we know they are connected with Soumialot as CNL [*Comité Nationale de Libèration*] leader for the eastern Congo. And that is the connection to CNL President [Christophe] Gbenye, presumably in Brazzaville. We don't know much more than that. Is this the same group that took Uvira and is threatening Bukavu?"

"This group doesn't appear to be from the same ethnic groupings in that area," David said. "My contacts told me that Olenga is a Batetela from the Maniema, not from the eastern region, and most of his troops are from the same tribe. I suspect also that many former MNC-L [*Mouvement Nationale Congolaise–Lumumba*] followers of Lumumba, those who have been to communist China or Soviet-bloc countries for training, have joined the CNL and are now trying to become a part of this movement."

71

Lumumba was a Batetela. The Batetela and the related Bakusu and Basonge were the principal groups the Zanzibari Tippu Tib had relied upon to gather slaves and ivory almost a hundred years before. They were then cannibalistic and ferocious. They defected to the Belgians and helped defeat the Arabs in the Arab Wars of the early 1890s. Many Batetela served in the old *Force Publique* that was transformed into the ANC at independence. Dissident ANC, mainly Batetela, had formed the main military force for the Stanleyville secession. As for the MNC-L dissidents who had been in communist countries, I knew that David had close contacts in this group. It was this sort of information I had anticipated would make David a valuable partner.

"All we really know for certain about the rebellion," I said, "is that it is against the central government, pro-Lumumba, led by Olenga, with Gbenye and Soumialot in the background. The troops, calling themselves Simbas, are made up largely of Batetela. They employ various rituals and fetishes to maintain discipline. The movement has undetermined support from communist China and possibly Soviet-bloc countries and is definitely antagonistic toward the United States and the United Nations."

"We can assume their intention is to continue advancing against the ANC, which did not show any inclination to put up a serious fight in Stan," David said. "Now that they have captured the largest city in the northeast, their next target will be Léopoldville. They will undoubtedly also attack Bukavu in the east. That would give them access to the outside world. But, the biggest question for us is what do they intend to do about the official representatives of the United States? We are, after all, the most visible supporter of central government forces."

"It's not a favorable omen," I said, "that as far as we know, the first place they attacked on their way into Stan was the American consulate."

Under normal circumstances, we would have written up our assessments and sent them to our bosses in Léopoldville and Washington. However, we had locked ourselves out of our communications facilities, and we were limited anyway by our laborious one-time pad code system. We could do little to "report from behind the lines," as I had assumed Ambassador Godley had wanted us to do.

We left all the lights on at the consulate and retired to the residence. The scattered firing that continued in the city was muffled by the sound of the evening rain shower. What would the Congo have in store for us in the morning?

Back in my own bed after two nights sleeping in a chair, I slept better than I had in days.

SATURDAY MORNING, 8 August, a few of our Congolese employees came to work. David's driver, the one who had whispered for us to be still during the attack on the consulate on Wednesday, said he had talked to the rebels at the time of the attack. He had told them the door to the vault was electrified, trying to keep them away from it. "It didn't do much good," he said. "They knew enough to go outside and turn off the power. Those in the vault next to yours were frightened into opening the door. They were sent home, unharmed." He said Tata Paul, the old cook, was killed by a stray bullet as he bicycled home that day. The consulate guard who had been beaten by the paracommandos came hobbling up the driveway. His face was swollen and his head lumpy from the blows. He could barely walk on his battered limbs, but he was cheerful, happy to be alive. His companion, Yetu, did not show up.

Two Simbas, with adjutant rank on their stolen ANC uniforms, came to visit. David told me they were ex-ANC soldiers who had been guards previously at the consulate. They had been fired over a year ago for "quarreling." They acted as if we all belonged to the same fraternity. "Don't worry about anything," they told us. "We'll take good care of you."

David's household servant arrived and said that Simbas had come to the house. They had found the driver's khaki uniforms and were convinced ANC troops lived there. They were now waiting at the house for the return of the vice consul and planned "to kill him when he comes."

Someone called to say that Simbas were harassing UN local

73

employees. "The Simbas were mad that UN vehicles were not running properly." This did not surprise us because we had seen the way the Simbas treated vehicles.

Patrick Nothomb arrived and took David and me to the Belgian consulate. There we talked briefly about the possibility of getting permission for a Red Cross plane to come in. There was little new to discuss, so Patrick returned us to the consulate, saying he would return for us in the afternoon.[11]

At noon, I made SSB contact with the embassy. Monty was on. "UN here is prepared to send aircraft on a humanitarian mission to Stan," he said. "They will bring doctors and medical supplies and take out foreign nationals who wish leave. Conditions for this mission are safe landing at airport or at the port if boats to be used. UN staff to have freedom of movement. See if UN rep can get local authorities to agree."

"Have not repeat not yet been able to make contact with local authorities," I said. "Will continue trying. Will be making another attempt with other nationals this P.M. Believe local UN rep here not in good position make démarche re flight. In any case, need more details of proposed mission."

Monty added, "Have request here from Greek chargé on status Greek community."

"In meeting this morning, Greek consul here said his people all okay," I said. "If you have nothing further, this is River Rat, out."[12]

In the afternoon, Patrick came again and I went with him to his offices. David and I had decided that he should stay at the consulate to handle anything that might happen there. I relayed the embassy's message about the proposed UN mission to the assembled group. They drafted a note on the subject for Olenga. Those who had already been in touch with the rebel authorities thought the terms proposed would be difficult for them to accept. No one expected them to authorize the evacuation of civilians. If some kind of flight was approved, however, we looked on it as a step toward opening the city up to the outside.

When I returned to the consulate, David and I decided conditions were stabilizing enough to regain entry to the vault. We wanted

74

to reestablish secure radio contact with the embassy. Don and Jim climbed up into the attic and quickly chopped a hole through the concrete ceiling. They dropped down into the vault and opened the door. Dust from chopping the hole covered the empty file cabinets and radio equipment. They fired up the radio equipment while I drafted a brief situation report. They encoded and sent it out.[13]

I made another SSB contact at dusk, but I had little further information to convey. Jo came on again for a brief chat. David, Jim, Don, and I had a few drinks, prepared supper, and went to bed. This had been the least disturbing day we had all week. I was encouraged with the few steps we had taken toward regaining our ability to function as a consulate.

DAVID AND I went to another meeting at the Belgian consulate on Sunday morning, 9 August. "Olenga appears to be backing away from contacting the European community," Romnée told us. "His only contact with the consular corps in the past day was with the Sudanese. They haven't been seen. We presume they left for the Sudan."

We were drawn to the window by the noise of a crowd of Simbas beginning to gather outside. They were running around the streets below, waving their weapons, excited about something. They fired a few shots.

"I'd better get you back to the consulate," Patrick said. We hurried down the back of the building and Patrick drove us to the consulate. He dumped us at the front door and sped off with his Simba guard.

After lunch, Patrick returned. "Things have quieted down," he said. "Come, we'll go back and continue our meeting." David stayed at the consulate. When we arrived, I suggested to Patrick, more as a thought than a request, that perhaps we should seek asylum at the Belgian consulate. Patrick indicated he did not think that was a very good idea, and I dropped the subject. He had problems enough of his own without taking on the Americans. We learned no one had been able to deliver the note, drafted the previous day, about the UN flight. Another note was drafted to present to Olenga; we requested a

75

guarantee of physical security for the expatriate community and his cooperation in returning economic life to normal. A group of consuls planned on presenting the note in person at Camp Ketele.

"That sounds fine to me," I said, expecting to be among those accompanying the note.

"You'd better not go to Ketele," Romnéc said. "It's a real mess out there. The Simbas are railing at the Americans even more." I respected his judgment, knowing his background as a paratrooper and his experience in the Congo. I returned to the consulate.

David had been on the SSB with Léopoldville and had relayed several messages from those evacuated from Stanleyville to those who had stayed behind.

Patrick called to say the consular group had not met with Olenga, but a general meeting with him was now scheduled for three P.M. Monday. "I think the authorities are ready to be cooperative," he said before hanging up.

I talked to Monty Stearns on the radio later that evening. "We think our stay here will be long and complicated," I said. "It will take time to sort things out. We may be able to carry on limited operations. Please tell my number one to go to Jerome." I was trying to tell him that Jo should return to the United States to join our other three children in Jerome, Arizona, where we had planned on spending our home leave.

I left the radio on. Jo came on the air later. "They were trying to locate a general you know here with the first name of Jerome," she said. "I told them it was where you wanted us to go. Why can't I stay here? I don't want to go home."

"It looks as if we are here for the long haul. You'll be better off with the kids." There would be many ups and downs, and I wanted her far away from the Congo. The Jerome they had tried to contact was General Anany, whom I knew from our work together liquidating our contract for ANC aviation.

I drafted a brief report and gave it to Jim to send.[14] "We had an incoming message," he said. "But it's for the system with the crypto machine we destroyed. Someone out there doesn't know there's an emergency here and is sending us normal traffic."

The evening rains came. It was quiet and almost peaceful. In spite of my contacts with colleagues, I still felt isolated. The rebels were treating the Americans differently from the other expatriates. Although we had been threatened, we had not been physically harmed. The dignity of the consulate and its personnel had been damaged in the attacks and by the theft of our vehicles. We were making some progress, however, in normalizing our status in our contacts with our colleagues. The painful knot of fear in my stomach eased. I felt that whatever was going to happen would take time to play out. I was relieved to think Jo and Evans were going home to rejoin the other children. I wanted them away from it all.

Persona non Grata

Days 6 and 7: Monday, 10 August, and Tuesday, 11 August 1964

MOST OF THE CONSULATE AND CULTURAL CENTER LOCAL employees and the residence servants came to the consulate Monday morning, 10 August, for work and pay. They had not suffered any serious harm, though it must have been widely known among their neighbors, and consequently the rebels, that they worked for the Americans. I admired their loyalty. Their presence was another sign of a return to more normal circumstances.

There was no work for them. They stayed around, waiting for me to tell them what to do. We made a list of our employees, personal servants, and stolen vehicles to give to Peter Rombaut, the honorary British vice consul, in case he took over for us. David Grinwis's driver walked to the Volkswagen agency in town and came back with a spare tire for Joan Allen's Bug. This would give the consulate one operating vehicle. "We can't use it until we get a Simba escort like Rombaut and Patrick Nothomb have," I said. "Meanwhile, all we can do is sit here and wait."

That afternoon, Nothomb took me to the meeting the rebel general, Nicholas Olenga, had scheduled with the consular corps and business leaders. When I arrived, the chamber of commerce meeting room at The Immoquateur was filled with a large group of expatriates seated in rows of chairs. They were facing several men, and I assumed the man seated behind a table was Olenga. He was dressed in a loose-fitting khaki Belgian red-tabbed general's uniform, a sword and pistol at his belt. He was tall and lanky with a small goatee. His small eyes peered out from under his visor cap into the crowd before him. Behind him were about a dozen rebel officers in ANC uniforms, adorned with palm leaves and animal skins. Next to them were a half-dozen older, amply-proportioned women. They wore U.S. Army helmet liners, painted UN blue, left over from the UN peacekeeping force. They wore bits of military clothing adorned with palm leaves over long dresses and waved fetishes on sticks. I quietly took a seat in the back.

Olenga made a brief opening statement in simple French. "I wish to establish good relations with the European community," he said. "I want to give assurances that you will be protected from harm. I ask for your cooperation. The present conflict is among Congolese and does not involve Europeans."

The spokesman for the civilian group was José Romnée, the tough former paratrooper. He presented a list of requirements to be met for the restoration of normalcy. "First is security. Guards are required to protect business and other installations around the city. Several Europeans have been beaten by the Simbas."

Olenga appeared disturbed by this assertion and said any Simba out of line would be punished. He agreed to provide guards for key establishments. For transportation needs, Romnée suggested each organization be allowed a minimum of one vehicle to continue operating. Olenga agreed to establish a mechanism to accomplish this. Romnée said the city needed to open up contact with the area around Stanleyville and beyond to supply the city with foodstuffs.

"We have six airplanes in our possession," Olenga broke in. "We

79

will be setting up an airline network in the area controlled by the Popular Army as soon as we can find pilots. But, no one can leave Stan until the whole country is conquered by the Popular Army. Telegrams to Léo will be permitted after submission to the PTT [post, telegraph, and telephone] for censorship. All messages should state everyone is in good health. I decree now that all priccs on goods will be at the price they were at independence. All taxes are hereby rescinded."

"Such a drastic move would disrupt commerce," Romnée claimed.

"We will establish a mixed commission to discuss prices and taxes," Olenga countered.

With that, the meeting broke up. I thought it had been a reasonable discussion of the issues between the rebels and the expatriate community. Everyone left except the UN and consular corps members who were to meet separately with Olenga. Present besides myself were the Belgian consul and vice consul, and honorary consuls for the United Kingdom, France, Greece, Cyprus, Italy, and the Netherlands. Rosso, the acting head of the United Nations, was trying to be inconspicuous. No one was there representing the Sudanese consulate general.

Nothomb, the Belgian consul, made the lead presentation, calling for the establishment of a secure environment for the European community by permitting consulates to operate normally. Olenga replied that there were too few of his soldiers in town to provide adequate protection for all.

At this point, I stood up and said: "I am the American consul. I would like to support what the Belgian consul . . ."

Olenga's angry shouts cut me off. "We have been fighting American troops in the field. We killed 250 soldiers from the United States at Wanie Rukula." He did not look directly at me but addressed the others. His small eyes narrowed.

The outburst stunned me. I tried to keep calm. I managed to voice an expression of doubt, in none too loud a voice, about the presence of American troops.

"I will show you the identity papers found on their bodies," Olenga roared. He raved on about thousands of American troops around Kindu and bombardments by American airplanes. He said he would invade the United States after capturing Léopoldville and obtaining the necessary transport. Each time he mentioned "The United States of America," the group around him, apparently recognizing only those words in French, would repeat twice in chorus "*Etats . . . Unis . . . d'Amèrique.*" The fat women screeched unintelligible words and waved their fetishes menacingly in my direction. I knew that during the Stanleyville secession, the women's groups had the reputation of being the most brutal against Congolese and Europeans alike. I had a brief flash through my mind of the claque of old women knitting and cheering at the guillotine during the French Revolution.

Then, abruptly changing back to a calm and controlled mode, Olenga said, still not looking directly at me, "We are breaking relations with the United States, and the American consulate staff will be expelled immediately."

"What about the security of the other Americans?" I ventured.

"I have nothing against American missionaries," Olenga said, still not meeting my eyes. "They can stay. We are only against the American military intervention in our country. I know that the American consulate gave advice to ANC military headquarters. The American consulate called for reinforcements from Léo."

The Simbas around Olenga shouted abuses at me. Olenga cut them off with a gesture. Nothomb asked Olenga—as a diversionary move I was sure—if he would approve the arrival of a World Health Organization (WHO) airplane.

"I can approve it, *en principe*," he said. Obviously not knowing WHO was a UN agency, he added, "But I will not tolerate any UN presence or operation." Olenga pointed to a black-bearded captain in his entourage and said he would be responsible for liaison between him and the consular corps. He would be specifically responsible for the protection of the American consulate. Still in a friendly vein, Olenga agreed to the free movement of consuls but made it clear the American consular personnel were "a special case."

Olenga then announced he was establishing a People's Republic with a civilian government headed by Alphonse Kinghis. Victor Benanga would be in the government with one representative each from Ulele and Kibali-Ituri provinces that, together with the truncated

Orientale, made up the former Orientale Province. This made it clear the rebels did not recognize the recent reorganization of the provinces. In an aside, Olenga assured the consuls that there were no Russian or Chinese advisers in his movement. Olenga promised to give a formal reply to a note from the consuls on all the subjects discussed and terminated the meeting. He and his entourage left.

The consuls gathered around and congratulated me on the prospect of leaving Stanleyville.

"You are sure lucky to be getting out," Peter Rombaut said. "I'll handle the consulate's affairs."

"That's very good of you," I said. "But we'll have to see if they really intend to carry out the expulsion order. I don't really see any practical way of getting out. Maybe if a Red Cross or WHO plane comes in. In any case, it's probably some time off."

We discussed the other topics that had been brought up. The consuls said they did not think they had made much of an impression on Olenga regarding the conditions necessary to reestablish economic activity. They were concerned about the cut-off in contacts with the outside. During other times of trouble in Stanleyville, effective, if not entirely free, links were maintained with Léopoldville and other points outside the area and country. We agreed the situation would not change soon. For now, we were all isolated and forced to live with the Simbas.

"I doubt the rebel military authorities will turn over any meaningful power to a civilian government," Michel Faeles said. "Kinghis is about the worst choice I can imagine as president." I was told Kinghis was a leader of the anarchist Kitawalist religious sect, a Congolese outgrowth of the Watchtower Society; he had just been released by the rebels from two years in prison. Kinghis had been mayor of Stanleyville under the secessionist regime. He was considered unbalanced, fanatical, and dangerous. Benanga, I knew, was leader of the most radical wing of the local MNC-L party. He was responsible for the 22 June raid on the *gendarmerie* camp. A quantity of arms undoubtedly went to the *jeunesse* and contributed to the rebel takeover of the city.

Returning to the consulate, I was still shaken by my encounter with Olenga. I learned that Jim Stauffer and Don Parkes had discovered their transmitter was not functioning, and they were not sure they could repair it. In view of the uncertain security situation, we decided to close the vault door again and wait for another time to attempt repairs.

The only way we could communicate now was by SSB radio. I reached Monty Stearns at the embassy in Léopoldville and quickly gave him the news. "Met with General Olenga today. He said he is breaking relations with the United States and wishes to expel the staff of the American consulate. However, do not believe you should make any special transport arrangements. I will contact you when I can learn anything more. This is River Rat, clear." I did not want to linger on the radio because I feared Simbas would come in.

David and I discussed the meeting. I told him Kinghis had been appointed president. "He's the guy who was caught trying to crucify one of his fellow government ministers when the central authorities came to arrest him," David said. "He's definitely not a nice guy." We agreed the composition of the government did not bode well for us, or for any improvement for expatriates in the city.

David shared my view that the expulsion order did not mean we would be leaving soon. "It just serves to further isolate us from our colleagues," I said. "What I'm afraid of is that the airing of charges that American aircraft and troops were involved in fighting might encourage roving Simbas to attack us at the consulate."

"American T-28s are certainly being used against them," David said. "And our transport planes are flying supply missions, but I'm not aware of any American ground troops."

"We have a few advisers from COMISH," I said. "An American officer was in Kindu with Lt. Col. Leonard Mulamba before its fall. As for the accusation that we were advising ANC headquarters, we certainly called there many times, and I relayed Commandant Banza's request for reinforcements. Léo evidently responded with that para company the day of the evacuation. All that information might have been relayed to the rebels by defecting or captured ANC troops." We may not have been guilty of all the charges, but the accusations were not entirely without foundation.

The anti-American character of the rebellion had become starkly

83

evident. It was beginning to sink in that we were potential hostages for such imagined or actual activity against the rebels by the U.S. government. I believed that being declared, in effect, *persona non grata* might not have any practical effect.

In contrast to his ranting against Americans, we noted Olenga's conciliatory attitude toward the rest of the expatriate community. He must have recognized that after four years of independence, the economic and commercial activity in the Congo was still totally dependent on European personnel and organizations. Without the active cooperation of expatriates, the economy would cease to operate. There would be no beer, no cigarettes, no petroleum products, no repair of vehicles, and little food. Petty trade was in the hands of Africans, but they depended on goods supplied by expatriates.

"As for Olenga's statement that he has no Russian or Chinese advisers," David said, "I have no evidence of that either way. What we know is that Soumialot and other rebels received money from the ChiCom embassy in Bujumbura. Also, many Congolese dissidents went to China or on Russian-financed overseas training missions, and they have undoubtedly gravitated toward this rebel movement. It remains to be seen how well they are received by these rebels."

David took careful notes on the day's events and our thoughts.

Because we no longer had our communications facility to maintain, I slept in my bedroom in the residence. David, Jim, and Don used the guest bedrooms.

THE CONGOLESE EMPLOYEES and servants who showed up Tuesday morning appeared more nervous than they had on Monday. They must have heard of yesterday's encounter with Olenga and knew about the anti-American flavor of the meeting. They remained loyal, however, and came to work. We intended to use the CIA money David had retrieved from his house to pay the consular and cultural center workers. I called Peter to give him further details about handling our affairs.

David called Dr. Alex Barlovatz and asked him to come to the consulate to treat an annoying bronchial cough I had developed from my resumed smoking. I also wanted him to tell us about conditions in the city. We had heard a rumor that executions were beginning to take place at the monument honoring Patrice Lumumba, as had happened during Antoine Gizenga's secession. From where Alex lived, he could see out on the plaza where the framed photo of the martyr was located; he would be able to keep us informed if events unfolded there.

Mr. Lambert, the contractor I had called to repair the damage done to the consulate by the rebel attack, arrived with his crew. Bullets had shattered almost all the glass in the windows along the front of the consulate offices. The crew started to replace the glass and repaired the broken door. I asked Lambert if he could have one of his men bring down the American flag that was still flying at half-standard.

David and I composed a message in French on a PTT telex form detailing the meeting with Olenga and his decision to expel the members of the American consulate. "We have been ordered to be expelled by the authorities," we said, "but do not recommend that any special transportation arrangements be made." I gave the telegram to my driver who walked to the PTT office. He returned a short time later saying that it had been accepted by the Simba officer in charge of censorship.[1]

I went to my office and made a rough draft of a note of protest to General Olenga regarding the treatment we had received to date at the hands of the rebels. It served to gather my thoughts on the events and get down specific complaints on activities of the Simbas. In it, I protested the attack on the consulate, the theft of our vehicles, and the threats made on our lives and property. I denied the presence of American troops in the field and demanded proof of identity papers allegedly found on their bodies. I also asked for official notification of our expulsion order.[2]

I saw a car drive up the driveway. Putting the draft in my briefcase, I went out to see who it was. Ernie Houle, with two Belgians and several Simba escorts, got out of the car. I had not seen Ernie since he had left for The Immoquateur on Tuesday, 4 August, the day of the evacuation. I had made no effort to get him to the consulate

85

after advising the embassy in Léopoldville against the helicopter res-cue. In the rush of other events, I had not thought of bringing him to the consulate, and he had not asked to come.

"It's great to see you," I said, embracing him warmly, welcoming him back into our family.

He mumbled something in reply, probably embarrassed by the unaccustomed show of affection.

Dr. Barlovatz arrived at that moment, alone in his car; he was apparently brave or brazen enough to dispense with a Simba escort.

Still standing outside the consulate, we had scarcely begun to talk when a car full of yelling Simbas drove up the consulate driveway. They pointed excitedly at the American flag that a contractor's man was bringing down from the pole. They shouted the usual "Simba! Simba!" and "*mai mai, Mulele mai.*" Then they yelled "ANC, ANC," pointing into the consulate, meaning, I gathered, that they must search the premises for ANC soldiers. I tried to explain this was a consular establishment, protected by diplomatic and consular immunity. "Gen-eral Olenga himself," I said, "told the consular corps yesterday that the consulates should be respected." Ignoring me and what I was saying, either unable or unwilling to understand my French, they streamed past me into the consulate, spreading out into each office. I followed. They came to the closed vault door. "*Fungua, fungua!*" they shouted.

"It can't be opened," I said. I pointed to the hole where the knob was shorn off. One of them swung back his rifle as if to hit me. I braced myself for the blow. He hesitated and exchanged some words with his comrades. They appeared undecided about what to do. I heard the words "Ketele" and "*général.*"

Leaving two of their force behind, the other Simbas climbed into their car and drove off in the direction of Camp Ketele. The five of us from the consulate sat on the front steps with our two guards. Lambert and his crew had left as soon as the Simbas arrived. Barlovatz and the two Belgians who had brought Ernie said they would follow the Simbas to Camp Ketele and try to contact Olenga.

The two Simbas who stayed behind muttered the word "*Amèri-kani*" in most disparaging tones and threatened and poked at us with their automatic rifles. We continued to sit quietly on the front steps. I had no idea what was to come next. What would the trip to Camp Ketele produce? Hopefully a reintroduction of some sense.

In about a half-hour, the car with the Simbas came back up the driveway, followed by a big truck. As they pulled up to the steps with a screech of brakes, about a dozen armed Simbas piled out of the truck, led by an officer with a major's rank on his shoulder. He had a large fur piece topping his cap and carried a heavy Belgian FAL automatic rifle, a standard North Atlantic Treaty Organization (NATO) weapon easily identified by its distinctive handle on top. He came up to me and glared in my face. I felt our fate would worsen, not improve.

"I fight Americans to get here," he said in barely understandable French. "But they not harm me. *Mulele mai* protects. We kill many Americans. Nothing touch me. See how." He opened the breech of his weapon to verify a cartridge was in the chamber, rammed it shut, cocked it, and laid it at my feet. The Simbas crowded around, yelling encouragement. "Pick up, pick up," he shouted. "Bullets no harm. Go! Do it!"

I stood still. "I can't," was all I could think of saying.

The major shrugged his shoulders in disgust, picked up the FAL and motioned me into the consulate. He headed straight for the locked vault door. "*Fungua, fungua!*" he shouted, pointing the FAL at me. I stood by the door, not knowing what to do. Someone handed me a cold chisel and a hammer. I put the chisel to the door and began to hit it with the hammer. My work was desultory, the chisel biting ineffectively into the steel of the door. The Simbas crowded into David's office shouted encouragement at my ineffective efforts. I received a few glancing blows on the shoulders from their weapons.

David came in. "They're beating the boys quite badly out there," he whispered to me. "Hurry!"

I began to work with more determination. I drove the chisel into the crack between the door and the jamb and pounded on it with the hammer, then pried it back. After several tries, to my amazement, the door popped open. I feared what the Simbas would do when they saw inside the vault. I had no idea what they were expecting, but I thought it would look exactly like the spy communications center it was.

87

The major pushed me into the room ahead of him, murmuring *"Mai, mai."* He peered in. The filing cabinets, desks, and racks filled with radio equipment were covered in ghost-gray dust from the hole punched through the ceiling. It looked spooky to me. The major took a quick look around, presumably looking for hiding ANC soldiers, and, finding none, came out.

"Search everywhere. Find ANC!" he shouted to the Simbas. He motioned for me to come with him. He pointed to the terrazzo floor and struck it with his FAL. "ANC! ANC!" he yelled at me, as if looking for a trapdoor in the floor. He pointed at my wristwatch, a gold one. I took it off to hand it to him. "No, no," he said and pointed to the ground. I dropped it there. He picked it up and put it into his pocket. He pointed at my glasses, and I dropped them to the floor. He lifted his booted foot and came down on them, grinding the glass into the floor. I was kneeling on the floor at this point, and he swung his rifle at me, hitting me on top of the head with the barrel. It bounced high. I felt only the shock, little pain.

Giving up on finding anyone underground, he pointed to the ceiling. I understood he wanted to search the attic. I found an opening in my bedroom closet, and he motioned for me to climb up. I did, and he followed. We walked on the uncovered rafters. I tried to steer him away from the hole punched through the ceiling into the vault, thinking he would find it suspicious. He pointed at the necktie I was wearing. I took it off and threw it away. He soon gave up on finding ANC soldiers and motioned for me to jump back down through the opening. In doing so, I caught my hand on a nail and tore it. Blood flowed.

We went outside. I saw the Simbas playing a game with my colleagues. David, Don, Jim, and Ernie were standing, and the four flag poles from the reception area and my office were by their sides; the ends of the two American flags and the two blue consular flags were stuffed in their mouths. Inside the circle, two Simbas were riding on secretarial chairs with castors, rolling back and forth like in carnival bumper-cars, crashing into them, shouting with glee every time a person was knocked down. The Simbas standing around forced the unfortunate victim to retake his place. They were yelling *"mangez, mangez"* ("eat, eat"), and beating them with rifles and with the flat of

88

bayonets, jeering and laughing at the sport. I was made to join the circle. I was jostled a few times by the chair-riding Simbas and a few blows struck me, but there were no other flags for me to chew on. Then the major motioned us to the large truck they had brought. The clasped-hand sign of USAID on the door showed it had been supplied under COMISH, our military assistance program to the Congo.

"To the Lumumba monument," screamed the major. That was where I had heard they were killing civilians and captured ANC soldiers. We were pushed and prodded, over the high stake panels, into the back of the truck. The flags and poles were thrown up after us. Several Simbas climbed in. As the truck started up and went down the driveway, a Simba tore a piece of dried fish, not normally consumed by Europeans, from the bundles strewn on the floor. He pushed the piece toward me. "*Mangez, mangez,*" he shouted. I picked it up and chewed on it. I tasted nothing. I was more concerned with where they were taking us. "Lumumba, Lumumba," our guards yelled as the truck sped down the road leading east toward Camp Ketele. I knew we were coming to the intersection with a road on the left leading to downtown and the Lumumba monument. I glanced down and saw the gold tie clasp still clipped to my shirt after I had taken off my tie in the attic. Jo had given it to me for my birthday last year. I pulled it off and threw it to the floor of the truck. "Not much use for this now," I muttered.

I looked up to see where we were headed. The truck was rolling at high speed toward the intersection. The Simbas in the back leered at us, waving their weapons, still shouting "Lumumba." They could either continue to Ketele or take the turn to the left to the monument. We reached the intersection and continued straight on without a pause. I thanked our luck—or something, anything—that led us away from the monument. I hoped General Olenga would be at the camp to deliver us from our tormentors.

When we drove into the camp, I realized any deliverance was not going to be easy. I had been warned against going there, but I had not imagined what it was like. Hundreds of motley dressed Simbas were milling around the large yard. When we drove in, they rushed the truck with howls of "*Amèrikani, Amèrikani.*" The truck drove on

89

with the crowd following. Dead bodies lay barely discernible amid the mud and debris. I saw the two Belgians, who had brought Ernie to the consulate earlier, by the side of a building. They gave us a look of helpless sorrow.

The truck stopped. The horde of Simbas pressed close. The major shoved them aside. We were pushed roughly out of the truck, along with the flags and staffs. I could see bodies writhing on the ground, caked with mud, trussed up like chickens, badly beaten, apparently still alive. A few yards away, several officers were seated behind a table and ragged men stood before them; it looked like trials were in process.

We were pushed to one side. Our Simba squad surrounded us, keeping the mob from getting too close. The major pointed to our feet, and we understood we were to remove our shoes and socks. When we did, they bounced their bayonets at our feet, forcing us to dance to avoid being cut. Luckily, it was not a serious game. No one was cut, and it did not last long.

I could not see clearly at that distance without the glasses the major had destroyed, but I thought I recognized the man behind the desk as the bearded captain Olenga had appointed the day before as liaison with the consular corps, specifically charged to care for the American consulate. "Aren't you the one who was to protect us?" I yelled over to him.

"You Americans are fighting us," he shouted back. "Why do you come to the Congo to interfere in our affairs?"

Some of the Simbas milling around us backed up his statement by describing and acting out how American airplanes had attacked them and how they had shot them down. "RAT-A-TAT-TAT," they shouted, pointing their weapons or fingers in the air. The major did his trick again with his big FAL automatic rifle, throwing it at my feet and demanding I pick it up. "I can't do it," I said again.

"Aha," he said, "that just proves it." He picked it up and strode off. For some reason the beatings ceased, and we gathered close to each other. A big black bearded Congolese in civilian clothes stood a short distance off. "That's Kinghis, the new president," David whispered to me. The bearded captain, Olenga's liaison man to the consular corps, strode over and motioned us gruffly through the door of the headquarters building. Our flags, shoes, and socks were thrown in after us. After he entered the room and closed the door on the mob, he said in a pleasant tone: "Don't worry about a thing. I'll talk to the general and get everything straightened out. Are you all right?"

"*Ça va, ça va*" ("okay, okay") was all I could manage. He left the room. It was a relief to be away from the noise of the mob and the beatings. I lit a cigarette and looked about. Everybody looked shaken but physically okay. I had some blood on my face where I had wiped my brow with my torn hand. The room, a sort of anteroom, was filled with what looked like booty—cases of food, furniture, radios. My heart rate began to slow, but the knot of pain in my stomach remained. We put our socks and shoes back on.

A young soldier of medium height and build came into the room. He was dressed neatly in an officer's uniform, devoid of Simba trimmings, with a white lanyard around his neck attached to his pistol. "I'm Commandant Sengha, Oscar," he said in French, "in charge of General Olenga's secretariat." His manner was open and cordial. "I'm glad to have the opportunity to talk to Americans. American policy in the Congo is most puzzling to us. Why are you interfering in our affairs?"

"We have no intention of interfering in Congolese internal affairs," I said. "We are supporting a strong central government and wish to help rebuild the economy." I guessed he was in his early twenties, sporting a scraggly beard, and probably educated at the lycée or high-school level. He talked to us in good French for perhaps a half-hour, asking questions about the United States. "All will be well with you," he said as he left. "Don't worry, I'll see that you are not harmed." Talking to him calmed me. The brutal treatment we had just experienced could easily have led to more serious harm.

General Olenga next came in, accompanied by the major who had brought us to the camp. Olenga looked drowsy, as if he had just been roused from sleep. He gave the major a small bag of something, perhaps hemp or money, which appeared to me to be a reward for something, perhaps for bringing us here rather than to the monument. Olenga turned to me, addressing me directly for the first time. "I am

91

sorry for taking so long to see you," he told me in a tired and soft voice, stroking his forehead. "I have a bad headache and so much work to do. I see you have blood on your head. Are you all right?"

"It's nothing," I blurted out. Then, thinking I should not make light of my wound, said, "It isn't too bad. It will heal."

"Major Nasor was drunk," the general said. "He was not following orders. I want to apologize for his behavior. I want you to operate normally. I am making arrangements for your protection. I do not wish to break diplomatic relations with the United States." He called in the major and told him to provide us with a twenty-four-hour guard at the consulate. They both left the room.

"I suppose that means he no longer wants to expel us," I said to David.

"Sounds like it," David said. "In any case, I don't see how they could have gotten us out of here."

Sengha came back in the room. "We're going to take you back to the consulate," he said. He led us outside, bringing our flags and poles. We climbed into two cars. A truck was behind us with a half-dozen Simbas. Arriving at the consulate, Sengha and the Simbas conducted another search of the premises. When he entered the vault, Sengha touched the communications equipment, handling a few of the knobs and switches.

"It's broken down and doesn't work," I said.

"I was a communications man at the PTT," he said. "I can repair it."

We returned to the residence side, and our servants brought out food and drinks. Sengha was relaxed and joined us. The guard squad sat apart and refused to take anything. Sengha said they would be using the kitchen to prepare their own food. After some discussion, it was decided the Simbas would sleep in the consulate, and we would stay in the residence. In a cheerful mood after the drinks and food, Sengha said good night and left. The Simbas guards hovered around us, trying not to be intimidating but making it clear they were our guards. They spoke almost no French. We communicated with gestures. For the more complicated discussions, our servants translated.

We had some more drinks and relaxed without saying much. We had achieved one goal after our ordeal; we now had guards at the consulate, but we still could not leave the consulate. We were under house arrest.

I could not use the ssb while the Simbas were in the consulate. We had heard tales of Simbas looking for radios they called *phonies,* which they claimed could be used "to call in troops."

Before we could settle in for the night, a car drove up the driveway. David and I went outside to see who it was. It was the newly appointed president, Alphonse Kinghis, who climbed out. He was an impressively large man, with a full black beard, and talked in a deep booming voice.

"Where is the vice consul's big car?" he asked.

"All our vehicles have been stolen by the Simbas," I told him. Kinghis turned and got back into his car and drove off without another word.

I finally found a chance to tend to my wounds. I washed the blood from my hand and discovered it was only a scratch. My head ached from the rifle barrel hitting me, and I could feel a few sore spots from the blows. The important thing was that we were all alive.

Before turning in, David and I went over the day's events and he jotted down notes. We had no difficulty in remembering vividly all the things that had happened to us that day. There had been some moments during the day when I had thought we would not survive. The knot of fear had returned in my stomach. I realized there would be no escape from our tormentors, no quick expulsion. We would be staying in Stanleyville to see things to the end. We could do little to influence events. We had to meet each day as best we could.

The night rain brought stillness and calm. The river flowed calmly on.

House Arrest

Days 8 through 16: Wednesday, 12 August,

through Thursday, 20 August 1964

"I DON'T LIKE HAVING THE SSB AROUND FOR THE SIMBAS TO find," I said to David at breakfast on Wednesday, 12 August. Sam, our number-two household servant, had taken over cooking duties after the unfortunate death of Tata Paul. "The rebels are so spooky about *phonies*. It's just too dangerous for us to use the radio or even have one around. I'm calling the camp to see if we can get rid of it."

When I called Camp Ketele, President Alphonse Kinghis answered the phone. I did not want to talk to him, but I had no choice. "Can you arrange for someone to come to the consulate to pick up our radio, our *phonie*?" I asked.

"I'll come pick it up," he said brusquely and hung up.

With our wireless radio not working, and my reluctance to use the SSB voice transceiver, the only way we could now communicate with our embassy in Léopoldville was by commercial telex. Yesterday we had telexed Olenga's remark about our expulsion while we were at the chamber of commerce. I had also confirmed it by SSB. Now, I wanted to inform the embassy of Olenga's decision not to expel us and that guards were at the consulate. I typed the message in French on the PTT telegram form and requested instructions.

"I'm requesting instructions," I told David, "to encourage the embassy to communicate with me. Also, assuming the rebels read the message, it conveys the impression I don't make decisions on my own."

"Yes, that may come in handy in the future," David said. "We're just lowly functionaries here, unable to act on our own, even under pressure."

I gave the cable to my driver to take to the PTT building. When he returned, he said, "They took it and figured up the cost, but then they said the PTT was closed down and gave it back to me. Here it is." I put it in my briefcase for use when and if the PTT opened again.

Commandant Oscar Sengha, our protector yesterday while we were at Camp Ketele, drove up the driveway and strode briskly into the residence. "I have just come from the vice consul's house," he said. "Would you be interested in making a deal with me to use it?"

"Certainly," David replied readily. "We need to draw up a written agreement for you to rent the house. You can pay me for any of the food or liquor you use." He asked the receptionist, Antoine Lingili, to go to the house to make an inventory. "I might eventually like to buy the refrigerator and other appliances and furniture," Sengha said as he was leaving.

"I had already written off the house and its contents to roving Simbas," David told me. "The property would now be protected. Besides, we're doing a favor for the one rebel who seems to show us basic respect and treats us decently."

David and I had decided, and had gotten Sengha's approval, to send Jim Stauffer, Don Parkes, and Ernie Houle to their apartments at the Immoquateur. It complicated matters to have them around when there was nothing for them to do, and we felt they would be safer and more comfortable there. Patrick Nothomb, who had stopped to check on us at the consulate, agreed to take them. Patrick had heard about our rough handling by the Simbas yesterday. "It doesn't look like you are leaving after all," he said. "Since you can't leave the

95

consulate, Peter Rombaut and I will look after Americans around here. We will come by here as often as possible." He left with our three staff members.

In the early afternoon, a car drove up the driveway, and President Kinghis got out. "Are you the only ones here?" he asked without formality. When we said we were, he told David and me to get into his car. He did not mention the SSB I had phoned about earlier. Our guards made no move to object to our leaving. Without a word, he drove us into town and pulled up alongside a large red brick building that I had not seen before. To me it looked suspiciously like a prison.

"It's the Stanleyville Central Prison," David whispered to me. It was like a castle, with a block-long, faded red brick front wall, topped by crenellated edges and towers at the corners. I had never been in a prison and in no way wanted to go into this one. Kinghis shoved us quickly through a small door cut into the large wooden gates of the entryway. Inside was a small reception area. We were hurried through another door leading into a vast interior courtyard. Kinghis turned us over to someone who appeared to be in charge.

"But this is no way to treat consuls, diplomats," I started to say.

Kinghis paid no attention. "I will see to your case later," he said and left.

"The prison was cleared of prisoners this morning," the prison director told us as he led us to the left, across the courtyard. "They were all killed. The last few days have been bloody and awful. All is quiet now." This in no way put to rest my foreboding at being in prison.

He led us to a door, opened it, and ushered us in. On a table in the middle of the room, lay two young Simbas, asleep, clutching spears. They woke up as we entered, grabbed their weapons, and staggered outside. The official told us to make ourselves comfortable and left, closing the door and locking it. I looked about. The walls appeared to be splattered with blood. The plaster was dirty and cracked, revealing raw brick beneath. It looked like a dungeon of a medieval castle.

I looked at David; we exchanged sighs, helpless. There was nothing to say or do. We could speculate on our fate, but we had little to go on. Kinghis's reputation was such that we could expect anything. Was he acting on Olenga's orders or knowledge? What were his intentions? We slumped on the dirty floor, our backs on the crumbling wall, clutching our knees.

We did not move. There was no noise.

"I'm glad we sent the others to the apartments," I said in a low voice, more to break the silence than to make conversation. "How would they have reacted?" I could imagine they would have been even more unnerved or frightened than we were at being thrown in prison. I was thankful not to have that additional burden to worry about.

"I worry about what they may do next," David said. "If they can put us in prison, they can do anything. With Kinghis in charge . . . God knows what he has in mind."

What we did not verbalize was what "anything" meant: beaten, killed, mutilated, . . . anything.

I sat, not talking further because all thoughts led to where I did not want to go. There was nothing constructive to say.

About midafternoon, someone poked his head in through the door. "What are you doing here?" he asked. David whispered to me that it was a local radio announcer.

"I don't know," I said. "You know diplomats should not be treated like this."

"Yes, but . . . ," he muttered, looking confused. He left and shut the door.

Our stark cell turned chilly as evening approached. There was no furniture other than the table and no bedding. It was quiet outside. The shock of being in prison began to wear off, and anger and frustration welled up in me.

To break my thoughts, I got up to explore our surroundings. A small courtyard gave out from an open door in our cell. It must be a private exercise area for what was undoubtedly the VIP quarters. Maybe Patrice Lumumba, who had been in this prison, had stayed here. This area was probably reserved for more important prisoners, Europeans probably, I thought. Exercise was far from my mind. I came back to sit on the floor in silence.

97

The prison director opened the door and said for me to come with him. He led me along the vast open courtyard, through the guard station, and outside to a parked car. Inside were Commandant Sengha and several companions, all well armed.

"Well, what are you doing here?" he asked. "I came by the consulate, and they told me you were here."

"I have no idea," I said. "President Kinghis brought us."

"I don't see any reason for you to be here," he said. "It's wrong for anyone to put diplomats in prison. Come along, and we'll go somewhere to eat dinner."

"Sure," I said, grateful to be out of the prison. "But, let's get the vice consul to go with us?"

"Sure," he said. He followed me to our cell and led David and me back outside. The prison authorities made no move to stop us. Apparently they recognized Sengha as someone with enough authority to release us. We left with as little formality as Kinghis had gone through to put us there. We crowded into the car. Sengha suggested we go to the Sabena Guest House at the airport to eat. After going a short distance, he stopped. I saw we were in front of the Congo Palace Hotel, the biggest, newest, and best hotel in the center of town.

"General Olenga is staying here," Sengha said. "I'll go and see if he knows anything about you being in prison." He disappeared inside the hotel and returned a few minutes later. "The general said he knew nothing about the prison. He gave permission for you to return to the consulate."

On entering the consulate building, I felt an immense relief. I wanted to forget the gloom of the prison.

"I'd like to see your communications room again," Sengha said. He examined the radio equipment, apparently to confirm it was not operational. "I will send two operators from the PTT to fix it," he said.

We went over to the residence and had drinks with him and his companions. David brought out his Polaroid camera and took pictures. They were delighted at seeing themselves instantly.

I asked Sengha if he could take us to spend the night at our apartments at the Immoquateur. I continued to believe we were too exposed at the consulate. Sengha readily agreed, and he drove us to the Immoquateur where he dropped us off at the door. When we went to our apartments, no one was there. Someone told us that a squad of Simbas had taken Jim, Ernie, and Don away some hours earlier. No one knew where they had gone. David and I found Nothomb at his office, and he agreed to go find them. He dropped us off at the consulate on the way to Camp Ketele.

"I worry about the boys," I told David. "They don't know much about what is going on and must be most apprehensive over what is happening to them. They're not accustomed to dealing with the Simbas. We've done all that. Ernie's Canadian French isn't much good around these guys who speak only marginal French at best. I wish there was some way we could help them."

Nothomb came back in less than a half-hour with the missing three. He had found them in the Central Prison. "They were taken there by Joseph Kitenge," Patrick said. "He claimed to be head of the *sûreté.*" This was the criminal police service, now under Kinghis's control. I rushed to greet them and gave each a bear hug.

"How were you treated?" I asked them.

"Not bad," Jim said. "It wasn't that big a deal."

I slapped each of them on the back in my exuberance at being reunited. My fears of them not coping without David's and my help had proven groundless. They had survived their brush with prison better than we had. It lifted my spirits to have them back with us.

We decided once again they would be safer at the Immoquateur, away from the action at the consulate. David and I would stay to handle whatever came along. Patrick took them to the Immoquateur.

"It seems that each time I decide on a move to the apartments," I said to David, "something happens to prevent it."

I was relieved to be out of prison but depressed over the thought that someone could put us there so easily. We were vulnerable to the whims of many different people. We had no control and could only await the next bizarre event.

I wrote more on a continuing letter I had started a few days earlier to my wife Jo and turned in for a fitful night's sleep.

THE NEXT MORNING, a rebel major with military police markings
came to the consulate offices. "You Americans," he snarled in a menacing tone. "I've come to take you to Camp Ketele at General Olenga's
orders. Where are the others?"

When I told him they were at the Immoquateur, he sent Simbas
to bring them. They came back with Don, Jim, and Ernie in tow,
along with a Halicrafter short-wave radio receiver set they had found
in Jim's apartment. "It's a *phonie* used to send messages to your
brothers," they said. They loaded the five of us, with the radio, into a
car and drove to Camp Ketele.

We drove through the open wire gates of the camp. A crowd of
Simbas swooped down on us, the same way they had two days earlier, and surrounded the car, shouting curses at the "bad" Americans.
We were ordered out and told to stand on the steps of Olenga's office.
"No talk," shouted the Simbas. "Just kill them. They have been killing
our brothers." They acted out again the shooting of American aircraft,
rat-a-tatting, with fingers pointed in the air. However, they were
kept at a distance by our guards.

Kinghis walked up. "How did you get out of prison?" he asked me.

"On General Olenga's orders," I replied.

"Well then," he said. "You have been using your *phonie* to talk to
your brothers."

"I telephoned you yesterday to come get our radio from the consulate."

"You addressed me in the '*tu*' form?" he said, referring to the
demeaning Belgian colonial practice of addressing all Congolese in
the familiar form, as one would with children.

"I never talked to you in that way," I said, emphasizing the "*vous.*"
I started to try to explain I learned French as an adult and did not use
the familiar form with anyone. He had no time for that.

"We will see about you later," he snarled as he strode off.

Maj. Lambert Nasor arrived and repeated his weapon trick for
the assembled crowd. He picked up the weapon I had again refused
to pick up, walking off in triumph, much to my relief.

Patrick Nothomb, vice consul Paul Duqué, and Peter Rombaut
drove up and stood to one side, hoping their presence would provide

protection. A few minutes later, all of us were ushered into the ante-room to Olenga's office and told to wait.

"Why did you send a message to Léo telling them the general had ordered your expulsion?" asked a rebel officer in the room. "That is why he ordered you here."

"I sent that telex Tuesday with the approval of the officer at the PTT," I responded. "I was just informing my embassy of the general's decision made at the Monday meeting at the chamber of commerce."

"The general is very angry," said the officer. He directed Peter, Patrick, and Paul into Olenga's office. They came back out a short time later.

"The general has ordered you to the Central Prison for the time being," Patrick said.

Before we could get organized and leave, another rebel officer came in; he was well dressed, a commandant. "I am confidential sec-retary to the general," he said. "I will be making all arrangements for the personnel of the American consulate. I know that you are part of the diplomatic corps and should be well treated."

"That's Prospère Amici. One of my people," David whispered in my ear, close enough so no one else could hear.

"We have been trying to think of ways to evacuate you to Leo," Amici continued. He had apparently not heard of Olenga's change of heart; yesterday Olenga had told me he did not want to break rela-tions with the United States. "We thought of sending you down the river in an outboard boat but decided that would be too dangerous. For now, you should return to the consulate and The Immoquateur to gather some personal belongings to take to prison. You will have your own guards to protect you. The British and Belgian consuls will supply you with food. I will go find some Simbas and be back." He left the room. I had been on the Congo River in an outboard motor boat when I had visited an American lumbering operation below Coquilhatville. One feels very small on the big river in such a small craft. It is not designed to travel the great distance it would have been required to cross into territory not yet overrun by the rebels. That was truly not the way to go.

I was stunned by the idea of returning to prison. This time there

101

would be no appeal since there was no rebel authority higher than Olenga. I was heartened by what David had whispered to me. I gathered Amici was one of David's paid informants.

Amici came back and took us outside where there was a car and a half-dozen Simbas. David and I, with the other consuls, left for the consulate in Patrick's car. The others went with Amici and the guards to The Immoquateur. David and I packed some belongings, and Patrick then drove us to the Central Prison. At the prison office, located through a door cut into the high front wall of the prison, Patrick said he had come under orders of General Olenga to put the American consular staff in prison.

"But I can't accept prisoners just like that," the director said. "I need a written order from the proper authorities."

I did not want to stay and argue with him. "Drive us back to your office before he changes his mind," I told Patrick. When we got there, I asked him again about staying there.

"That's not such a good idea," Patrick said. "I'll go back to Camp Ketele and try to persuade Olenga to allow you to stay at your consulate." I agreed that was the best alternative. The other three staff members had not yet left their apartments so we all returned to the American consulate, and Patrick set off for the camp.

He arrived back at the consulate shortly with the word that we were now permitted to stay at the consulate with another guard squad chosen by Amici.

"What with all this happening," Patrick said, "Peter and I think it best we take turns with Paul staying at the consulate with you at night. If anyone comes to take you, we will know about it right away and can try to do something about it." We readily agreed. Duqué would stay with us tonight.

After the others had turned in, David and I talked before going to bed. "What's with this Amici?" I asked. "Can he do anything for us?"

"He is one of my best men," David said. "I am confident he will not betray me. That would reveal our own relationship. But that doesn't mean he is in a position to help us very much. I think he will do all he can for us. Unfortunately, he doesn't have many options."

"It's good to know we have someone among the rebels potentially able and willing to be well disposed toward us," I said. "Sengha has been helpful, but I don't think he has the status in the army that Amici has."

SENGHA CAME TO the consulate Friday morning, 14 August. "The general and his party left last night to join the battle to take Bukavu," he said. "They're going first to Kindu, Kasongo, and Albertville to gather troops for the assault." He left with Antoine to complete the inventory, which would be attached to the lease of David's house.

Jim, Don, and Ernie relaxed in the backyard sipping beer while our new guards sat around looking at them. There was nothing else for them to do. The guards were friendlier than the last group. I used the last roll I had for an old movie camera to film Sengha and the guards. In the background, between the river and us, I caught on film people streaming into town on foot and on bicycle. Some semblance of normal life was returning to the city.

An older man with a small goatee headed our guard squad. His hat was an Australian style with one brim tied to the crown. He carried his heavy FAL rifle with him everywhere. His name was Yoni, a former schoolteacher, he told us in rudimentary French. He said he had been personally chosen by Amici to ensure our protection and, of course, to ensure our house arrest. The young Simbas under his command spoke no French. One of them was surly and suspicious. The others appeared glad to be on such soft duty. I could imagine that conditions at the consulate were infinitely better than on campaign. Although they prepared their own food, we gave them drinks, cigarettes, and cigars and tried to make them feel relaxed.

Yoni was eager to talk. We had long discussions in which he talked freely about the rebel movement. He confirmed that almost all higher rebel officers and noncoms, including himself, were Batetela, from Kasongo and other parts of Maniema Province. They formed Olenga's most trusted entourage. We learned that Olenga had been active in organizing political support for Lumumba's party, the MNC-L, in Kindu during the Gizengist secession. Olenga had no military background until he became involved in the fighting to take Uvira and Kindu and the campaign for Bukavu. Yoni spoke of him with

103

respect. During our conversations, Yoni continued to talk as if the plan for our evacuation from the city was still in effect. I had by now dismissed this as a possibility.

I raised privately with David what possible further action Amici could take on our behalf. "The problem is," said David, "that we have no way of communicating with him. We have to rely entirely on him to take any action. Anyway, if he is Olenga's confidential secretary, he is probably with him now on the way to Bukavu.

"With Olenga and Amici gone," I said, "we are left with the likes of Kinghis and Nasor or any other rebel who might take it into his mind to harass the Americans. Sengha is our best protection at this point."

Sengha stopped by again and brought a stereo tape recorder he had found in Jim's apartment. He wanted us to show him how to use it. After we showed him, he departed.

In the evening, Nothomb came to take his turn spending the night. Rombaut dropped by and told us he had not been able to contact either the British or Belgian embassies to arrange for a Red Cross or WHO aircraft to come. It had been a day without incident, and I slept easier.

Joseph Kitenge, Kinghis's *sûreté* chief, came to the consulate on Saturday. He did not appear to have a specific purpose for his visit and wandered around the offices and residence. David whispered to me what he knew of his background. "He was the principal *fétisheur* for the Popular Army," he said. "He would baptize the local youths into the movement before they took over Stan."

I thought this would be a good opportunity to get rid of our *phonie* and asked Kitenge to take the SSB equipment to Kinghis or anybody in authority. "Certainly," he said. "And you can give me a box of cigars and ten thousand Congolese francs." I gave them all to him, thankful to be rid of the cursed machine.

In the afternoon, Sengha took David to his house to review the inventory and make final arrangements for the lease. On the way, David told me later, Sengha told him the story of how his young "cousin" had been shot and killed by Simba MPs after they found him driving Sengha's car without proper authority. They found in the glove compartment a copy of the commercial telegram we had sent 11 August about Olenga's decision to expel us. "There was no explanation of how or why he had the telex. Sengha did not seem overly concerned over the message or the death of his cousin," David said.

"That explains our summons to Camp Ketele to see Olenga," I said. "They are so nervous about any kind of communication we have with the outside."

During the day several groups of Simbas came to visit, having heard the consulate was a source of free booze and other goodies. They further engraved the word "Simba" in our minds with their shouts, but they appeared to enjoy talking to us. They treated us like some strange oddity and sometimes discussed the most bizarre topics. One of them told us about the marriage problems of the Belgian royal family, a topic on which we had no information and that concerned us less. Although the presence of the Simba guard and the continual visits kept us on edge, we were not otherwise harassed or mistreated. Olenga or Amici must have passed the word that we were not to be abused.

Peter Rombaut arrived for his stint at spending the night. "I visited the American, Canadian, and British missionaries at Kilometer Eight yesterday," he said. "Al Larson told me to tell you that they are all safe. He and the rest of them are very nervous. They hope that at least the women and children can be evacuated as soon as possible."

Early Sunday, 16 August, Peter left for Wanie Rukula to check on the British missionaries there. Later in the morning, yet another former guard at the consulate, now a Simba captain, came by to see us. He was quite drunk but articulate. He kept repeating David's name and said he would kill anyone who harmed him or any other American. He told us about the rebel taking of Bunia, on the extreme eastern end of Kibali-Ituri Province, close to Lake Albert. "I led the troops that took the city without firing a shot. President [Jean Foster] Manzikala ordered the ANC to lay down their arms and not fight the Popular Army." We could not verify his story, but we appreciated his expressions of concern over our safety. "Do not harm them," he told our guard as he left. "They are international diplomats and should not be touched."

105

In the afternoon, Dr. Alex Barlovatz visited, ostensibly to treat us. He recounted what was going on in the city. "Some killings began to take place before the Lumumba monument after the rebel takeover," he said. "But that was nothing compared to the scale of savagery that is going on now that Kinghis is in charge. With Olenga's departure yesterday, Kinghis presided over a mob scene of ritualistic murders and blood sacrifices. Important members of the previous administration, captured ANC officers, and other 'intellectuals' are being tried and executed. The former president of the PNP [*Parti Nationale du Progrès*, accused of being tied to the Belgians] was dismembered alive and his liver was eaten while it was still warm. President Aradjabu was not among the victims, but many were killed in horrible ways. I could see this all from my clinic."[1]

"That might have been our fate if we had remained in the prison where Kinghis had put us," I said. "We would have been easy pickings without Olenga's protection."

Barlovatz said that he knew of six Europeans who had lost their lives at the hands of Popular Army forces. He said communications of all kinds had now been cut off with Léopoldville and the rest of the outside world. He did not believe a Red Cross or WHO plane would be permitted to land in Olenga's absence. "Conditions in the local hospitals are chaotic," he said. "I had to fight witch doctors to treat Simba patients. We have little in the way of medicines. Roving Simbas keep trying to take away my car despite the fact that I have the general's written permission to keep it.

"Earlier in the day, a small, fast reconnaissance-type airplane flew close to the city. It made the Simbas very nervous," he continued.

The doctor gave me medicine for my bronchial cough, brought on by my continued smoking. Life appeared too short for me to worry about the health hazards of smoking.

Security chief Kitenge showed up again in the evening, asking for another ten thousand francs. He said he had given our SSB radio to Kinghis. "I have become very rich today," he said as he left.

We maintained telephone contact with Americans and other expatriates in the city. It kept us abreast of events and lessened our feeling of isolation at the consulate. Our guards insisted on being present while we talked on the telephone but did not object to our speaking in English, which, of course, they could not understand.

In the evening David and I reviewed the previous days' events and tried to come to some conclusions on future trends. The main conclusions we came to were that economic and commercial activities were limping along but supplies would soon run out without contact with the outside world. The European population was becoming increasingly nervous and apprehensive. We could not determine for certain what communist influences there were on the rebel movement. There was no evidence of direct aid or supervision, but the Soviet Union and China were considered "good" countries and the United States was "bad." We concluded that

> In general, the attitude of the new authorities towards the American Consulate staff and by extension Belgians and other foreigners is not yet clearly defined. It is possible we are regarded simply as hostages who must be ransomed, although the ransom "price" or its character cannot yet be determined. It is difficult to believe the authorities will permit our evacuation without receiving in exchange for that evacuation something of equal value to them, particularly in the military sphere.[2]

THE REBEL CAPTAIN who was a former consulate guard paid us another visit Monday morning, 17 August. "I am going to Paulis on military operations," he informed us. "You guys," he told our guards on leaving, "take good care of my friends." Paulis was a large town approximately one hundred miles to the northeast of Stanleyville. We thought the rebels had already taken it.

Taking a chance that it would be sent in spite of the word that communications had been shut down, I sent one of the Congolese staff to the PTT with a message to the embassy in Léopoldville. I wanted them to know that all five of us Americans were at the consulate. The text stated, "ALL PERSONNEL ARE WELL SHELTERED TOGETHER IN THE CONSULATE." A copy of the message came back with a receipt indicating it had been accepted and presumably sent.[3]

107

Professor Loewen, the Canadian vice rector and head of the University of Stanleyville, called me. "I'm very worried about you," he said. "We have heard rumors that you are to be executed. I hope this is just talk, but take care."

Rombaut stopped by the consulate and told me he was going to a meeting Kinghis had scheduled with the consular corps that day. He advised me not to attend. "The anti-American propaganda over the radio has been increasingly virulent," he said. "The local population is confused and frightened, and the Simbas keep shouting abuses at the Americans. There could be ugly incidents if you traveled the streets. Kinghis could use your presence to create an ugly incident." I agreed that I should not try to attend.

He also told us about his visit to Wanie Rukula the day before. "It was a most unpleasant experience," he said. "We encountered eight roadblocks on the way. Heavily armed, nervous, and unfriendly Simbas guarded them. Each crossing was a harrowing event, in spite of my written credentials and accompanying Simbas. The missionaries I finally reached were safe and in relatively good spirits. I'm thankful to be back in the relative calm and safety here in Stan."

The Red Cross representative and Dutch honorary consul Franken telephoned. "Nothing can be done about getting permission for a Red Cross aircraft to come to Stanleyville during Olenga's absence. He is not expected to return until August 22nd. All cables on this subject are being refused at the PTT."

During the afternoon, several groups of Simbas came by, announcing their arrival with the inevitable cries of "Simba! Simba!" We were forced to listen to their rantings. They claimed the Americans were so clever that they were able to hide a radio transmitter in a matchbox. Therefore, they had to be diligent in searching. Every group had its tale of how it had fought the Americans in battle, claiming they had killed hundreds of American soldiers. They said the only reason Bukavu had not yet fallen was because of the presence of American soldiers and military assistance. We repeatedly were subject to the pointing of fingers to the sky, the rat-a-tat-tat chant, and the inevitable pantomime of the downing of an American airplane.

We heard about a raid on the Victoria Hotel, a residence hotel near the Central Prison, by Simbas looking for ANC soldiers supposedly hidden there. A group of Europeans was taken to Camp Ketele, but they were soon released unharmed by Col. Joseph Opepe, who had been left in charge of the city garrison.

In the evening, Peter Rombaut told us about the meeting Kinghis had called. Kinghis himself did not show up but was represented by his *chef de cabinet,* Charles Ifefe.

"He seemed reasonable and relatively intelligent," Peter said. "He asked for the cooperation of the European community and acknowledged the 'vast European contribution to the development of the Congo.' Ifefe agreed in principle to establish communications with the outside world by both aircraft and wireless but said nothing concrete could be done for the moment.

"He asked if the American consul was present," Peter continued. "When I told him you were under house arrest, he said he would try to visit you himself. Also during the meeting, Ifefe took a telephone call from former President Aradjabu. From the part of the conversation we heard, we gathered Aradjabu would be appointed to a minor post in the Department of Public Health. Ifefe promised assistance to those Europeans needing it. He said he would be touring the communes in the city to install new mayors. Each would be provided with a Simba guard to serve as the communal police force.

"In all," Peter concluded, "the meeting served to calm many of the Europeans. But, they remain skeptical the Simba soldiers and *jeunesse* could be controlled. Up to now, the *jeunesse* has not bothered the European population, but memories of their excesses during the Gizenga secession lead them to fear the worst."

Rombaut said he intended to go to Kilometer Eight again the next day. "Larson," he said, "has shown great steadiness and usefulness during these trying circumstances."

"Tell him I have been trying to contact them by phone but have been unable to get through," I said. "I would welcome any further news you have of the American missionaries."

Into the late evening, Simbas continued to visit the consulate. This was becoming almost routine, and it was reducing our stock of goodies to a dangerous level. We tried to maintain good relations with our guards and all who came. The only item that was in good supply was the locally brewed beer, both Stanor and Simba brands, in brown quart bottles.

We spent the next three days in similar fashion. On Tuesday, a PTT employee delivered a telex. It was from our embassy in Léopoldville, a routine message asking for the status of American citizens in Stanleyville. I drafted another message giving a full rundown on the Americans I knew about in Stanleyville and sent it to the PTT. The PTT employee came back and said the people at the PTT had told him the Léopoldville PTT was now refusing to accept traffic from Stanleyville, and they would not accept our message for transmission.

Someone called to tell us there was an overflight of a four-engine aircraft near the airport. "It spread panic among the Simbas," he said. "Fortunately, most of the troops were gathered at the airport and Camp Ketele, and were not around Europeans in their excited state."

Paul Duqué visited and told us he had received permission to visit civilians in the interior and would check on any Americans he found. He said Nothomb was trying to persuade the rebel authorities to reestablish contact with Léopoldville. "It seems," he said, "that the PTT here cut off all communication with Leo after receiving a provocative message from Nendaka." Victor Nendaka was the central government security chief. He had been in office since independence and was notorious for his ruthlessness. "We received a message at the consulate from our embassy before the cut-off," Paul continued. "It asked after you, disguised as an inquiry about a family with an unusual Flemish surname that we knew referred to the Americans."

Sûreté chief Kitenge came by again, this time asking for fifteen thousand francs and a bottle of gin. "My duties are exhausting me," he said. "I need some amusement." He talked freely about what was going on. "The city is calm after the flyover of an American plane," he said. "The general is due back in the city by Monday." He left with his bottle and money.

We received several phone calls from Simba officers complaining about American planes and troops that were "helping [Prime Minister Moïse] Tshombé fight the Popular Army."

Thursday, 20 August, was perhaps the quietest day we had since the arrival of the Popular Army on 4 August. No Simbas came, and our guards kept to themselves.

We listened discreetly to a small portable short-wave radio receiver. The Voice of America (VOA) and the British BBC broadcasts carried news of rebel and ANC military activity in the Congo. VOA made no reference to the American consular staff in Stanleyville and was sparse and measured in its reports of military activities in the Congo. It avoided exaggerated claims of victories and defeats on either side. BBC broadcasts stuck to facts it could verify. We heard of fighting in and around Bukavu, and there were references to U.S. assistance in the fight against the rebels. We did not know what news sources the rebels listened to or had access to, but I was worried such references supported rebel claims of U.S. assistance to Tshombé.

That night there was news of heavy fighting in Bukavu. There was a brief mention of American consular officers missing in the forests near the city. David and I discussed the possible repercussions to us because of the fighting. A rebel defeat at Bukavu would not be good news for us.

Last Words

Days 17 and 18: Friday, 21 August, and Saturday, 22 August 1964

"YOU NEED TO WRITE YOUR LAST WORDS," PATRICK NOTHOMB, the Belgian consul, shouted excitedly as he bounded up the residence steps Friday morning, 21 August. We had enjoyed a quiet morning and were just about to have lunch when Patrick careened up the driveway in his Land Rover. Vice Consul Paul Duqué and the Greek honorary consul, Dr. Hagis, were with him.

"Just what's going on?" I asked.

"Hurry," Patrick said. "A message from General Olenga has just been received over the CFL's radio. We came right here with it. They're holding up delivery to Camp Ketele. We don't have much time. Olenga is ordering the military command here to take Americans and 'try them without mercy.' Here, look for yourself."

I read the papers he handed me hurriedly. There were two messages. One was a rambling diatribe by Nicholas Olenga against American leadership of the imperialist camp against the Popular Army and told of his intention to call upon the socialist countries to assist in the struggle against them. The other one concerned us. It instructed his officers to arrest all Americans immediately, including those in the American consulate, and bring them to Camp Ketele where they were to be tried by a military court and "judged without mercy."[1] This must have been Olenga's reaction to his defeat at Bukavu. In his frustration at not taking the city, I thought, he had ordered our execution. My worst fears had been realized, but I had no time to dwell on them.

"He used similar language before when he wanted some of his own followers killed," Patrick said. "Makaroff brought the message to me. He cannot delay sending it to Camp Ketele much longer."

Paul and Dr. Hagis went into a consulate bedroom with Jim Stauffer, Don Parkes, and Ernie Houle to begin writing their messages.

"Let's see if we can figure out something to stave this off," I said to Patrick and vice consul David Grinwis. "I don't see much sense in writing out any last words."

Before we could discuss it further, Commandant Oscar Sengha drove up.

"I met him in town," Patrick said. "I told him of Olenga's message and asked him to come see if he could help."

"This is very serious," Sengha said. "I know the general can get very upset over any reversal. We must do something very quickly."

"We're just trying to think of something," I said. "The message will get to the camp pretty soon, and they could be here shortly."

"Why not send a message to your embassy and to Washington?" Patrick asked. "You can tell them what a bad situation you are in. Maybe that would put things off."

"That's a good idea," said Sengha. "You should appeal to them to stop American military assistance to Prime Minister Moïse Tshombé. That is what is endangering your lives."

I hesitated to advise my government against its policy of supporting stability and unity of the Congo. I had directed all my efforts toward this over the last two years. We were now hostages to that policy.

"We're certainly in a pickle," I said. "Our bosses need to know

113

that." A message would do that and it just might put off our execution, a pretty important consideration at this point.

"Mr. Nothomb and I will go to Ketele and bring back Colonel Opepe," Sengha said as he turned to leave with Patrick.

"David and I will start drafting the message," I told them.

I wrote out on a note pad in French an initial draft, addressing it to the embassy in Léopoldville and the State Department in Washington. It said that U.S. military assistance to the central government was endangering the lives of all Americans in Stanleyville.

Patrick and Sengha returned with Colonel Opepe. Joseph Opepe was older and fatter than most Simbas. He was a former ANC major based in Stanleyville and had been dismissed after he participated in the Gizengist secession. He had held Banza's position as chief of staff. A Batetela, like Lulumba, Opepe was apparently trusted enough by Olenga to be put in charge of the Stanleyville garrison and had specific responsibility for relations with the Europeans. Patrick had told me he was friendly and cooperative with the Europeans who had dealt with him. He was said to be a heavy drinker, a propensity he shared with most of his fellow officers, including Olenga.

Opepe sat on the sofa in the library room of the residence. Sengha translated because Opepe appeared to speak little French. "The colonel asks if you sincerely believe the United States should stop its assistance to the central government, and do you admit the United States is interfering in Congolese affairs?"

I did not know if these were Opepe's or Sengha's questions, but I did not want to make a direct response. Instead I tried to steer the conversation to the subject of sending a message. Sengha turned to Opepe and said something that seemed to satisfy him.

"The colonel is willing to consider sending a message," Sengha told me. In an aside, he added, "He says sometimes General Olenga says or does things in anger or when he is drunk that he regrets later. He has been known to reverse such actions. If we send your message we can probably delay your execution and wait to see what happens when the general gets back."

Just then another rebel colonel, later identified as Kifakio, drove up the driveway with some fellow officers. He was a follower of

Alphonse Kinghis and just as unstable. He was dressed more like the Simbas, with palm leaves and animal skins on his uniform. It was obvious from his manner that he was ready to carry out Olenga's orders and take us to Camp Ketele. He was motioning for us to follow him when Opepe intervened. I could not follow the conversation between Opepe, Sengha, and the new colonel, but I knew we did not want to fall under the control of the newly arrived contingent. The shouting match between them ended when Opepe pointed his finger at the door and bellowed something in Lingala or Swahili.

"Colonel Opepe will be taking charge of you," Sengha said. "You will be placed in detention." Kifakio stomped out angrily, took his men and left, muttering something about his getting the *Amèrikani* later. "Now we need to finish that message," Sengha said.

Patrick took my draft, cleaned up the French, and added a few words about the consequences of continued American military assistance that should be "reconsidered." With a nervous hand, I typed out a new draft, adding President Lyndon B. Johnson's name as an addressee at Patrick's suggestion. He thought that would impress the rebel leadership. It now read (in translation):

TELEX

AMERICAN EMBASSY LEOPOLDVILLE

FOR THE AMERICAN AMBASSADOR FOR TRANSMISSION TO THE

DEPARTMENT OF STATE AND PRESIDENT JOHNSON

Pursuant to a message from General Olenga, we ask you in a most insistent manner for reconsideration of the policy of American military assistance to the central Congolese government. It is a matter of the lives, repeat lives, of all Americans residing here as well as of the personnel of the consulate. Up to now, we are all in good health, but continued American military assistance would without any doubt put in immediate repeat immediate danger the lives of Americans living in the area controlled by the Popular Army of Liberation that has the situation perfectly under control and maintains order in the better part of the Congo. We await your response most urgently, repeat most urgently.

HOYT AMERICAN CONSUL IN STANLEYVILLE

115

I had added the phrase about Olenga's role to make it clear the initiative came from Olenga. I handed it to Sengha, hoping he would not notice.

"Sounds good," he said. "Let's add something about how well the Popular Army is doing." He wrote out, "The discipline of the Popular Army is remarkable. The Popular Army, in addition, collaborates in perfect harmony with the civil authorities." He circled it and indicated it should be added to the end of the message. The addition made it even clearer that it was not my message, but a dictated one. I typed a final draft, adding another sentence, just before the last one requesting authority to enter into negotiations with the new authorities in Stanleyville. Everyone read it again. I signed it and made copies for everyone.

Our last coded message had been sent on Sunday, 9 August. We lost our teletype communications capability the next day. Our last voice SSB contact was on 10 August when I reported on Olenga's decision to expel us. I had sent several telex messages in the open since, with the information on our on-and-off expulsion. After that, we had sent or received nothing. With this message, if it went out, everyone would know that we and the other Americans in Stanleyville were in very grave danger.[2]

SENGHA AND OPEPE ushered all of the consulate staff out into the cars waiting in the driveway. Patrick said he had to leave as he had just learned that his people were also being rounded up. Reprisals for the rebel defeat at Bukavu had apparently spread to the Belgians.

"We're going to the PTT to send the message," Sengha said as we settled into a Volkswagen bus. "It's closed down, but I called some people to come and open it up." Arriving at the huge gray building downtown, we entered by the back door and mounted the steps to a vast hall where dozens of teletype machines were arrayed in rows. We gathered around one machine as a technician turned it on.

I was standing by David, with the others of the staff close by, watching them prepare the equipment. My knees began to tremble. I felt I would collapse. Olenga's message was affecting me. I looked about for support, saw a chair nearby, and slumped into it as my legs gave way. I stood up, but my knees still shook. I sat again. No one seemed to notice my distress, focused as they were on starting the machines. As the teletype began to clatter, I stood up to watch. The activity calmed me, and I was able to remain standing.

A tape of the message was made while the machines were warming up. "I'll get the American embassy on the line," a PTT technician said.

When he made contact with the embassy, a message began tapping out. I saw the address "AMCONSUL STANLEYVILLE" forming on the paper. It apparently had been a message stuck in the system when the PTT had closed down. Or, maybe the embassy operators were taking advantage of a line open to Stanleyville to send a message they were holding for us. To my consternation, I saw five-number groups of a classified message begin to form. The text appeared in neat groups across the page. I was certain the rebel officers, or the PTT employees, seeing the coded groups, would know we were being sent a secret message. But they ignored it. When the short incoming message finished, they concentrated on getting our message out. The tape went through the machine and appeared on the page in French. "It was acknowledged in English as having been received directly by the American embassy in Leo," the operator said.

Everyone appeared pleased with the task accomplished. I had no idea what was to come next. Opepe and Sengha led us downstairs, out into the street, and across it to the provincial offices. We were ushered into the president's office. Kinghis sat behind a huge desk. Sengha and Opepe exchanged a few words with him, explaining, I gathered, what had occurred with the message.

"You Americans are so stupid," Kinghis burst out. "You are like children. You cannot understand the Congolese or Africans. Take them out to the airport and put them under the control of the contingent there."

117

As we were hurried out, I saw Simbas herding, none too gently, a group of European men. I heard someone say they were waiting for the Belgian consul to arrive. We were loaded back into the vw minibus and driven to the airport. I knew that Maj. Lambert Nasor commanded the airport Simba group. We could expect no better treatment than when he led the squad at the flag-eating incident at the consulate ten days before.

Arriving at the faded pink stucco airport terminal building, Opepe ordered us out and put us into the hands of a motley crew of Simbas. As they herded us into the terminal, Sengha and Opepe drove off.

The airport Simbas greeted us with shouts of glee and blows to the body. We were led into the baggage claim area where they had set up operations. Weapons and gear were strewn around; cots and chairs were set up. They poked and shoved us with rifle butts, more to humiliate, I suspected, than to hurt us. The anticipation, however, can be as bad as the reality. Similar to a dentist's drilling, you don't know exactly when the real pain will come.

The Simbas danced around us, and then pushed us down a short hallway that led to the rest rooms. They opened the door to the women's side by twisting the tip of a bayonet into the hole where the doorknob used to be. They shoved us inside. In the gloom of dusk I saw it was a small bare room, about six by ten feet, with two open cubicles with toilets without seats or covers at the end opposite the door. There was a small window high on one of the painted peeled walls. It was incredibly filthy, and the stench rose strongly from the toilets. The smell, mingled with the pain of fear in my stomach, almost made me retch.

We were too shocked to think of anything to say. After a few minutes passed, the door opened and we were ordered outside. The Simbas taunted us and pushed and beat us. We were forced to remove our shoes and socks. They bounced bayonets on the floor to make us dance. We jumped and danced to avoid the blades. They made us take off most of our clothes and pushed us back into the filthy toilet room. I was relieved to be away from the bayonets.

I heard the bayonet tip twist open the door again, and six Congolese civilians were shoved in. They had been beaten and they had been well dressed before their clothes were torn. They were as frightened as we were. We exchanged a few words. They were apparently small businessmen, held hostage by the Simbas until their friends and relatives came with ransom money. They kept to one side of the room as a way of trying to show they were not friendly with the hated Americans. They had their own problems, and we had ours.

We were taken out, taunted or shown off to visiting Simbas, and put back in the rest room a half-dozen times. "We're going to kill you," they shouted in rudimentary French. They acted out the various ways they would kill us: by knife, rifle, or bare hands. Their gestures were specific enough not to need translation. They kept repeating the word "*mateka.*" I didn't know what it meant, but it was associated with death in some way. I could not see much blood or other signs of serious injury on any of us. Ernie, Don, and Jim kept silent and made no move other than those ordered by our guards. David and I spoke softly during the few moments of peace we had in between our comings and goings.

"This Simba contingent is set up for the extraction of money from the people caught in town and brought out here," I said.

"Yes," David said. "It looks like they have instructions to protect us and keep us under guard. We have to depend on their sense of discipline to survive."

"Still, we can't be sure where it will end," I said. "At any time, they or others could lose control."

With nightfall and the start of a light rain, the tempo of our outings eased. We were called out once more to the baggage room; the Congolese civilian prisoners remained in the rest room. The Simbas motioned us toward some chairs. We had been standing for most of the day and welcomed the chance to sit. They gave us back our clothes and shoes and socks. They offered us a dish with a typical Simba's ration of rice and fish. I was suddenly hungry, having been interrupted before lunch. It didn't taste bad. The others refused to eat. Eating took my mind off thinking about our problems. We were offered beer. Jim joined me, but the others declined. During all this, the guards continued to taunt us and I heard someone saying we would be killed the next day.

119

We were ordered back into the toilet room with the Congolese hostages. There were a dozen of us in that small room. No one could lie down but some squatted. The rest of us stood, leaning against the wall. It was quiet outside except for the soft distant beat of drums. It was a long and uncomfortable night. I must have dozed off and awakened abruptly a dozen times before the dawn came. The thought came to me that I would never have trouble sleeping in an airplane seat again.

IN THE MORNING we were let out of the women's rest room and allowed to stretch our cramped limbs. But not for long. More Congolese prisoners were brought to the airport, and we were shuttled in and out of the toilet room. The Congolese numbered eleven at one point, which made sixteen in the room. We were crowded and could only stand, pressed next to each other. We would be taken out occasionally into the baggage room to be shown to visiting rebels and to be knocked about, threatened, and have graphically demonstrated again how we would shortly be killed. Our guards would point out which parts of our bodies they would particularly like to eat. The word *mateka* was repeated many times.

This lasted into the early afternoon. The fear in the pit of my stomach was not enough to quell a growing sense of hunger. Except for the small amount of the Simba ration I had the night before, we had eaten nothing since the morning before. I had not seen Major Nasor so I asked a Simba commandant, who had acted more reasonably toward us than the others, if there was any way we could get something to eat. He reacted with surprise and concern that we had not eaten. He said two of us could go to the consulate to pick up food. David and I were taken there by car with a few guards. The Simba guard under Yoni was still there. They greeted us as if nothing unusual was going on. While the servants cooked a meal, I shaved and changed my shirt. We ate and drove back to the airport with food for Jim, Don, and Ernie. The town was quiet; there were not many people or cars in evidence. With food and clean clothes I felt better able to face whatever came next.

In the late afternoon, I began to hear a faint rumbling noise building up in the distance. It soon became discernible as the sound of a huge angry crowd. There was only one Simba with us, a younger fellow, left on guard by the officers who had gone off on this quiet

Saturday afternoon. He ran toward us, picking up a rifle as he came. In a serious manner, he motioned for us to go into the toilet room, putting his finger to his lips for us to be silent. He then closed the door.

We heard the wild noise of the mob outside, which was now closer. A wave of shouting filled the room. I could sense something was exciting the crowd to a frenzy. An occasional shot rang out. We had no way of knowing what was happening, but I thought the anger of the crowd was somehow directed toward us.

The door opened and we were motioned outside. I saw a white couple, with two small children, being shoved toward us. Simbas were hitting them. The woman was young and pregnant, carrying a small child and leading another. The young man was kept from helping them. We were pushed back into the toilet room with them and the door was shut. We crowded together with the couple, the kids, and several Congolese hostages. I motioned the woman to sit on one of the bare toilets in the cubicle and stood in front of her. She sat there with the two children clinging to her, looking frightened and bewildered. We had not yet spoken, and I did not know what nationality they were. I started to say something in French.

"I'm Chuck Davis," broke in the man in an American accent. "We are American missionaries. The Simbas came to get us this morning. It was an awful trip. They killed a man at the camp outside of town. He just dropped at our feet. The Simbas told us we were being taken to see the American consul in Stanleyville."

I hesitated to respond, knowing they did not want to hear what I was about to say. I forced out the words in a low hoarse voice, "I'm the American consul." I could see the news drained them of any hope they had of relief from their tormentors.

The door burst open and Major Nasor appeared in the doorway. He looked as menacing as he had on the consulate lawn when I first met him last week. He pointed rudely toward the woman and the children. "Come!" he shouted. There was a lot of yelling and gesturing. They were reluctant to move. "Come! Come!" he bellowed menacingly. Davis was about to intervene.

"Let her go," I said. In that split second, I had decided we could do nothing to prevent her leaving and sensed it would be better for her than staying in this miserable and threatening situation. Major Nasor represented a level of authority that might save her from the mob outside. The woman and her children were hustled out and the door closed.

Davis appeared devastated. "The Simbas are not known to harm women and children," I said. "She's better off in Nasor's hands than at the mercy of the mob." I could not be certain I was right, but I tried to put the best light on it for her husband's sake. We had no time to discuss it further. The Simbas came after us again, bringing us into the baggage room, but leaving the Congolese behind. They forced us to strip to our shorts. They pounded on the floor with their bayonets to make us dance. They struck at us with sticks and weapons. This was more serious than the game played earlier at Camp Ketele. We had difficulty evading the sharp blades. Blood, oozing from our feet, began to appear on the floor.

"Stop that," shouted a Simba officer who had returned from his Saturday afternoon outing. It was the commandant who had let us go for food. The Simbas stopped their beatings and put away their bayonets.

"Are you all right?" asked the commandant. I was too startled to answer. They went through our clothes and returned them to us. We were permitted to dress. Everything was returned to us except the money we had in our pockets. About one hundred thousand Congolese francs, mostly from David and me, were spread out on the table. The commandant offered us beer from their seemingly inexhaustible supply. I was grateful for the warm beer that cleared my throat, which had dried to cotton from fear.

The commandant found something for us to eat and said we could sleep that night out in the baggage room. "If you pay us one hundred thousand francs for each of you," he said, "I will see that your treatment will be most favorable."

"To raise such sums we have to contact our consular colleagues," I said, seeing an opening to get Nothomb's help.

"We'll see about that," he responded. "General Olenga has returned to Stan and will see you at eight in the morning."

I didn't know if this was good or bad news. Olenga had given the order for our execution. But he represented more order than the mob. I thought we had been saved only by our lone Simba guard's quick action with the rifle. We might not be so lucky next time.

The five consulate staff members and Chuck gathered in a corner.

"I don't have anything like one hundred thousand francs," Chuck told me. "What can we do?"

"Don't worry about it," I said. "We'll take care of it." That was the least of our worries.

The rest of the evening was peaceful. Several groups of Simbas came by to see the Americans. They taunted us as usual, but they were not permitted to touch us. Chuck had time to tell us his story. The Davises had been at the missionary station in Bangwade, he said, fifty kilometers north of Stanleyville. They had arrived only a week before the rebels took Stanleyville and were the only Americans there.

"The Simbas came about noon," Chuck said. "We had heard on Radio Stan in the morning that Kinghis had put out an order for all Americans in the vicinity to be picked up. The Simbas had apparently missed the turnoff to Kilometer Eight because they had a paper with Al Larson and Del Carper's names on it. When they found out we were Americans, we were told we were to be taken to Stanleyville where we would be evacuated with the staff of the American consulate.

"The trip to Stan was a horror. Every few miles, we were stopped at roadblocks manned by *jeunesse* or Simbas. Each time our escorts were forced to explain their mission and negotiate their way past. When we arrived at the camp outside of town, a huge crowd of Simbas and *jeunesse* surrounded our car. The mob clamored to get at us and rocked the car. The officer in charge shot several who got too close. One body just dropped to the ground by the car. That broke the crowd's hold on us. We drove to the airport with the mob following behind. You know the rest."

"Why were you staying at the station?" I asked. "Didn't you get some warning from the embassy through your radio network after the rebel takeover of Stan?"

"No, nothing like that came," Chuck said. "We knew the rebels were anti-American, but we did not dream they would harm us. The

123

others at the station are Canadian or British. They were nervous about the Simbas, but they had no thought of leaving."

The Simbas offered us more beer and food, and I accepted. The warm liquid tasted delicious and took the edge off my worries. We tried to make ourselves comfortable for the night on chairs in the baggage room. We were able to stretch out. The Congolese prisoners, meanwhile, remained locked up in the rest room. Chuck was inconsolable about the fate of his family. I tried to reassure him that they were in less danger than we were. I somehow had faith that Major Nasor would take care of them.

As midnight approached, drums began to beat outside the terminal, much closer than the night before. It sounded like empty fifty-five-gallon drums. The drumbeats slowly increased in intensity. It was dark inside the building now and I could see lights flickering outside. Although we had been well treated that night, the day had been filled with threats. Anxiety continued to increase the knot of pain in my stomach.

The drums kept beating. The lights from outside flickered in the darkened baggage room. The sound of the drums continued. Were they preparing for our fate in the morning? I had no way of knowing. The drums continued to beat their cadence from the darkness of the forest surrounding the airport. Soon exhaustion and the beer eased me into a troubled sleep, the sound of drums mingling with my heart beating in the darkness.

> The vision seemed to enter the house with me—the stretcher, the phantom-bearers, the wild crowd of obedient worshippers, the gloom of the forests, the glitter of the reach between the murky bends, the beat of the drum, regular and muffled like the beating of a heart—the heart of a conquering darkness. (Conrad, *Heart of Darkness*)

Michael Hoyt (*far left*) and Catholic nuns, with church and assistance officials,
distribute flour, provided through the U.S. Agency for International Development program, in Stanleyville before its fall to rebel forces on Wednesday,
5 August 1964.
U.S. Information Service Cultural Center, Stanleyville.

Cultural Center and consulate local employees with Simba guard in front of
U.S. consulate in Stanleyville on 11 August 1964.

David Grinwis answers the telephone in reception area of the U.S. consulate in Stanleyville.

Michael Hoyt manning the telephone in the U.S. consulate office in Stanleyville.

Cell number eight (*far right doorway*), where the American consulate staff were held prisoner 9 October to 20 November 1964, in Stanleyville Central Prison. Photo taken during author's 1971 visit.

Interior view of cell number eight, where the American consulate staff were held prisoner in Stanleyville Central Prison. Hoyt's plank was the one to the right of the prisoner standing. Photo taken during author's 1971 visit.

Rebel triumvirate leadership at the Lumumba monument in Stanleyville during 18 November 1964 demonstration. Gen. Joseph Olenga (*center, standing*) and unknown officer greet Christophe Gbenye and Gaston Soumialot (*left to right in back seat of car*).

"Major" Carlson and some of his cohorts at Governor's Palace, 18 November 1964. Hostages, *from left to right*, are Don Parkes, David Grinwis, Jim Stauffer, Dr. Paul Carlson, Jon Snyder, and Hoyt.

Demonstrators marching on 18 November 1964 in Stanleyville. The placard translation is

Down with the Yankee aggressor and his lackeys
Death to the mercenary Carlson and his acolytes
The sold-out Kasavubu, the corporal Mobutu,
policeman Nendaka, and the traitor Tshombé
will pay for their crimes
Down with the nazi army of the Congo
A.N.C.

Hostages at the 18 November demonstration. *Left to right:* Dr. Paul Carlson, Jon Snyder, Hoyt, and Ernie Houle.

Hostages on the road to the Stanleyville airport on 24 November 1964.

News conference at Ambassador McMurtrie (Mac) Godley's residence in Léopoldville on 24 November 1964. *Left to right:* Godley, Hoyt, and David Grinwis.

Each of the five members of the staff at the American consulate in Stanleyville that were held hostage in 1964 received the Secretary's Award on 9 June 1965 for outstanding courage and dignity.

The General Returns

Days 19 through 32: Sunday, 23 August,
through Saturday, 5 September 1964

I AWOKE WITH THE DAWN ON SUNDAY, 23 AUGUST. THE DRUMS
were silent. Sunlight streamed through the filthy windows of the airport's baggage claim area. Stiff from sleeping on the chair, I stumbled
up to eat a few morsels of the Simbas' breakfast of dried bread and
cold rice. A few passing Simbas shouted the usual curses against the
Americans, but they appeared more curious than threatening. The
meeting with Gen. Nicholas Olenga foretold for that morning did not
materialize, and I did not inquire into it. We sat on our chairs, grateful for the quiet in contrast to the previous days.

At noon, Jim Stauffer and Ernie Houle were taken to the consulate to pick up food. At three o'clock, the commandant—the deputy
commander of the airport guard—told us the Americans would be
moved to the Sabena Guest House across the street from the terminal.
After some confusion in organizing the expedition, we were marched
with our few possessions to one of the cottages close to the Guest
House headquarters and dining building. The cottage had a small

veranda and a single door in front, a simple pleasant building painted in the usual pink of buildings at the airport. We went in through the screen door. Six made-up beds were jammed into the small room built for two. We settled in, grateful to have a place to lie down after the filthy rest room and hard chairs at the airport. I looked forward to sleeping between sheets again. The cottage would help insulate us from passing Simbas. I hoped our guards would keep away bothersome guests.

Chuck Davis looked into our small bathroom and said the toilet was stopped up. He reached into it and soon had it flushing, much to our relief. We had been reluctant to use the stopped-up toilets in the women's rest room.

David Grinwis and I sat on my bed and brought our journal up to date. Whenever we could find the time, we continued to record the events of our ordeal.

23 August. . . . The Commandant, for unknown reasons, had decided to be as pleasant as possible and arranged for a simple meal of rice and sardines to be sent over from the Sabena Guest House kitchens; and he allowed us to purchase beer from the Guest House bar. A Simba guard of six was stationed immediately outside the door of the cottage, but during the evening we were not bothered by them.

24 August. On Monday a routine began which repeated itself for the next several days. We were served breakfast of bread and coffee at about nine o'clock in the morning. During each morning we would receive many visits from Simbas who were passing by the area and who wished to come in to see the strange Americans. At no point however in this initial period were we beaten by these individuals, although frequently we were made to stand at attention and listen to diatribes against Americans and announcements of what was in store for us.

The Commandant continued to be amiable and during the afternoon offered to help us. We requested him to try to find out where Mrs. Davis had been taken. He was also asked to try and obtain permission for Dr. Barlovatz to visit us as Consul Hoyt had developed a severe bronchial cough.

During the afternoon and evening we received many visits from

Simbas but no violence developed. We were asked to retire at ten o'clock in the evening and it was requested that a light be left burning in the room. All windows were closed but fortunately the ventilating system in the air-conditioning unit was still operable and there was some circulation of air.[1]

I was disturbed, and Chuck even more, about the lack of news about what had happened to Chuck's wife, Muriel, and the children. I thought she was probably okay and said this to Chuck, but he was unconvinced and inconsolable. Our inability to obtain any news was frustrating. I kept asking the commandant what had happened to them, and he always answered that he would try to find out. That, and our inability to communicate with our consular colleagues and our final unknown fate, was marring our otherwise stable and secure existence at the Sabena Guest House.

Chuck Davis, tall and angular—and cheerful when not thinking about his wife and children—told us more of his background. He was to be a seminary teacher, and this was his first missionary posting. He and his family had spent several months in Uganda learning Swahili before coming to Bangwade in late July. Although they had been in touch with Al Larson and the other missionaries at Kilometer Eight, approximately twenty miles away, they had not been advised of the availability of evacuation planes in Stanleyville. He said they had heard no warnings from the embassy passed over the missionary radio network of any danger posed to them from the rebels.

"I had hoped that at least following our August 21st message the embassy would have alerted the missionaries in the region," I told him. "We knew the Simbas spread quickly beyond Stanleyville in all directions immediately after the fall of the city on August 5th. You may not have been able to leave even if warned."

There was little to do during the day. We had nothing to read. Chuck organized some prayer sessions. David and one or two others participated. Chuck also explained his ideas on African masks. He said they represented the devil and sketched some examples to prove his point. I failed to see the connection between African masks and the Christian concept of the devil.

127

IN THE EARLY MORNING of Tuesday, 25 August, a large group of people came to the cottage. It was Alphonse Kinghis with an entourage.

"Come with us," he said, pointing to David and me, "you must make a statement over Radio Stan." He turned and left. David and I were loaded in a car and driven to his offices in city hall. We waited in an anteroom for an hour before being ushered in. Kinghis was seated behind his huge desk and harangued us aimlessly in the usual anti-American jargon. His black beard tumbled over his chest, and he waved his arms as he spoke. "Take them to see the minister of the interior," he told our guards after he had his say.

We were taken to a nearby conference room where the rebel minister sat. David whispered to me that he was Dominique Gbagbeu, one of the more radical leaders of the MNC-L *jeunesse*. He glared at us while playing with an automatic pistol on the desk in front of him. His small black beard bobbled as he spoke.

"You will read a message over Radio Stan denouncing American military aid to the central government," he said. "You must say that continuation of this interference in Congolese affairs jeopardizes the lives of Americans in the area. These are some journalists to help draft a message," pointing to the two thin young men in dirty white shirts seated on the other end of the table.

"We already sent such a message on the 21st through the PTT," I said. "It was sent to the American embassy and to President Johnson. I have a copy of it right here." I handed him the cable that I still had in my shirt pocket. He glanced at it and turned it over to his journalists. They read it and wrote a new text. Gbagbeu looked at it and handed it to me. It was similar to the previous one, with one notable exception. Instead of starting with "Pursuant to a message received from General Olenga," it had "Pursuant to the military policy of interference of the American government in the internal affairs of the Congo."

"I cannot say the United States is interfering in the internal affairs of the Congo," I blurted out.

Gbagbeu reared back in surprise. I dogged on. "Don't you see?" I said. "I am the official representative of the U.S. government and a soldier like yourself. There are certain things I cannot do just as you cannot act against your commanders." While I was saying this,

128

another part of me was thinking, Why am I making this stupid argument? These points are irrelevant, beyond this joker. Besides, it's dangerous. This guy is quite capable of simply shooting us!

Gbagbeu turned angry and ugly. He picked up his gun and began waving it about, shouting that I must do as he said. Before I could think about caving in and acceding to his language to spare our lives, he suddenly calmed down. "You might say," he said, "Pursuant to the policy of military assistance by the American government. . . ."

"That would be fine," I said quickly, much relieved at the compromise.

He put down his gun and asked his journalists if that sounded right. They agreed. He told them to write it out in final form. It came out much like the message of 21 August except the threat to all Americans in the area at the end was made more explicit. I signed it. Everyone appeared pleased with the results of our discussion.

We were taken to the studios of Radio Stanleyville, where, after some delay in finding the right equipment and technicians, I read the message into a tape recorder. I tucked my copy into my pocket.

"Your message will be played after a speech by the president," the director of the radio said. "He is announcing the arrest of the staff of the American consulate for ignoring the pleas of the popular government for a cessation of military aid to the Tshombé regime. The president will promise to keep the population informed of the status of the American consulate and give them the results of its pleas to stop American assistance." David and I were then driven back to the Sabena Guest House cottage.

"That was a bit of bravado that was perhaps unnecessary," I said to David.

"What would you have done if Gbagbeu had insisted?" David asked.

"I don't know. He caved before I did. I don't know that it made much difference what the message said, but I feel better for having succeeded in avoiding the interference bit. The Simbas harp on it so, and it makes me furious."

"You made a dangerous move in a dangerous place," David said. "You got away with it. Maybe next time you won't be so lucky."

129

"I assume the embassy or someone is monitoring Radio Stan the way they did during secession times," I said. "My little speech is in reality a report on the situation here. It's the only way we can get news out. After all, isn't that why Mac told us to stay?"[2]

"With our message of the twenty-first and this one," David said, "they must know for sure we're in deep trouble. It represents what the rebels are thinking. Maybe that will prod them into some kind of action to save us. I don't know what they can do, but at least they know that we, and anyone in rebel hands, are in terrible danger. I hope all missionaries that can get out have been warned."[3]

"Mac put us here," I said. "He should figure out some way of getting us out. Maybe we would have been better off taking our chances with Operation Flagpole. I was just afraid that the Simbas had us surrounded with all their guns."

"I'm convinced if it had been successful, they would have taken terrible reprisals against Ernie and the Europeans," David said.

At the end of the day, I asked the commandant again for news of Mrs. Davis and requested that he telephone Dr. Barlovatz to come attend to our various health needs.

The next day, on Wednesday, 26 August—the twenty-second day since the rebel takeover—we received three visitors. General Olenga came with a large entourage early in the morning. I recognized him only when he came close; without my glasses, which had been crushed at the consulate on 11 August, I could not see well. I did not know what to expect. Was he here to follow through on his order to try and execute us?

"Are you all right?" he asked in a gentle voice. "Are you well? Are you getting enough to eat?" He continued without waiting for a response. "I have been in contact with New York through the PTT. I expect to speak to Washington today. I will be in touch with you when we have learned the results of my conversations."

"I would be glad to accompany you," I said, wanting to get more involved.

"That won't be necessary," he said. An officer in his entourage approached him and whispered something in his ear. "They tell me that the PTT equipment has broken down." With that he turned and left.

"I can only guess that he was checking up on us," I said. "He might have wanted to see that we were still alive. I assume he has thought better of his order to try us after his defeat at Bukavu. Strange man. He must have plans for us. Maybe he thinks we are more valuable alive as hostages than dead in vengeance."

Thinking the general's visit may have improved our status, I asked the commandant again for news of the Davis family. He again promised to find out something.

A little later, our second visitor arrived. I was overjoyed to see Alex Barlovatz, the first person on our side we had seen since we were forced from the consulate on the previous Friday, 21 August.

"The best news," he said, "is that Kinghis and his government have been dismissed, replaced by a group of nonpolitical technicians called commissioners. The president's man, Colonel Kifakio, was killed by Olenga, right out on the street in front of the Congo Palace. The general just pulled out his pistol and shot him. It was said he had tried to take over from Olenga."

"Glad to get those two out of the way," I said. "Kinghis sure had his sights on us. If he had had his way, we would have been a part of the slaughter that Olenga apparently didn't approve of. As for Kifakio, I'm sure we wouldn't have survived if he had taken us to Ketele that day Olenga's message came in."

"More good news," Alex said. "Albertville has been retaken by the ANC, and there are rumors that the ANC was attacking in the vicinity of Kindu. I have no way of verifying any of this information."

"Kindu is a long way from Albertville," David said. "I doubt the ANC could advance that quickly."

"Radio Leo tends to anticipate victories for the ANC," the doctor said. "And you," he said, turning to me, "how is your cough coming along?"

"Not too good. I'm still smoking," I replied. "Somehow it doesn't seem worthwhile to quit at this point."

131

Barlovatz gave me a shot, deliberately in full view of our Simba guard, to justify his visit.

At dusk, our third visitor appeared. A young Simba, obviously drunk, burst open our door and barged into the cottage. "You're trying escape," he shouted in rudimentary French. "Everyone, on bed."

There wasn't much space between the six beds, and he maneuvered unsteadily to get at us. He slapped at Ernie, who remained silent and still. The Simba turned to Chuck and struck several blows to his head with his fist. Chuck offered no resistance. The Simba moved to Don and hit him repeatedly about the face and head. Jim was in the corner, apparently out of sight. David and I were on the front row and obvious targets, but the Simba did not even look at us.

Ernie keeled over, in an exaggerated movement, and dropped to the floor with a heavy thud. At this, the Simba's demeanor changed. Instantly sober, he bent to Ernie. "Are you all right?" he said. "I no mean hurt you." He laid Ernie on the bed and soothed him. "Have you eaten supper?" he turned to us and asked. When we told him no, he went to the Guest House kitchen and returned with our meal. He then left, extending more apologies.

We examined the wounds he had inflicted. Chuck had a cut on his scalp, and Don had a cut over his right eye. Ernie was unhurt. We washed the wounds and the bleeding stopped. We picked desultorily at our meals, shocked by the violence and worried about what more was to come. It brought home to us how vulnerable we were to random acts of violence. We congratulated Ernie on his quick thinking in faking a faint. He had no comment. The rains came. That, as usual, calmed the Simbas. All was quiet and dark outside.

The commandant arrived first thing in the morning. "What happened last night?" he asked. "I heard someone disturbed you."

"Yes," I said. "One of your Simbas beat us quite badly, as you can see." I pointed to Don and Chuck. We had heavily covered their wounds with bandages to make them appear more serious.

"I'll put that Simba in the *cachot*," he said, referring to the small solitary confinement punishment cells all prisons had. "Also the two Simbas responsible for your security."

"As you can see," I said, pointing to Ernie, "he is an old man, fifty-three years old, and is suffering. Can't you let him go to our apartments at the Immoquateur? Here his health is in serious jeopardy."

"I'll take him to Colonel Opepe and see if he can arrange that," the commandant said. He left with Ernie and returned within the hour, saying Opepe could not be found. "Nothing can be done to change his situation until we can find some officer in authority," he said. "Meanwhile, he stays with you."

During the morning, the servants from the residence came with food to supplement the Sabena Guest House's monotonous fare of rice and sardines. They brought news of Mrs. Davis and the children and had a note from her to Chuck. He read it, and his mood changed to elation. "She's safe," he said. "Here, read it."

Muriel wrote that she and the kids were fine at the Evangelical Library (LECO) store. They were with the Jenkinsons, an older English couple. Major Nasor had taken them around the city looking for a place to leave them. She finally remembered someone mentioning the LECO bookstore and Nasor dropped them there, she wrote. She and the children had not been harmed. She said the Jenkinsons did not have much space and were not accustomed to children. She requested money to pay her share of the expenses. David and I sent some with the servants. Chuck was bubbling over with relief and joy. He kept talking and talking, rambling on about anything that came to mind.

The last journal entry for this day, 27 August, reads:

> In the afternoon we received a visit from a Simba Adjutant who had recently returned from "operations in the city." The Adjutant said the Kinghis government had been "neutralized" although he did not know why. The Adjutant also gave us an interesting description of how discipline was enforced among the Simbas: Simba discipline consists essentially of murdering out of hand any Simba who disobeys his superior officer. The Adjutant informed us that the Popular Army Forces were now very close to Coquilhatville. He complained that the discipline problem was provoked mainly by new recruits from among Jeunesse elements in towns captured by the Popular Army. The Adjutant furthermore stated that the new Jeunesse elements enrolled in the Popular Army were creating tension between themselves and the hard core of the Popular Army, Simbas from Maniema Province and most of whom, at least in Stanleyville, were now assigned to military police units.

"It's good to hear some discipline is maintained in the rebel army," I said. "Our lives depend upon it."

"It's the Maniema Batetela who are holding things together,"

133

David said. "Their loyalty is to Olenga. Now, we have to see what he has in store for us."

The next day, I sent a note to Peter Rombaut with the servants who brought food and clean clothes. I asked him if he could arrange with the rebel authorities to return Ernie to The Immoquateur and to have the Davis family reunited.

Later in the morning, Opepe came to ask about our health. I asked him about the two requests I had made concerning Ernie and Chuck. He said he could not allow the moves, but he would issue a *laissez-passer* for Mrs. Davis to visit her husband. He also said that Rombaut or the Belgian consul could obtain permission to visit.

"You are being kept under close guard, incommunicado," said one of the Simbas who was translating for Opepe. "This is to prevent you from calling your brothers to come and rescue you."

A short time after Opepe left, Muriel Davis and Peter Rombaut arrived. The reunion of the Davises was joyous. After their initial greetings, David and I questioned her on what had happened to her and what she knew of the rebel treatment of the missionaries. She said Nasor had been very helpful in trying to find a place of safety after bringing her out of the horror of the airport. It was only by chance that she remembered hearing someone in Bangwade say something about the Evangelical bookstore. Someone in Nasor's group knew about the library and located the Jenkinsons.

The Jenkinsons, she said, had heard that most of the approximately 150 missionaries in the area to the north and east of Stanleyville had managed to get out to Uganda. The three they had left in Bangwade were still at their mission. The missionaries in the Bunia region had said over the radio that everyone should leave as the situation appeared to them far worse than in 1960. She had no knowledge of any warnings issued by American embassies or the State Department. She said that she thought there were about twenty-five American missionaries left in the Stanleyville area.

We squeezed Peter for all the news he had.

Mr. Rombaut gave us the following information: that he had no news on United States reaction to the situation in Stanleyville; that Mali, Chad and other small African States were attempting to arrange a

cease-fire between the ANC and the Popular Army; that Albertville
had fallen to the ANC and there were rumors of fighting in the streets
of Kindu; that Tanganyika troops were sealing off the Tanganyika-
Congo border to prevent Simbas from crossing over into Tanganyika
territory as they fled from the ANC; that both Gaston Emile Soumialot
and Christophe Gbenye are expected to arrive in Stanleyville in the
very near future; that President Kinghis is under house arrest for
unknown reasons; that a Simba Major was shot in front of the Congo
Palace Hotel by Olenga himself for spreading rumors that Olenga had
been killed in recent military operations near Bukavu; that François
Sabiti, a local MNC/L radical and an "Arabisé," is now acting as a kind
of Civil Governor under Olenga's control; that economic chaos is
threatening Stanleyville and the region held by the Popular Army
and that cash in the hands of large companies with many Congolese
employees is already running short. Rombaut also revealed that the
European community had not yet established any effective organization or found leaders who would be responsible for treating with the
new authorities. Baron Nothomb, the Belgian Consul, has not yet
attempted to organize the Consular Corps into some kind of useful
mechanism. It appears that the problems from minute to minute and
day to day are so arbitrary if not desperate that it is impossible to create any sort of significant organization of the European community.
Rombaut believes on the basis of Stanleyville rumors that when
Gbenye arrives he will set up a "national government" and attempt
to obtain international recognition of it. Rombaut also believes that
the local authorities will do nothing drastic to the members of the
American Consulate at the present time because the situation is too
confused; he does not think any specific plan concerning the American Consulate has been evolved by these authorities.

"I can understand the lack of effective action by the European
community on our behalf," I said to Peter, "given the fear and isolation imposed by the rebel authorities. But I want you to realize that
if we can be treated this way today, they can turn on you next. By
making protests you may prevent this from happening to you. I
know you have little control over events, and you are in a delicate
position and doing the best you can. I am frustrated by our inability
to act, and I appreciate all you have done for us."

This was the first opportunity I had to talk freely to someone on

135

the outside and found it difficult to measure my words. I felt a twinge of jealousy over Peter and Patrick Nothomb's ability to move about and perform their functions, while we were stuck here. In performing their tasks, in the midst of the rebels, they were in as much or more danger than we were. But, at least they were active; all we could do was sit and wait.

Peter was gentle in responding. He said he would confer with Patrick, and they would do whatever they could. As he was leaving, I was startled when he said with a twinkle, "Keep a stiff upper lip." I realized I had been so tensed up that I had not laughed at his attempt to joke and lighten the mood.

After he left, David and I, most grateful for all this news, digested each morsel and reflected on the consequences for us.

"Sabiti is much better for us than Kinghis," David said. "Gbenye, being a minister in several central governments, should be inclined to treat diplomats properly. One thing not promising, however, is Gbenye's treatment of Frank Carlucci when he was covering Stanleyville for the embassy during the 1961 secession. That was before the consulate was established. Gbenye, as minister of the interior and number-two man to Gizenga, locked Frank in his hotel room, holding him hostage. The international reaction was so intense that Gbenye released him after a few days. During the time of the secession, contact was always maintained with the outside world. Pressure could be brought to bear."

"We don't have a handle on events," I said. "We have no way of influencing them. However, things should look up with a new government, one hopefully willing to deal with diplomats rather than locking them up."[4]

THE NEXT FOUR DAYS were spent much like the previous ones. No one came to see us except passing Simbas. I had asked Peter to try and arrange for Nothomb to visit. Peter was a businessman and a British honorary vice consul. With Patrick I felt I could have a more professional discussion because he was the Belgian consul. Not that I had any solutions to our problems, but at least we could coordinate what little we did. However, Patrick did not appear.

We heard from our guard that Gaston Soumialot had arrived. We saw there was activity at the Governor's Palace, which was located behind the Guest House. We heard that former President François Aradjabu would be named an extraordinary commissioner for Stanleyville. Later, the rumor circulated that he might be named governor again.

One afternoon, a large crowd of civilians gathered outside our door; they were somewhat hostile, but not particularly threatening. Our guards kept them from getting close to us. They sang songs that included words—those we were able to catch—that linked the American consulate with the "bad PNP party," which was widely thought to be a tool of the Belgian administration.

We received a large box of books from Barlovatz, a welcome gift that helped take our minds off what might happen to us. We heard several rumors on different days that aircraft were about to arrive. Once we were told an airplane was circling the city. The airport was almost deserted; we only saw a few Simbas run around with spears.

Another day, a twelve-year-old Simba told us an American airplane was to arrive that day to evacuate us. The prospect was tantalizing but not believable. The manager of the Guest House told us his food supplies were running low, and he would be unable to supply us with anything but limited amounts of bread, coffee, rice, and sardines. I was becoming quite fond of the rice and sardines. We had a supply of catsup and mustard that I thought made a tasty dish. The others disdained it. There was an uncertain supply of goodies from the consulate when our servants were permitted to visit.

David and I analyzed the rebellion and our relationship to the rebels as we saw it at this point. Our journal entry read:

1. The Popular Army is clearly dominated by members of the Bakusu and Batetela tribes. Their chief collaborators in Stanleyville are "Arabisé" elements. . . .

2. A basic inspiration of the Popular Army, aside from its reliance on witchcraft, concerns revenge for Lumumba's death—Lumumba had been a member of the Batetela tribe. The Simbas have also been promised by their leaders like Olenga, very high salaries, important jobs after the Popular Army conquers the whole Congo. . . .

137

3. Concerning the situation of the Consulate Staff, we assume that our detention is probably explained away to Europeans as either a preventive custody device or required to protect us from the "wrath of the population. . . ." It certainly is confirmed that we are regarded by the authorities as hostages for the behavior not only of our own government but also that of Prime Minister Tshombé. The most difficult aspect of the situation for us is that we cannot affect our fate. . . . Our greatest personal disappointment is that we are unable to get any solid news on local or international activities concerning our situation in Stanleyville. We are also very disappointed that we do not receive relatively regular visits from our consular colleagues and have no news of any efforts being made locally on our behalf.

Our assessments were based on our limited view of the world from our cottage room and from what we could glean from passersby. We had overheard Simba soldiers discussing by the hour how much they were making in pay, how much was piling up owing to them, and speculating on what positions they would have once victory came.

"This sounds very much like ordinary working people, discussing their present and future prospects," I said. "While I am most disappointed that our colleagues don't come more often, I realize they have their own problems to face and have been most generous with their time and efforts on our behalf. We owe our lives to Peter and Patrick. Now, I sure would like some indication they are doing something for us. They have the freedom to move around; we don't."

I woke on Thursday, 3 September, to the sound of an aircraft flying above the city. It flew away. Nothing else happened in the morning. We lay on our beds, reading our books. Later in the day, I asked a servant to contact Peter to see if Muriel Davis could visit her husband again.

In the evening, Henri Bablon came to visit. David said he was an influential radical youth leader in Stanleyville. He came, I thought, to see the local celebrities. Our guards apparently placed no restrictions on who could visit us. Bablon was now an officer and had some political function in the Popular Army. He talked freely and frankly about the military and political situation, much as someone would talk to us as consuls, and seemed to want to inform us about what was happening. He treated us as equals and with respect.

138

"The Popular Army is besieging Coquihatville and approaching Luluabourg," he said. We had heard these same stories for the past few weeks. We suspected these points represented the furthest expansion of the rebellion and not where the rebels were now.

"In Bukavu," he continued, "[Lt. Col. Leonard] Mulamba [commander of the ANC Third Army] is calling for more reinforcements and will evacuate the city if he does not get them."

Bablon told us the PTT was functioning and was receiving and sending messages normally. He said the authorities had decided in principle to allow a Red Cross plane to land at the city, but formal approval had not yet been granted. "They are angry with the Red Cross for requesting approval from Nendaka for the flight from Bangui to Stanleyville," he said. Asking permission of Victor Nendaka, the security chief in Léopoldville, for a flight to Stanleyville was an obvious slight to the rebel regime.

"The local government is being run by Sabiti, two Simba officers, and two women from the National Women's Organization," Bablon continued. These were presumably some of those women I had seen at the meeting with Olenga, so long ago, at the chamber of commerce offices. He said no foreign state had yet recognized the rebel government, and Christophe Gbenye, the president of the *Comité Nationale de Libèration* (CNL), was expected to arrive soon. "This should improve our chances for foreign recognition." Throughout the discussion, Bablon expressed concern over the general state of the rebellion and disapproved of the violence and primitivism he saw around him.

After Bablon's departure, two of the officers in the airport guard came to tell us a World Health Organization plane was expected "in the near future." I asked what that might mean for us, but they had no comment.

The next day, a servant delivered a letter to Chuck from his wife. In the letter, she relayed the information Peter had asked her to send us. She said there had been a consular meeting with Sabiti and the Popular Army on 1 September. The consuls were told that no Europeans would be permitted to leave Stanleyville because if they did the city would be bombed by the central government and its Belgian and American allies. The rebels said that when Europeans left Uvira after the rebels took it, the city was bombed by ANC aircraft. Muriel

139

said it was possible she and the children would be allowed to go to Kilometer Eight and join Al Larson and the English, Canadians, and Americans at the station there.

Saturday, 5 September, the thirty-second day since the attack on the consulate, passed uneventfully until about five in the evening when Rombaut, Nothomb, and the Swedish honorary consul arrived at the cottage. They said they were taking David and me to a consular meeting with the new revolutionary president, Gbenye, at the Governor's Palace. I was pleased with the prospect of being involved again. Our guards did not oppose our departure. We arrived at the Palace and started to go inside with others of the consular corps. Before we could enter, several cars filled with Simbas drove up. Olenga got out and ran up to block our way.

"I have not given permission for the Americans to be released," the general shouted. "Take them to the Central Prison immediately."

His Simbas pounced on David and me, hitting us with their rifle butts, and threw us into a Land Rover. The rest of the consular corps stood in silence, stunned, knowing they could do nothing but watch.

We were driven to the airport terminal and then shoved roughly into the same toilet room we had been in before. Again, I noted that violence accompanied our worsening situation. The pain in my stomach returned. The Simbas told us our time had come, that our last hours were upon us. They laughed as they taunted and knocked us about.

After a few minutes, we were dragged to the front of the terminal where the other three members of the consulate staff and Chuck Davis were in another car. David and I were put back in the Land Rover, and we sped off on the road into the city, accelerator to the floor, with Olenga's car in the lead. There was no question now, I thought, that we could work with or be allowed to deal with the rebels. We had to await our fate; there wasn't much else we could do.

We arrived at the prison and were shoved into the entryway. We were forced to remove our belts, shoes and socks, wallets, and other items in our pockets. We had no other possessions with us. Everything was given back but our belts. We were led into the central courtyard and put into a cell on the left, just opposite to the one where Kinghis had put us on 12 August. It was bare except for six narrow boards on the incredibly dirty floor. A window on the wall facing the street was too high for us to see out. Simba soldiers, prisoners themselves, came to peer in to see the Americans through the open door. They started their usual chants of how bad the Americans were and how they had shot down American planes.

It was too familiar. In prison again, but this time put in by Olenga, with no appeal possible to a higher authority. We had come tantalizingly close to participating in a meeting with our colleagues and the authorities. Instead we were thrown into a bare cell, beaten and helpless. There was nothing to do but make ourselves as comfortable as possible on our hard boards.

The night was long and cold.

Red Cross

Days 33 to 53: Sunday, 6 September,

through Saturday afternoon, 26 September 1964

OUR PRISON CELL, MARKED CELL NUMBER ONE, WAS THE FIRST ON
the left and faced a paved courtyard. It was one of the upper-grade
cells forming the front corner of Stanleyville Central Prison. From
the doorway, we could see the vast quadrangle of the main yard.
Across from us was the cell where we had spent an August afternoon
when Alphonse Kinghis had imprisoned us. The medieval aspect of the
place struck me again. Surrounded by crenellated walls, it reminded
me of the Quadrangles at the University of Chicago, where my father
had taught physics and I had attended. Both had that strong look of
solid stone and brick construction, blackened with age. I knew this
was different, vastly different, and dangerous. We had nowhere to go.
There would be no escape.

I slept little that first night, partly because I was not used to our
beds, which were boards laid on the rough brick floor. Imprisoned
Simbas kept coming into the cell to gawk and say nasty things about

142

the Americans. Thankfully, they did not hit us. Sunday morning, 6 September, dirty, scraggly pallets—ticking filled with foul-smelling lumpy straw, sorry excuses for mattresses—were brought in. We were told we could use the toilets and showers located in our corner of the prison. They were reasonably clean, but we had to pass a gauntlet of Simba prisoners each time to reach them. We could not have blankets, razors, or knives, we were told.

We had not eaten since leaving the airport the previous evening. A prison official said our servants could bring us food twice a day. They arrived around noon. They said they had gone to the Sabena Guest House and were told we were at the prison. We picked at the food. Who could be interested in eating in such dismal surroundings?

David and I hunched in the corner of our cell to talk about our predicament. "What do you come up with?" I asked. "What is Olenga trying to do?"

"I don't know," David said. "He must consider us valuable. He may not want us to talk to our colleagues. Maybe he's afraid of us, thinking we might encourage them to be uncooperative. Or, it might simply be in retaliation against American support in the defense of Bukavu."

"It could be he fears we could somehow subvert the civilian authorities he's put in place," I said. "Basically, I think Olenga sees us as hostages and wants to be sure we are safely tucked away and can't be used by anyone else. We are prizes of war. Somehow, he believes we also may be useful in case the city is attacked."

"The Simbas are in here for infractions of discipline," David said. "They are capable of anything and may turn on us. I've not put my contact lenses back in after taking them out at the airport last night. I can't risk being beaten about the head with the lenses in. It could injure my eyes permanently."

"Now we both have problems seeing," I said. "Since Nasor crushed my only pair of glasses, I've had trouble recognizing people at a distance."

"I can't recognize anyone more than a few yards away," David said. "Be sure to tell me when you can identify people coming."

Simba prisoners, the higher-ranking ones in cells next to ours

143

and others in dormitory cells around the large quadrangle, continued their tirades against Americans. Each Simba had his own tale of how he had killed American troops on the battlefield. They followed the ritual of pointing their fingers into the air, rat-a-tatting, and imitating the shooting down of American airplanes. The Simba prisoners, however, quickly became accustomed to our presence and became perfunctory in their taunts. We were left alone most of the time. Certain Simba prisoners took responsibility for controlling the others if they felt they bothered us too much.

We spent most of the time in our cell. The door was not locked. It was shut only when there was activity in the yard that someone decided we should not see. Otherwise, we came in and out of the cell as we wanted. I did so from time to time, from nervousness or from being tired of staying inside doing nothing.

We swung into a rhythm of simple prison life. Our basic needs were met. Toilet facilities were available, and simple meals were sent in. We had nothing except the clothes we arrived in. Our servants brought soap, toothbrushes, and towels, sent by Alex Barlovatz and his wife, Lucy. Many other prisoners did not have these simple luxuries. Congolese civilian prisoners were forced to clean the yard and the toilets, pick up trash, and chop weeds with long steel machetes. We were not forced to join them.

Most of the time Chuck, Jim, Don, and Ernie kept their thoughts to themselves, still in shock, I thought, produced by our bleak surroundings and prospects. David and I did not feel much better, but we were interested in arriving at some understanding of our fate. We welcomed anyone outside our group who appeared willing or able to talk to us.

Such a person was Charles Ifefe, a fellow prisoner, who had been the *chef de cabinet* of the Kinghis government. He came to our cell and claimed he was put in prison because he had tried to protect Europeans. He said he had stood up to Olenga and the other authorities for proper treatment of civilians and diplomats. Others told us that while he had been moderate toward civilians, he had been arrested for appropriating funds for his personal use. Although we learned

144

little new from him, he was intelligent and articulate; David and I enjoyed conversing with him.

On the third day of our incarceration, General Olenga came into the yard. Someone had closed our cell door, but through the cracks I could see Simba prisoners lined up before him. At times he motioned for some prisoners to take their things and leave, presumably freed.

A rebel officer came to our cell and told us to come out. "Line up and stand at attention," he said.

Olenga came over and stood before us. "My forces have captured 108 American mercenaries at Bukavu," he said, not looking me in the eye. "They have not been killed. I will have them brought to Stanleyville and put in prison with you. This proves American troops are fighting with Tshombé forces against the Popular Army."

I could think of nothing to say in response to virtually the same accusations he had made at the chamber of commerce meeting on 10 August. I did not want to provoke him and was certain I could not convince him Americans were not involved in the fighting. American involvement was extensive and well known on the logistical side, but I still had no way of knowing if any Americans, civilian or military, were involved or if any had been captured.[1] Olenga did not wait to hear my thoughts on the matter and strode out of the prison with his followers. I feared the Simbas in prison would have heard Olenga's statement and retaliate, but they did not. Perhaps they had heard the story so often it was no longer new.

THOUGH SIMBAS WERE incarcerated, they maintained their status as soldiers and did not appear particularly worried about their imprisonment. They were anxious to have their "case" adjudicated and return to duty. Their friends, usually other Simbas, were free to visit them.

One visiting group came from the fighting around Beni and Butembo on the northeast border of the Congo. They were delighted to see the Americans they had heard so much about and lined us up at attention. Pushing and yelling at us, they forced us to run around the large courtyard. It was about a 440-yard run, and Ernie began to lag behind. A Simba shoved him, and he fell to his knees. Charles

145

Ifefe called the prison officials, and they chased the Simbas off, returning us to the calm of our cell.

The next day, Colonel Opepe came into the prison. He paid no attention to us. He appeared to judge Simba prisoners and dealt with some civilian detainees.

We guessed there were about two hundred inmates in the prison, about equally divided between civilian and military. There were almost daily releases and additions. The civilian prisoners wandered about the courtyard, downcast and discouraged. They awaited the arrival of some functionary to "judge their case." Some were women, we were told, but we never saw them. The civilian prisoners did not bother us. Perhaps they sympathized with someone who was in the same situation as they were. One cell along the wall close to us contained mental patients. They carried on an almost continuous chorus of shouts and ravings. We could not distinguish what they were saying, but an occasional word could be recognized, like *"Amèrikani,"* which led us to believe they knew we were there.

A short, bearded Simba colonel we had not seen before came into the prison on Friday, 11 September. I thought he had come to deal with the Simbas, but he was pushed around and treated as a prisoner. A Simba told us it was Martin Kasongo, arrested at Olenga's order, for some unknown reason.

"He was minister of interior in the rebel government of Albertville," David told me. "He was with Soumialot in Bujumbura as an agent of the CNL [*Comité Nationale de Libèration*] mission to the eastern Congo. You remember that one intercepted message from Olenga in Kindu to Gbenye and Soumialot warned them that Kasongo was a *sûreté* agent. I met him in Stanleyville some time ago."[2]

Kasongo came to our cell and went right up to David. "I want you to write a note saying that I was invited to a consulate reception, but I did not attend," he said. "You must say that I refused in writing to accept the invitation. Give as the reason that I said the consulate was trying to 'emasculate Lumumbists by subverting their nationalist fervor.'"

"Sure," said David. "I'll write you a note. Get me pencil and paper."

They were produced, and David wrote the note. Kasongo took it, thanking David profusely.

"I wrote as he said," David said. "Maybe proving Kasongo is a good nationalist will do us some good. I have no idea whether or not he worked for Nendaka. I doubt it."

"He must have learned the words from the Chinese," I said. "A most peculiar character, not very stable. He sure looked pleased with your note."

Later in the afternoon, Olenga came to the prison. He mingled easily with the prisoners. Again we were ordered to line up at attention in front of our cell. Olenga came over and made a speech about American interference in Congolese affairs by supplying mercenaries to fight against him. "I have heard that one of you is a missionary," he added in a completely different tone. "I have no quarrel with missionaries."

"Yes, Chuck Davis here is a missionary," I said.

"Missionaries have a special status," the general said. "He should be permitted to rejoin his family." He motioned to one of his entourage to take Chuck away, and they left.

"Now we're back to the hard core," I said. "The Davises landed in this trouble, not knowing the Congo. They were thrust into other people's problems. At least we knew something of what we were getting into. Anyway, I'm glad Chuck's out of here."

The next day was quiet except for a brief intervention from Kasongo. He barged brusquely into our cell with two other officers. "You will sing," he ordered. "Dance around the room and sing 'I like Lumumba.'" We did as he said, murmuring *"j'aime Lumumba"* as we did a desultory dance. After a couple of minutes, Kasongo left, and we slumped back to our pallets.

After a few minutes, Kasongo came back alone and stuck his head in the door. "I will save you," he whispered.

147

"Was that supposed to make us feel better?" I said. "Does he want us to believe he is a friend? I doubt he'll turn out to be another Sengha."

On Sunday families come to bring food and see their relatives.

No one came to see us. We heard Kasongo record a speech in the director's office, located behind our cell, on Monday. We could not hear what he was saying. Charles Ifefe came by for a chat. We learned on Tuesday that Kasongo had been put into a *cachot*, a lightless cell that is too small for a man to either stand up straight or lie down. Earlier we had seen him wearing the prison uniform, blue cotton shorts and a yellow-and-blue striped jersey tank top. It was the first time we had seen it worn by a military prisoner. Ifefe told us Opepe had been to the prison early in the morning to promise that all Simba officers would be taken from prison and placed in more comfortable surroundings, under some form of house arrest.

Later in the morning, a short, thin Congolese, sporting a trim goatee and wearing an animal skin cap, entered the prison yard. A table was set up in the courtyard, and he began disposing of prisoners brought before him. "He's the minister of defense," a Simba told us. "Soumialot, Gaston."

Soumialot released many civilian and Simba prisoners in quick succession. When he finished, he came over to our cell from where he must have seen me watching the proceedings. I could see he was balding under his cap. He stared straight ahead with small beady eyes, not looking at me. He started with the usual lecture on American interference in Congolese politics and participation in military operations against the Popular Army. He repeated Olenga's assertion that American mercenaries had been captured and would be brought to Stanleyville to be imprisoned with us. Then, changing his tone, he asked, "Are you in good health?"

I was too surprised to say anything and instead gave him one of my best bronchial coughs. Before I could reply further, he turned and went out the door. One of his entourage came back and poked his head in. "We will look into your case," he said.

148

"We've heard that one before," I muttered.

Twenty minutes later, Dr. Barlovatz came into the prison and to our cell. "Soumialot sent me," he said. "Here, let me look at you." He examined all of us, making an elaborate show of treating us. He gave David an unwanted flu shot and me some cough medicine but was hurried off before he could talk further to us.

About nine in the evening, the same officer who had poked his head into the cell after Soumialot's visit came again. "You are to be released from prison," he said. "You will be placed under house arrest. Where do you want to go?"

"To our apartments in the Immoquateur," I said quickly, pushing this desire one more time. There we would be with our friends. I could almost feel the comforting walls of the luxuriously laid out multistory apartments.

"It is too late to go there," the officer said. "I will take you back to the Sabena Guest House."

I knew it would be difficult to move once we were installed again at the airport, but we had no choice. We gathered our few belongings and followed the officer. We passed through the entryway without formality. When we arrived at our cottage, we found it had been sealed shut after our departure. Nothing had been disturbed. After planks and straw pallets in the prison, it was a relief to be able to sit on a chair and stretch out on a bed. We took turns at the bathroom, bathing and shaving. My pepper-shaded ten-day growth of beard came off without difficulty. Our Simba guards had remained and gave us a warm welcome. They ordered beer and food from the Guest House kitchen, and we celebrated our return.

THE NEXT DAY, 16 September, we remained in the cottage. Chuck's bed was removed to give us more room. We were treated better than before; the Simbas were relaxed. Dr. Barlovatz brought us books and playing cards, and he talked to us at length to catch us up on events since we had been incarcerated. We had access now to our briefcases and took notes. David and I recorded what the doctor told us in our journal:

> (1) that our release from prison was due to the intervention of the French correspondent [Joseph Gerlache] who has daily contacts with Gbenye and is promising the latter French aid for the Popular Army; (2) that the Belgian consul and vice consul had visited Gbenye and were preparing for him a copy of the 1961 Geneva Convention concerning diplomatic and consular privileges; (3) that there is a certain easing of tension in the European community and that Europeans

are circulating on the streets for the first time. Barlovatz said however that European women were in a nervous state generally, that there were no grave illnesses, either mental or physical, among the European population except for 2 or 3 cases. Three Catholic priests had been arrested yesterday on the complaint of a witch doctor but had been released this morning.[3]

Gerlache was the *Agence France Presse* representative and French honorary consul. "You tell him we are most grateful for his intervention," I said to the doctor. "I suspect our release has something to do with Olenga's presence or absence."

"Yes, Olenga has left again for the eastern front," Barlovatz said. "He released Mr. Davis after Peter Rombaut explained to him the distinction between mercenaries and missionaries. Davis rejoined his wife at Kilometer Eight. The American and other missionaries in the area are all right, frightened, but bearing up well in spite of harassment by the Simbas."

"We last saw the general in prison five days ago," I said. "Opepe and Soumialot appeared in prison to judge prisoners on the fifteenth. I guess that was because Olenga had left."

Barlovatz said the rebel government formed by Olenga on 5 September was called the *République Populaire du Congo,* with Christophe Gbenye as president. He had arrived in Stanleyville, coming from Brazzaville via Brussels and Bujumbura. Gbenye was proclaimed the "spiritual successor of the martyred Lumumba" and the CNL was the successor to Lumumba's party, the MNC-L. Barlovatz confirmed that Soumialot had preceded Gbenye to Stanleyville by several days. Soumialot had been in charge of the rebel administration of Albertville and was given responsibility for information and interior in addition to defense in the new republic. François Sabiti was minister of public works.

150

According to Barlovatz the original six provinces of the 1960 Congo were restored, and local governments were being appointed. Stanleyville was proclaimed the capital. "While civilian authority is put in place," the doctor said, "everyone agrees that the military is still firmly under Olenga's control and holds the real power."

Opepe came to the cottage the next day. I reiterated my desire to move to the Immoquateur. "I will discuss it with Soumialot," he told me with the help of one of his officers. "I want to know if you are eating well?"

"Fairly well," I said. "But the Sabena Guest House kitchen is running out of food. It is becoming difficult for us to get proper meals."

After Opepe left, David's driver arrived. He told us that although food supplies in the town were low, he thought our servants could feed us adequately from stocks left in the consulate and our apartments. He also confirmed for us that the word was that Olenga was in Kindu planning another attack on Bukavu.

"Now we have to think of what happens if he is frustrated again in taking Bukavu," I said.

The next day, Friday, we heard an airplane flying over the city, some distance away. In the afternoon, another aircraft flew over, this time drawing fire from the Simba airport garrison. "It was a WHO airplane," a Simba lieutenant told us. "Firing at it was a mistake. Gbenye was at the airport, trying to stop the firing. Another plane is due to arrive Monday or Tuesday."

That night, there was a particularly heavy rainfall. Our guards opened our door and slid their weapons in to keep them dry. I stared at the pile of assorted loaded pistols, rifles, and automatic weapons with ample ammunition. I was not tempted. It just showed how relaxed our Simba guards were around us.

Wounded Simbas convalescing at the nearby hospital came by the cottage to harass the Americans. We were brought outside and made to stand at attention to listen to their tales of how they had killed many Americans in the field. There was the familiar rat-a-tat as they shot down American planes. Sunday was a day of celebration for the Simbas and their friends at the airport. Palm wine and beer flowed freely. Several groups of celebrants strolled by and shouted at us. In the afternoon, our guard was reinforced because, we were told, "your American brothers are coming to try and rescue you." On Monday our servants did not show up with food. One managed to come by on Tuesday and told us that the authorities had ordered

151

everyone off the streets so they could conduct identity checks in the communes. Anyone who did not have an MNC-L identity card was supposed to be arrested.

On Wednesday, Soumialot arrived, accompanied by Sabiti and a few officers. "Are you eating well?" he asked. Without waiting for a reply, Soumialot said to me, "Come with me to the consulate." I followed him to his car and got in beside him in the back seat. "We have received a message from [Cassius] Senn, the Red Cross representative in Bujumbura. I knew him here and in Bujumbura. He asked if the American consulate would like to leave Stanleyville."[4]

"Well, what do you think?" I asked, not wanting to show my eagerness. "What is our status here? Why aren't we allowed to move about? What are we going to be permitted to do?"

"I will have to look into your dossier," he said. The rest of the trip passed in silence. On reaching the consulate, Soumialot said he would like to see the offices and residence. "I am thinking of using them for myself," he said after the tour. It was more a statement than a request, and I did not respond. "What about the communication facilities?" he asked.

"I gave our *phonie* to Kitenge, the head of security," I said. "Our teletype equipment was damaged during the attack on the consulate on August 5th and is inoperative."

"I will send technicians to repair it," he said. "If the American staff is evacuated, I will take over the building."

"Yes, you can certainly do that when we leave," I replied.

We were seated by this time out on the back veranda, by the drained pool. The servants served us gin with water, the only mix left. I described the various attacks on the consulate staff, detailing the beatings and humiliations we had suffered at the hands of the Simbas. "The protection accorded diplomatic and consular personnel has been a mark of civilized behavior among men and nations throughout history," I concluded.

152

Soumialot acted surprised by my revelations of our treatment. "These are unfortunate incidents and come from General Olenga's lack of sophistication," he said. "He is a military man and concerned only with fighting. He does not understand how consuls and diplomats need to be treated. Your situation should improve because military rule is drawing to a close, to be replaced by civilian administration. You should understand the Simbas have a negative attitude toward you since they are encountering American soldiers in the field against them."

"I can state unequivocally that this is not the case," I said.

"Would you stake your life on that?" he asked.

I did not reply.

"The United States should not support fathers against sons in the one family that forms the Congo," he said.

"American policy is to work for a strong and united Congo," I said.

The conversation was carried on in a friendly fashion, but I felt we were not talking directly at each other. We each said what we were supposed to say.

"By the way," Soumialot said as we were getting up, "a Red Cross airplane will be arriving soon."

He said nothing further about this tantalizing bit of news he had dangled before me.

He took me to where he had his offices and living quarters a few blocks away. It had been Gizenga's residence during the 1960 and 1961 Stanleyville succession. People of all descriptions were milling around the house, waiting for an audience with the minister. Several young and pretty girls were also there. Soumialot conferred with some people and then came to where I was standing. "I will try to improve the lot of the American staff," he said. "Drive the consul back to the airport," he told his driver. "Give everyone a separate cottage."

At the airport, the guards opened four more cottages for us. Two guards were assigned to each cottage. "This is putting quite a strain on my personnel," the commandant said as he placed the additional guards.

For the first time in six weeks, we had our privacy. We spent most of the time together in one cottage but slept apart as ordered. I was free to wander among the seemingly endless rows of Sabena Guest House cottages. Each was made up and empty, waiting for guests who were no longer transiting to or through Stanleyville.

153

THURSDAY PASSED WITHOUT incident. On Friday, 25 September, Antoine Lingili, the consulate receptionist, appeared. He told us Soumialot had come by the offices early in the morning and told the employees, who came each day, to be ready for his occupancy by eleven o'clock in the morning.

While Antoine was still there, we heard the noise of an airplane flying low; it was in a landing pattern for the airport. Shortly thereafter, a DC-3 aircraft with Red Cross markings taxied up behind the terminal and stopped. We all crowded around my window because from there we could see the front of the airport terminal, which was about a hundred yards away. This was the first aircraft to arrive in Stanleyville since the rebel takeover. I thought only of when we would be permitted to see the members of the mission. I almost stopped breathing with anticipation. It might not mean liberation, but the prospect of contact with the outside world gave me hope the end of the nightmare was in sight.

"That looks like Senn, the Red Cross rep," said David, who had resumed putting in his contact lenses. "I know him from his many trips here. If anyone can do something for us, he can."

A crowd of rebel officers mingled with members of the arriving group. We watched them get into vehicles and drive off toward town and out of sight. It was quiet now. I began to feel that perhaps we would not meet with them after all. Maybe they would see the rebel leaders, and then, surely, hopefully, would come to see us. No one spoke. Our hopes were there, but as time passed, I felt optimism fade.

No one came to talk to us and nothing happened. The night was long. The next morning passed slowly. Shortly before noon, two of Opepe's officers came to the cottage where we were gathered. They handed us small forms marked with a red cross with lines for a brief message, the standard Red Cross "we are well and safe" form. "Write twenty-five words in French," said one of them. "This is for the Red Cross mission."

Before I could react, David hissed in my ear, "Don't take them! Don't write anything!"

I knew he was right. "No, we won't write anything," I told the officer.

"But you must," the officer said, surprised and puzzled. I shook my head. They appeared pressed for time. Realizing they could not force us to comply, they strode off.

"We should not accept anything less than a full ability to communicate with the mission," David said. "Writing a message the rebels obviously could see would indicate we agreed to the restrictions imposed on us."

"Yes, you're right, David," I said. "Besides, maybe it will lead to a meeting with the mission. And when they see we won't send a message, they should know things are not all right."

About an hour later, we saw vehicles return from town and drive up to the terminal. As far as we could determine, only those who had arrived with the mission got out of the cars. We had watched medical supplies being unloaded and taken away previously. The engines started, and the plane taxied away from the terminal. We heard it take off and fly away.[5]

The realization sank in that they had flown in and out without seeing us. None of us spoke. The silence lasted all that sullen afternoon. We were neglected, isolated, alone with our thoughts. If black is the color of despair in the heart of darkness, it was now its most impenetrable.

> Never, never before, did this land, this river, this jungle, the very arch
> of this blazing sky, appear to me so hopeless and so dark, so impene-
> trable to human thought, so pitiless to human weakness. (Conrad,
> *Heart of Darkness*)

Gbenye and Soumialot

Days 53 through 66: Saturday afternoon, 26 September,

through Friday, 9 October 1964

LATE IN THE AFTERNOON ON SATURDAY, 26 SEPTEMBER, SAM, THE replacement cook from the residence, came to the cottage. He said Dr. Barlovatz had come to the consulate and asked him to tell us that he had seen Mr. Senn of the Red Cross at the Congo Palace Hotel. From what Sam said, I gathered that Senn had spent a good deal of time discussing the "situation of the American consulate" with the rebel authorities. Barlovatz had given Senn details about the "mistreatment of the American staff." The Red Cross mission had apparently drawn up a list of people to be evacuated for medical reasons and received tentative agreement for their evacuation in a future flight.[1] Sam also said Soumialot had told him he intended to occupy the consulate "very soon."

In the evening, the deputy commander of the Simba airport guard came to see us. He said President Gbenye had told Colonel Opepe this morning that they must "show respect for the American consulate prisoners." The president told him their officers should talk to the Americans "because they are so intelligent."

"That sounds like fallout from the Red Cross mission," David said after he left.

"I can't imagine where he got that 'intelligent' bit," I said.

On Sunday, an officer came to take me to see Soumialot. "I have decided that I will use the consulate and residence for myself," the minister said when I was ushered into his office.

"I can agree to that," I said. "You mentioned before this would be conditioned on the evacuation of the American staff. Is that going to take place?"

"*D'accord*," he said. "Yes, I can agree to that."

"While waiting for evacuation we should be permitted to live in our apartments at the Immoquateur," I ventured, making this my umpteenth try.

"I will consult with President Gbenye on that," Soumialot said. "For now, we need an inventory of the premises."

"The vice consul should take care of that," I said. I thought David should get involved.

I was sent to the airport to get David. We were driven back to Soumialot's office and waited outside, amidst the usual hangers-on. People were drinking on the terrace. Some were dancing on the lawn, in a festive mood. It looked like the usual gatherings I had seen outside African chieftains' houses. When Soumialot emerged we went to the consulate. We waited in the residence while someone went to look for an employee to bring a key to the offices. In the small library, Soumialot sat, studying papers a secretary had brought.

When he finished, he looked up at us. "Many houses and offices are being requisitioned by this new central government established for the Congo," he said. "We are finally being freed from colonial status."

"Did you know that the United States was once a colony of Great Britain?" I asked.

Soumialot acted surprised. He may have thought only Africa had been colonized by Europe.

"You can gather your personal belongings here," he said. "Put them into suitcases and leave them here until you are ready to go."

157

I put clothes and other things in several suitcases. I brought the silver flatware from the kitchen and included it. It was Jensen luncheon silver, and I did not want to lose it. I remembered a small pistol I had left on a closet shelf, right by where I had climbed into the attic with Nasor when he searched the residence in August. If it was discovered, it might provoke an incident. I decided to leave it where it was.

After Soumialot left, one of his officers took us to the airport. We learned Dr. Barlovatz had been there during our absence and had briefed the others about the Red Cross visit. He said he had an "unauthorized" contact with Senn at the bar of the Congo Palace Hotel, where the group had stayed under close guard. Barlovatz said he was the only European they saw. The rebels told the mission members that they could return in ten days, but no one would be allowed to leave Stanleyville. The doctor was convinced no one would be allowed to leave, and all Europeans were considered hostages by the rebel authorities. Barlovatz said the rebels had confiscated all the medicines the Red Cross had brought.

That evening, while we were relaxing after dinner, Jim Stauffer mused out loud, "You know, I have Congolese friends in the commune. I could easily slip out of here and go to them. I know they would welcome me and hide me."

"That might well be possible," David said. "But have you thought what they would do to us when they discover you've gone?"

"Yes," I said. "There should be no thought of doing that."

AN OFFICER FROM Opepe's staff came to the cottages at eight the next morning and told the five of us to gather our "things" (*vos choses*) and come with him. He drove us to Opepe's office at staff headquarters at Camp Ketele. Through his officer, Opepe asked me where we wanted to be housed. Again I said we wished to go to the Immoquateur. He said that would not be possible. Then he asked why we had refused to send out messages with the Red Cross.

"We did not know enough about our situation or our status to make a statement," I said. "How could we say we were well or not?

And the officers bringing the message forms did not make it clear what we were supposed to do."

"You should write a message now saying that you are alive and well," he said. "I will send it by CFL's radio to Bujumbura. But for now, we must go see the president."

We were ushered into Christophe Gbenye's office with our boxes of books and clothes. He was seated behind a large desk, a tall, large man. His thick black beard dominated his round face, and he was going bald in the front.

"You people in the American consulate are victims of misunderstandings and lack of contact with the nationalists," he said without formality or greeting. "You do not appreciate the nationalist point of view." He continued his speech in this vein for some time.

"Before coming here, I was in Bujumbura and met your Mr. Devlin in late August." I tried not to act startled and avoided looking at David. Larry Devlin had been CIA station chief in Léopoldville, and David's boss, until about a year before. "We were about to reach an agreement about what should be done with the American consular staff," Gbenye continued. "We were to meet the next day to make arrangements. But, I had to hurry over to the Congo, to Uvira, which had just been bombed by an American airplane. I then came here and did not see him again."[2]

I knew Larry had established close connections with Mobutu and had been involved in some way in Lumumba's transfer to the Katanga, where he was assassinated. Gbenye had been the recipient of grants from the embassy. These grants had been funded by the CIA and probably involved Devlin, as well as Monty Stearns. I thought it possible, but was not sure, that Gbenye might know or suspect Devlin's and even perhaps David's affiliations with the CIA.

"I arrived here on September 4th," Gbenye went on without a pause. "I was not aware you were under house arrest by military order when I included you in the invitation for the consular corps to be presented to my government. We can envisage the evacuation of you and other civilians from Stan when normal air communications are established. It was impossible for you to leave by the Red Cross plane

159

due to the bad psychological effect this would have had on the population. For the moment, no Europeans or other foreigners will be permitted to leave the city. It is possible that they will be allowed to depart eventually if they sign attestations they are abandoning their property or that they sold their properties at prices fixed by the authorities.

"As for you," he continued, "you can be assured that I am aware that you have diplomatic status and ought not be executed. I also know that by diplomatic practice, you should have been evacuated from Stan eight days after the Popular Army took over. But for now, I will make arrangements for you to have better living conditions. You may leave now."

We were ushered to the anteroom. Opepe remained behind. Soumialot arrived and went into Gbenye's office. Opepe emerged shortly afterwards and drove us back to the Sabena Guest House cottages. We were told someone would be back at seven in the morning to take us to "new and better quarters."

A consulate employee arrived later and said that Soumialot had moved into the consulate and residence that day. "The things you packed in suitcases are still there," he said. "They broke into Mr. Hoyt's bag to take the utensils because there were no others."

A Congolese civilian came to the door. I did not recognize him. He handed me a typed note labeled "CONVOCATION." In essence, it stated that the American consul should appear before a military tribunal to answer questions on back pay and other benefits due. David informed me that the man named in the note was a driver employed by the consulate and fired by John Clingerman, my predecessor, last January after being caught red-handed stealing consulate funds. There was no date or place on the paper telling me when or where I should appear.

"I will see to it," I told the driver. He left, apparently satisfied.

160

"I don't know whether to be encouraged by our contacts today with Gbenye and Opepe," I said to David. "Nothing much has taken place, lots of words, but there may have been some movement toward a better status for us."

"At least it has been a busy day," David said. "Maybe we will be less isolated in our new quarters and be in touch with our colleagues."

"What do you make of Gbenye's meeting with Devlin?" I asked. "Larry is just the guy to pull something like that."

"They must have known each other in Léopoldville when Gbenye was a minister. I can't imagine what Larry told Gbenye before they got interrupted," David said. "It shows there is someone interested in our fate."

"This is the first indication we've had that the department or your agency have made any move on our behalf. I'm sure they are doing something else, but this shows someone's concerned."

We recorded our impressions of our meeting with Gbenye in our journal:

> From this first meeting with Gbenye it became clear the man is not interested in discussing anything substantive with the American Consulate. He carried on a long monologue during which it was impossible to interject any response whatsoever except "yes" and "no" and those words had no visible effect on him. It was also obvious that Gbenye regards us as objects to be used and is not interested in any thoughts we may have on our immediate situation or the activities of our Government.[3]

No one came the next day to take us to "new and better quarters." The only news we had was that the airport commandant had gone to Kasongo in the Maniema to visit his family. On Wednesday, there was a disturbance when a Simba was run over by truck driven by a civilian. The Simbas ran through the nearby settlement, beating people and demanding the execution of the driver.

When the servants arrived on Thursday, 1 October, with our food and some books from Dr. Barlovatz, they said Soumialot had informed them that we had been moved to new quarters. I told them to tell Soumialot we had not been moved. I also asked them to try and bring the suitcases we had packed.

In the early afternoon of the next day, a man came; he said he was Placide Kitungwa, *chef de cabinet* to Soumialot. Soumialot's function as minister of information was allowing him to occupy the consulate. Kitungwa said he had come to take all five of us to the consulate to take inventory. We rode down to the consulate and began a room

161

by room inventory. "The minister has given me orders," Kitungwa said when we came to the communications vault, "for you to repair the radio equipment so that you can communicate with your government."

"Our communications system is quite complex," I told him. "Our transmitter is out of order. Our *phonie* was taken by Kinghis. It should be around somewhere. In any case, we can communicate only with our government through our embassy in Léopoldville. That is the way embassies and consulates work." I did not want the rebels to know exactly what our communications capabilities were in case we could find a way to use them in the future.

"Come with me," Kitungwa said, "and we will look for your *phonie*." He took me downtown, and we entered a room filled with confiscated radio equipment. I could not see ours but noticed the United Nations' radio with its UNOC label.

When we returned to the consulate, David took me aside. "Jim and Don are most reluctant to work on their equipment," he whispered. "They feel for some reason that it should not be repaired."

"I sensed something like that when the transmitter went out originally," I said. "Jim was not eager to make repairs then. We'll discuss it later. For now, tell them to make it look like we're going along with whatever the rebels want."

When we went out on the back patio, by the pool, Kitungwa noticed the lawn blackened by fire. The destruction barrels were still there. "Why did you burn so much material?" he asked me. I wondered how he knew we had destroyed documents.

"We only had a normal amount of unimportant papers," I mumbled. "The fire got a little out of hand and spread to the lawn."

We were taken to see Soumialot after the inventory was completed. "We have not been moved from the Sabena Guest House," I told him. "Living conditions there are really poor." Gbenye arrived before Soumialot had a chance to reply. They discussed some matter that apparently did not concern us.

I managed to intercept Gbenye before he left. "Do you know that we are still at the airport?" I said. "We are coming to the end of our strength. I appeal to you to do something to provide us better living conditions and better security."

"I will appoint an officer as liaison between my office and the American consulate," he said. "However, you must remain under house arrest." We were then taken back to the airport.

Kitungwa brought us back to the consulate the next afternoon. David and I were ushered in to see Soumialot. He had established his office in the room that had been my Belgian secretary's office.

"The Americans plan to bomb Kindu," Soumialot said in an excited voice. "The control tower intercepted a message from the tower in Leo that a flight plan has been cleared for an American air-craft to overfly Kindu. I cannot agree to such machinations that can provoke serious incidents against American citizens. You should send a message to your embassy in Léopoldville to stop these things. Here are the details of the flight. Write a message that the bombing endangers the lives of Americans here."

I sat at the typewriter at my desk and typed in French what Soumialot had told me. Translated, the message read:

American Embassy Bujumbura for transmission to
American Embassy Leopoldville
    Just been informed by MinDefense Soumialot that he has
learned that an American aircraft R.47 is going to overfly Kindu at
11:55 this 3 October STOP. He told me that he does not agree with
such machinations that can provoke serious incidents against American citizens STOP. Told me to demand you do the necessary that
such incidents are avoided. FULLSTOP.

                                    HOYT
                                    AMCONSUL STANLEYVILLE
                        Stanleyville, October 3, 1964

Soumialot's secretary typed it on a fresh sheet, handed me a car-bon copy, and gave the original to Soumialot.[4] He took it and motioned us out of the office.

We waited for two hours. Kitungwa came in at one point to chat with us. "Perhaps we will lose this war," he said, "but sooner or later the nationalists will triumph."

After we returned to the cottages, David said, "You know, that's the first time that any rebel indicated they might not conquer the whole country. Remember when Olenga said he would take on the United States after taking Léopoldville?"

LATE IN THE AFTERNOON of the next day, Sunday, 4 October, the newly appointed mayor of Stanleyville, a short man with evasive and wild eyes, came to the cottages waving an elephant tail wand. "I've come to take you to the Congo Palace," he said. "Gather your things and come with me."

By that time we had accumulated enough possessions—clothing, books, food, playing cards, etc.—to fill several boxes. We loaded them and ourselves onto a yellow school bus. We sat in the bus in front of the airport terminal, which gave our Simba guards time to come out and see us off. They could not resist taunting us, saying we were going to be given a bad time where we were going. "They must not know we're scheduled for an improvement in our condition," I remarked. "When we're going to a better place, they do it gently, but when we go to a worse place, it's done roughly. Let's hope we're going to the hotel and not prison."

We drove off and arrived at the Congo Palace, the largest and newest hotel in town. We registered at the front desk in the lobby and were led to the second floor. Each one of us was given his own room with a clean, large king-sized bed. We luxuriated in the sumptuousness. The hotel staff apologized that they had not been alerted to the fact we were coming and would only be able to give us a light supper. Two Simbas from the airport contingent were stationed at the end of the corridor, presumably to ensure that we not leave the floor and that only authorized people had access to us.

Opepe came the next morning to tell us we had to move again. This time it was to the seventh and top floor of the hotel. It was less fancy than the second floor, but comfortable enough. "You will be the first victims in case of an attack by air," one of Opepe's men told us.

"Can we have our bags from the residence?" I asked him.

"I'll see to it," he said.

The hotel staff informed us they could not provide us with food. "Can't my cook bring our meals to us?" I asked.

"The Simbas tell us they are busy taking care of Mr. Soumialot and cannot be spared to feed you." For the moment, the feeding problem remained unresolved.

David, Jim, Don, and I went to a room to discuss the problem of the repair of our communications equipment. "What I don't understand," Jim said, "is what the rebels want to do with our equipment."

"The only thing I can come up with," David said, "is that Soumialot might want his own communications capability."

"I tried to convince them our equipment was only designed to contact our embassy in Léopoldville," I said. "It could not reach Moscow or Peking or any other place."

"I just don't like the idea of working on it," Jim said. "And I certainly don't want to operate it. It seems that every time we do something, it just irritates the Simbas, and we wind up in more trouble."

"Yeah," Don said. "I'm for just lying low, keeping out of trouble."

David did not say anything. I was vaguely aware that communicators were recruited separately and worked under only the nominal control of the CIA. Thus I thought David might not have complete authority over them.

"Look, if they want to communicate with communist countries, they can do it through the PTT," I said. "We've got a problem here that we have to resolve. My view on dealing with the rebels is that we should try to do anything we can to return us to a more normal operating mode. That is preferable to being stuck aside somewhere, neutralized, and exposed to all sorts of danger that an isolated position puts us in. Restoration of communications would mean a step in that direction, admittedly at some risk.

"In any case, we can't outright refuse to carry out rebel orders without the gravest consequences," I continued. "I think you should at least give the appearance of working on the equipment. Find out what the possibilities are of reestablishing communications, and then, at that point, we can decide on how to proceed."

"I think we ought to do what the consul says," David finally said. The others grudgingly grunted approval.

Kitungwa arrived Tuesday and said he wanted Jim and Don to go to the consulate to join technicians from the PTT to repair the communications equipment. I said I needed to come as translator. We got to the consulate before the technicians and waited all morning doing nothing. Jim and Don had a chance to check their equipment but told me they could not tell yet if it could be repaired or not.

165

We were returned to the Congo Palace. Our suitcases had not been released but my cook had brought a box of canned food from our stock at the residence. Soumialot, we were told, had taken all the cans of meat, and we were left with vegetables and fruit. The hotel kitchen heated canned brussels sprouts. They tasted terrible, and we passed bad gas the rest of the day.

We were informed that Dr. Barlovatz had come to the hotel but had not been permitted to see us because we were being held "incommunicado." A pass signed by either Soumialot or Opepe was required. This, however, did not prevent stray Simbas from coming.

That evening, the head of the two-man Simba guard, a young, short, clean-looking kid, approached me in what I perceived as an attempt to be friendly. He offered me a bottle of his beer. I accepted. Alcohol had otherwise been forbidden to us. In halting French, he tried to make conversation, talking about mundane matters. His position as our guard apparently gave him status and perks, including food and beer, but also, as he proudly showed me, a pretty Congolese girl, about thirteen, lying naked on his bed. Her coal-black skin shone against the white of the sheets. The thought crossed my mind that he might be offering her to me. I backed out hurriedly and returned to my room.

Jim, Don, and I were again taken to the consulate the next morning. After working on the radio for a while, Jim told me he thought it might be possible to get it operating.

"Continue working on it, giving all appearances of being serious about it," I whispered to him. "Delay actually getting it online until we know more about what is going on." We were returned to the hotel at about one in the afternoon.

The next day was spent quietly in the hotel. The following day, Friday, passed similarly, until about six-thirty in the evening. We heard the sound of boots stomping noisily up the stairs to our floor. A squad of Simbas burst into our rooms, shouting "Americans, Americans. Gather your things! Come!"

We packed a few pieces of clothes and picked up some books and playing cards. We were pushed downstairs, hit with weapons, and shoved into a waiting vw minivan. The back compartment was battered and stripped bare. We sat on the floor with our bundles, knocked from side to side as the driver drove at floorboard speed. It was a short drive. We screeched to a stop and were unloaded before the familiar crenellated walls of the Stanleyville Central Prison.

"The general came back this morning," a Simba said. "He ordered you back to prison. That was where you were when he left. He wants you back here, now."

I guessed he had been frustrated once more at taking Bukavu.[5]

We trooped into the prison office where our things were searched. Shoes, socks, and belts came off again. Everything was returned to us except our belts and briefcases that belonged to David and me. In my briefcase I had various papers, including my continuing letter to my wife Jo, copies of messages, and my desk diary. David's briefcases contained our journal notes and the considerable amount of money left in Congolese francs he had retrieved from his house before the rebels took the city. We had locked our briefcases and were not asked for the keys. "We will keep these safe for you," the prison director said.

We were led none too gently by our Simba squad to the double doors forming the entryway to the prison. The mayor of Stanleyville was there. "What are you doing here?" he asked us. As if we knew. "This is Georges Kokoyange," he said, pointing to a miserable heap of a beaten man at his feet. He had been the interior minister in the provincial government before Aradjabu's administration, David told me later. "We captured him in the forests with a group of ANC soldiers. They had been hiding since the fall of Stanleyville. We will be shooting them all." I was sure they would.

While waiting in the entry, through the doorway to the prison courtyard, I could see prisoners being moved out of a cell to our right, opposite to cell number one where we had been placed on 5 September. Someone went through the door with a broom. He came out, sweeping trash into the courtyard.

We were led there with our possessions. I read "No. 8" on the sign above the door. The room was about twenty feet wide and thirty feet long. A small barred window high up gave a view of the courtyard. A single electric bulb shone inside, just above the door. Planks about a foot and a half wide rested on ledges along the two walls and

167

on two-foot-high walls, forming a corridor down the middle of the room. The room was otherwise bare.

The door was closed behind us with a bang and was noisily locked. Silence. Too stunned to talk, we each put our belongings by one of the planks that we assumed were our beds. We had been through this before. There was nothing to say. Each was enshrouded in his own dark thoughts.

Today was 9 October, the sixty-sixth day since the Simbas took Stanleyville. The inevitable evening rain beat on the corrugated tin roof over our cell. The noise filled the cell. The echoes reinforced and deepened my despair.

Stanleyville Central Prison

Days 67 through 104: Saturday, 10 October,

through Monday, 16 November 1964

AFTER ARRIVING AT CELL NUMBER EIGHT IN STANLEYVILLE CENTRAL
Prison late Friday night, 9 October, I slept little during the remainder
of the night. We had no pillows, no blankets, nothing to cushion the
hard boards that served as our bed. As daylight arrived on Saturday,
I inspected our cell. I saw that it had been swept clean of debris but
was filthy. Bugs crawled about; the walls were cracked and caked
with dirt or blood or things I did not want to imagine. At least the
boards raised us off the dirty floor. I had picked my spot, located about
half-way down the room, on the right. From there I had a view of the
room and faced the door, which was located in the corner.

The door opened and a guard called for me to come outside. He
led me to the entryway to meet an elderly white-haired man. I could
tell he was an Englishman when he started speaking. "The Simbas
came to me this morning to say that five of our brothers had been in
the prison for two days without anything to eat. Here is something

for you. I am Kinso Jenkinsons from the LECO Christian bookstore across the street from the prison." I recognized his name and remembered that he and his wife had taken care of Muriel Davis and her children in August after they were released from the airport, while Chuck Davis remained incarcerated with us. "I apologize for not bringing food sooner, but we did not know you were here."

"We're not as bad off as that," I said. "We arrived only last night. Thank you very much for the food. I hope it's not too much trouble."

"We are happy to do this for you," Kinso said as he left. "Every day I will bring sandwiches in the morning and a bigger meal in the afternoon."

Guards examined the tray and said I could take it. I brought it back to the cell. We were still too shocked to do anything but pick at the food.

The guards told us we could leave our cell only to use the toilets at the far end of the courtyard. Simba prisoners shouted abuses as we passed. The latrine was a series of holes in the floor. An overpowering stench came from excrement spilling out onto the floor. Next door there was a rudimentary shower, consisting of a thin stream of water coming from a pipe high up the wall. I thought that constipation would be a problem and that cleanliness would be difficult to maintain.

Guards came with a bundle of clothing. I recognized the blue shorts and the yellow-and-blue striped wool sleeveless jersey of the prison uniform, worn only by the most humble prisoner. The only rebel I had seen in it had been Martin Kasongo. Simbas gathered to force us to shed our clothes and don the uniforms. They told us it was General Olenga's order. I persuaded them to let us keep our undershorts, shoes, and socks. My long white boxer shorts extended well beyond the blue shorts, which were too small for my almost-six-foot hefty frame. I knew I looked ridiculous.

170

"That does it," I said to my colleagues after the Simbas left. "After days of trying to work with the rebel authorities, dealing with Soumialot and Gbenye, pretending there is some basis of discussion between us, negotiating for use of the consulate, trying to repair our communications equipment, and all the broken promises for better treatment, it comes down to this, this humiliation. I can no longer pretend our detention is in some sense for our protection against angry Simbas. I will ask nothing further from the authorities and will not deal further with them. We will take what they give. I will not beg for anything. Let them do what they please!"

David Grinwis said, "I agree with the consul."

Jim Stauffer and Don Parkes looked relieved. Ernie Houle was silent, as usual.

"I won't even ask for blankets or pillows," I concluded. "We'll make do with what we have without complaint." I felt more relaxed after making my resolves. Some of the tensions and frustrations building up over the past weeks eased. The jersey made a fine padding for my hipbones against the plank. A bunched-up shirt served as a pillow. I used my trousers as a blanket.

Our door was unlocked and opened at six in the morning and closed and locked at about six-thirty in the evening. When we left the cell for the latrines, we were told to speak to no one. The door was closed during the day if something was going on in the prison that they thought we should not see. At night, the only sounds we heard were the soft buzz of talk by the Simba prisoners, the intermittent ravings of the mental patients, and the drum of the evening rain on our tin roof. The light bulb above the door burned night and day.

Breakfast, consisting of sandwiches, coffee, and boiled drinking water, came early. The main meal was thoughtfully prepared. It usually was a stew with meat and other goodies, and arrived in the middle of the afternoon. We had enough to save leftovers for an evening snack. I thought the Jenkinsons must be having a difficult time in keeping us supplied every day. I did not know how they did it with the shortage of food in town. I thanked Kinso each time I picked up what he brought.

From the window looking out on the courtyard, we monitored what was going on in the prison even when our door was closed. We were able to identify some of our fellow prisoners, including former President François Aradjabu. I encountered him on one of my trips to the toilets. "I've been here since September 21st," was all he managed to say before the Simbas chased us apart.

Our old friend, Charles Ifefe, was still there. He was not afraid of

171

being seen talking to us and came into our cell on occasion. He said Aradjabu was there for unspecified peculation. Henri Bablon, the former *jeunesse* leader who had come to see us at the Sabena Guest House, was in prison now. He risked some limited contact. Ifefe identified for us a former president of Maniema Province, and an MNC-L politician from Bunia, a collaborator of Moïse Tshombé. David knew or had heard about most of these people. We were told Oscar Sengha, who had contracted to occupy David's house, was also in prison, but we did not see him. David had difficulty identifying people without his contact lenses, which he was leery of wearing after our last rough trip to prison. I did little better without my glasses.

Most helpful to us were a half-dozen civilian prisoners located in a building just opposite our cell. They appeared to be nonpolitical long-term prisoners. We called them trusties. They knew the routines and were confident enough of their status to be friendly with the Americans. We communicated through the window when Simbas or guards were not around. They had a short-wave radio receiver and kept us informed of news they thought would interest us. This included the progress of military operations against the rebellion as reported by Radio Léopoldville and by the international media, such as VOA, BBC, or Radio Moscow. They also relayed the latest prison gossip and activities.

ON THE SECOND DAY after our arrival, our door was closed as Soumialot came to judge prisoners. He made no sign he was aware of our presence.

Two Simbas on the way to the toilets stopped Jim on Monday, 12 October. They wanted him to do pushups, but he hurried away. This was the first instance of physical harassment by the Simbas.

At dusk the same day, the guards brought an Englishman to our cell. He was a large muscular young man with a bushy black beard. He introduced himself as Jack Siggens and said he worked for Peter Rombaut at the BAT factory. "A Simba saw me with a short-wave radio receiver he claimed was a *phonie*," he explained. "He took me to Soumialot, who ordered me put in here. I don't speak French or Lingala, so I don't know exactly what happened."

"What's going on with Peter and the other Europeans in town?" I asked.

"Gee, I don't know," he replied. "I've been working out at the factory. I don't know much of what's going on in the city. Peter is away most of the time, and he hasn't told me much. I've been running the factory, making cigarettes."

"Do you still have a good supply of American tobacco?" I asked.

"We've been able to keep up with demand so far and don't anticipate running out. Up to now, we haven't had any difficulties out at the plant. What's going on here?"

"We're just sitting here in the pokey, waiting for something to happen," I said.

Jack was strong and athletic-looking, taking in stride the ridiculously undersized prison shorts and singlet they had given him. He played cards and told bad dirty jokes; in all, a welcome breath of outside air.

Two days later, another European was put in our cell, the Greek manager of the Equateur, the city's third-ranking hotel. He had been accused of harboring a spy. He thought he was arrested because the rebel authorities had discovered that a local Greek businessman, who had been permitted to make trips in rebel-controlled territory between Bunia and Stanleyville, had disappeared over the border into Uganda on his last trip. He was not forced to wear the prison uniform.

Early the next morning, 15 October, the rebel mayor of Stanleyville came by our cell. "What are you doing in prison uniform?" he asked. "That is not proper."

"Don't ask me," I replied with a shrug of my shoulders. "We just do as we're told around here."

Soumialot came into the courtyard at noon to judge prisoners. Several officers, including Martin Kasongo accompanied him. A Simba came to the cell and called for "the Englishman" to come out.

"He needs an interpreter," I said. "He speaks no French." I went out with Siggens, and we stood with a large group of prisoners. The Greek was also brought to stand with us.

Soumialot called us to come forward and asked Siggens a few

vague and pointless questions through me. "He is completely innocent of anything," I said. "He merely had a radio receiver."

"He is free to go," Soumialot said. "The Greek can go, too," he
added. They were taken away. I was left standing there.

Soumialot looked at me with some puzzlement. I could hear him
say something to an aide that included the words "prison uniforms."
I also heard the word *espion* (spy) several times. I, of course, thought
of David who was in the cell and not visible.

I knew that if David were singled out, that would be the end of
him. I feared that some in Soumialot's entourage might suspect David's
CIA affiliation. Equally disturbing would have been if the Chinese
embassy in Bujumbura, or the Soviets, learned a CIA operative was a
rebel captive; they would be desperate to gain possession. This must
have been the worst nightmare at CIA headquarters in Langley, Virginia.[1] David had been in Stanleyville more than two years, a long time
in a small town. Kasongo, in particular, could be suspicious. But then,
the rebels must consider all of us spies, I said to myself. Otherwise,
why would we be in prison?

I stood, watching Soumialot judge prisoners. He released some.
Others, he ordered to the *cachot,* the punishment cells. Whenever that
happened, the prisoner was beaten and dragged off. One unfortunate
inmate, on being ordered to the *cachot,* ran directly there, hoping to
avoid the beating. They caught him and beat him anyway, confirm-
ing my theory that when conditions were worsened for us, it would
involve violence. Soumialot presided over the process with obvious
relish, his small body perched on a stool, his small beady eyes fixed
intensely on his victims. This was one of the rewards of power, judging
prisoners.

I suddenly realized Soumialot was addressing me. "That message
you sent about the airplane attacking Kindu," he shouted. "You made
it sound as if I were threatening the Americans. That was not what
I wanted. You are not cooperating with us. On the question of the
imprisonment of the American consulate, that is a military matter.
The general left last Friday night." This was the same day we were
put in prison.

Soumialot continued after a pause. "A CFL boat was bombed in

Kindu by an American Fouga Magister on October 9th." Soumialot ended his monologue and left without giving me an opportunity to respond. The Fouga Magister was a French aircraft supplied by France to Tshombé during the Katanga secession.[2]

I returned to our cell. A few minutes later, the guards came over and took our prison uniforms away, saying we could wear our own clothes. "That's a relief," I said to my colleagues. "People tend to treat you the way you are dressed. And, we achieved it without asking for it. It might even be a small step forward." Such are the elements of hope in the darkness of despair.

THE REST OF the day passed quietly. On 17 October we heard from the trustics that Gbenye had left on a trip to Buta and Aketi, his home area. On Monday, 19 October, five blankets and pillows arrived; we were told they were gifts from Dr. Barlovatz. Besides providing warmth, it meant we could cover ourselves completely to protect us from mosquitoes. The nights were cool after the usual rain and a light covering was welcome. The pillow, I found, worked well to cushion the hips from the plank.

Civilian prisoners flushed out the toilets about once a week. We tried to use them before they clogged up again. I feared that if I complained about their filthy state, we would be given the job of cleaning them.

I used items sparingly from my toilet kit, which I had managed to keep through our various confinements. There was little possibility of obtaining replacement supplies. I had a small bottle of bug repellent. I applied it to my only exposed areas, my face and hands, before going to sleep. I frugally used a sliver of special soap for my skin allergy. I took a quick shower every third day at the pipe flowing from the ceiling at the toilets. I hoped the soap would not give out before the end of our captivity. The relative tranquillity and security of prison life, compared to the stressful period of the previous weeks, allowed me to sleep most nights until dawn. The light bulb burning all night above the door and the howling of the mental patients began to no longer bother me.

Constantly on my mind was the thought of the impossibility of our position. I knew that there was not a moment when our lives were not in danger. I believed the Simbas would carry out the threat they repeated so many times: "If your brothers come, we will kill you."

On 20 October, we heard Gbenye had returned from Buta. On the same day, Bablon finally mounted the courage to visit us. He was eager to talk. "You should not be imprisoned," he told us. "After the real revolution, diplomats will be accorded full respect in accordance with international law. These leaders have betrayed the revolution. Soumialot is a despot. Most young intellectuals are lining up against him, as well as Gbenye and Olenga. They are waiting to mount a counterrevolution." Bablon went on to make a distinction between the intellectuals who followed Gizenga, the true successor to Lumumba, and those who spread the Lumumba "myth." The latter, he said, are "exploiting and debasing the original political program of Lumumba." I found this difficult to follow. After Bablon left our cell, David explained the situation to me.

"Everyone knows the martyr was Lumumba," David said. "The difficulty is in knowing who is the true and authentic successor. Many of the intellectual prisoners here have been either to China or the Soviet Union and received communist education, training, and indoctrination. This background does not appear to bring them favor with the rebel regime. In fact, their education and foreign experience appears to be against them."

I suspected that one of David's main duties for the CIA was to track these individuals. "Olenga, Soumialot, and Gbenye use anti-American and socialist rhetoric," I said. "If they succeeded in taking over the Congo government, they would undoubtedly recognize and favor the communist countries. The fact that Belgium and the United States are the principal backers in the fight against them would certainly mean they would turn to the East. But the rebel movement has primitive roots and a nationalist character. That, I think, would prevent them from becoming a true communist state. This is just not a communist movement."[3]

The next day, the director of VICICONGO, the company responsible for all transport facilities to the north and east of Stanleyville, came

176

into our cell. "I was arrested and brought here," he told us, "because one of my employees told the Simbas that I had said 'the Simbas' time is short because the Americans will arrive soon.'"

He gave us what news he had. "They took my last two trucks two days ago, so there is little work to do. Olenga, Gbenye, and Soumialot keep the best available automobiles, usually Mercedes, at their residences, guarded and loaded ready to flee. They have divided among themselves the gold they found at the Kilo-Moto mines. I don't think Gbenye has yet returned from his tour. There is another rumor that Olenga has left with his family for the Sudan, accompanied by the Sudanese vice consul. Others say Olenga is not fleeing, but is arranging for arms shipments with the cooperation of the Sudanese government."

"That would be news if the Sudanese have sent someone back into rebel territory," I said. "I heard their consular people fled early on. It would be serious if they decided to get involved in this rebellion. We have no evidence of this up to now. All sorts of rumors are flying around."[4]

The VIVICONGO director was released the next day, 23 October, and Ifefe informed us that Gbenye had definitely returned.

LATE IN THE AFTERNOON, a slight, dark-haired white man, carrying a small cardboard suitcase and a pith helmet filled with bananas, was led to our cell. "Another American for you," the guard said.

As he entered, I identified myself as the American consul. Similar to missionary Chuck Davis's reaction when we met in the women's toilet at the airport in August, his shoulders drooped as if all hope was now lost.

"I am Paul Carlson, a medical doctor from Wasolo missionary station near Yakoma in the Ubangi Province," he said after he regained what little composure he had left. "I was taken by the rebels at my station, beaten, first sent to Aketi, then to Buta. I've been there for the past month with the Belgian Catholic fathers. Gbenye learned of my presence during his visit. A young Simba who knew me from Yakoma told Gbenye I was a missionary doctor and a 'good man.'

177

Gbenye ignored him. He said I was a major in the American army, a mercenary, fighting the rebellion, and ordered me taken to Stanley-ville. I packed this cardboard case given to me by the fathers and was hauled off in a truck. They gave me these bananas."

"When we came into town," he continued, "we passed the airport. They told me they expected the arrival of a Soviet plane with arms and equipment. The runway was clear and ready for planes to land."

After getting him settled, I asked Paul for more details on why he had not left before the rebels arrived and took him. He said he and his family were at Wasolo at his hospital in early August when they first heard of the rebellion, far away, they had thought, in Stanley-ville. Some Europeans and ANC troops fleeing the rebellion had come through Wasolo, and they spoke of the danger from the rebels. The missionaries, he said, were more afraid of the nervous ANC soldiers than they were of the distant rebels. They had received no warning of danger from the rebels at that time, either from the Congolese authorities or from the American embassies in Léopoldville or in Bangui, the capital of the Central African Republic (CAR). Bangui was their normal contact since it was much closer than Léopoldville.

The missionaries in the region, Paul said, were in constant radio contact with each other over the SSB radio network. On 31 August they heard over the radio that Lisala, very close by, had fallen to the rebels. Then, he told us, "the word came from the embassy that we should evacuate at least women and children."

Paul continued with his tale. "I waited until September 4th to leave Wasolo for Yakoma to the north with my wife Lois and our two young children. From there we crossed the Ubangi River to Kemba in the CAR. I left my family there and went back to Wasolo to work in the hospital because I had so many patients who needed me."

"Did the embassy in Bangui give you any advice or warning on returning to the Congo?" I asked.

"No, nothing," he said. "They knew I was going back and forth. I was in Wasolo when the rebels took Yakoma on the eighth and cut me off from the CAR. I was stuck in Wasolo, with rebels between me and the CAR. I was in radio contact with my family and still working at the clinic. On the eighteenth, Lois said she received word from the embassy advising me to leave because of the danger from the rebels. By that time, it was much too late.

"The Simbas came to Wasolo looking for my transmitter. Someone had told them I had a *phonie*. They killed one of my assistants before my eyes. They took me and several Belgian priests to the prison in Yakoma. Five days later, after bad treatment there, two priests and I were taken by truck to Bondo and then Aketi. Along the way, we were severely beaten. I received many hard blows to the head. Each time I was careful to receive the blows on the top of the head. That was painful, but they would have been fatal to the base of the skull."

"At the Aketi prison, we were forced to cut grass with long machetes without handles. Our hands bled profusely. After a few days of this, I was transferred to Buta where I was put into the care of the Catholic mission there. I stayed with the Flemish fathers, recovering from my wounds, and was not bothered by the Simbas. Gbenye arrived on October 21st and sent me here."[5]

Paul had barely finished his saga when the prison guards came and said they had orders to take him to the *cachot*. In the morning, Paul was returned to our cell. He said he had not been mistreated during the night. They had left his door open and allowed him to stretch out to sleep. The only disturbance had been a lengthy anti-American tirade by one of Bablon's buddies.

Soumialot and Gbenye came at noon to judge prisoners. They called for Carlson and said he would be placed under house arrest at the Congo Palace. When he came to the cell to fetch his suitcase, I told him to contact Kinso Jenkinsons at the LECO bookstore if he needed food. Opepe arrived later in the day to judge prisoners and released a few.

When the food arrived from LECO on Saturday evening, there was a note from Lucy Barlovatz saying we would be moved to the Congo Palace on Monday. Nothing happened Sunday or Monday. We learned later from Dr. Barlovatz that there had been a meeting of the consular corps with Soumialot on Friday. He had asked the corps to send a message out saying that all were safe and well. It was pointed out to him that the Americans were in prison, and that fact must be included in the message to make it credible. Soumialot said the Americans

179

would be moved to the Congo Palace and held there under house arrest. The consuls then agreed to send the message, adding that the staff of the American consulate was under "house arrest."[6]

On Monday, 25 October, the former consulate driver who had visited us at the airport with his *"convocation"* came to the cell. He had an order from Gbenye's office for the consulate to pay him thirteen thousand francs in back pay and unused leave. "We are hardly in a position to pay anything," I said. "We are here in prison with nothing, no money." He shrugged his shoulders and left.

Later in the morning, Antoine Lingili, the consulate receptionist, appeared in the prison courtyard. Our trusty informants told us that Soumialot's entire staff at the consulate had been imprisoned because Soumialot and his entourage had taken off for Lubutu, about a hundred miles southeast of Stanleyville, without letting anyone know. It was assumed they had fled "at news of approaching central government forces." The next morning, we learned Soumialot had returned and had justified his absence. His staff was released from prison. Soumialot came to the prison twice that day, releasing almost all the Simba prisoners. He swaggered and appeared light-headed, almost hysterical.

Late that evening, after our door was closed, a silence fell over the prison. I looked out the window into the courtyard. I saw guards herding several dozen prisoners—small men, dressed in rags—from the *cachot* area. They jumped through the entryway, and we heard a truck drive off. This confirmed a rumor we had heard about a group of prisoners being kept in the *cachot* under harsh conditions. The next morning, the trusties told us the group had been members of the *Rassemblement des Démocrates Congolais* (RADECO) party, which had been formed by former Prime Minister Cyrille Adoula. They had been identified by a group picture on a poster and rounded up. Last night, they were taken to the bridge over the Tshopo, sewn into sacks, and thrown into the crocodile-infested waters far below.

LATE THAT NIGHT, 28 October, our door opened and Carlson walked in with his suitcase. He said Simbas had come to the hotel and brought him back to prison. He had heard a general arrest order had gone out that day for all Americans and Belgians. Women and children, often separated from the men, were taken to the Hôtel des Chutes. Many of the men were taken to Camp Ketele. We helped Paul settle in on a spare plank.[7]

The next morning, two more Americans, Jon Snyder and Gene Bergman, were put into our cell. They were young Mennonite conscientious objectors serving their military time with the PAX organization. I had last seen them when they had babysat my son Evans, an eon ago. They could not say exactly who had been included in the roundup or why. They thought those at the University of Stanleyville had not been included. That afternoon, a large group of Africans, called Senegalese—West African traders—was brought to the prison and placed in a cell far down the courtyard. The trusties told us two more Congolese political prisoners had been executed the night before.

The next day, Friday, Patrick Nothomb and Paul Duqué, the Belgian consul and vice consul, respectively, were brought to our cell. I had not seen Patrick since 21 August when Olenga ordered us to be arrested and brought to trial. I rushed to embrace them warmly. Patrick's clothing was rumpled, and he was pawing at his nose, which was obviously bothering him. "It's been bloodied," he said. I asked Carlson to look at it while he told us what happened.

"Wednesday," Patrick said, "I was taken to see Gbenye. He was in a rage over what he said was Belgian involvement in the defeat of rebel forces in Beni. He said he would arrest all the Belgians in the city. I offered to send a message admitting Belgian guilt in the matter and that this threatened the lives of the Belgians under rebel control. I had done this several times, and it had worked well. We composed a message, and it was sent out.[8]

"That did not prevent the Simbas from rounding up all the Belgians and Americans they could find in the city and in the immediate area," Patrick continued. "It was mass confusion. They brought hundreds of detainees to the Hôtel des Chutes; women and children were crowded into the rooms, and the men were laid out in the dining room. Colonel Opepe lived in the hotel and was in charge. He was drunk most of time but kept some order in the midst of the idiotic chaos.

181

"Thursday night, General Olenga returned and came to see me at the hotel. He said an intercepted ANC message 'proved the Belgian consul general in Bukavu had directed ANC operations against us.' He also said the Belgians had dropped an atomic bomb on Beni and killed one hundred thousand Congolese. He punched me repeatedly in the nose. Paul was beaten. We were dragged to the Lumumba monument as if to be executed. Then we were brought to the radio station where I broadcast a statement saying that all Americans and Belgians were being held hostage, to be released only if their two governments would cease military assistance to the Tshombé government. My message included the phrase, 'I have seen with my own eyes the most irrefutable proof of Belgian aggression in the Congo.' I added that the hostages were in danger of being killed. In the morning, today, Paul and I were brought here."

"Welcome to our little club, Patrick, Paul," I said. "We now have our consular offices together." Carlson pronounced Nothomb's nose intact and Duqué's beating had only caused bruises.

That night, Gleb Makaroff, a large bearded man, came through the doorway of our cell. I had last seen the manager of Chemin du Fer et du Lac (CFL) when he had given us Olenga's intercepted messages from Kindu in July.

"They have put me here because they accuse me of sending instructions over the radio for the Americans to bomb and destroy bridges on the railway," he told us.

I hugged him, too. I showed him our humble quarters. Older than the rest of us and long in the Congo, he seemed to take his imprisonment lightly. He settled next to me on one of the additional planks brought to accommodate the increased population.

"Many Belgians are being treated badly by the Simbas," he told me as we made up his bed. "The men in the military camps are under tough conditions. Women are being separated from their children, and at least four women have been raped at the Hôtel des Chutes. I don't want to tell Patrick that. He has many matters to attend to and should not have to worry about things he has no control over."

I told Patrick what I had decided when we were last put in prison, that it was senseless to deal with the rebels in any normal way. "We no longer ask anything of our captors," I said.

"I don't have any problem saying anything the rebels want me to say," Patrick said. "If they want me to say Belgium is interfering in their affairs, I'll do it. I've done it enough times. And, it seems to work. I've saved lives doing it. That is what I was sent to Stan to do."[9]

"I have resisted saying the United States is interfering in the internal affairs of the Congo," I said. "That may not be relevant now. After all, we need to let the outside world know of our plight.

"The arrest and imprisonment of Belgians and other Americans represents a serious deterioration in the situation for all of us," I continued. "While we were the only ones being held, I felt we were vulnerable to random violence and if the city were to be retaken, we would be killed. With all of you here now, this creates a certain safety in numbers. What I mean to say is that I'm sorry you are here, but it has its advantages for us. Again, I say, welcome!"

"If the rebels fail to realize we are valuable as hostages, we could be in serious trouble," Patrick said. "Killing us would make us lose our value. I'm willing to do anything that tells them we're worth something."

"The way I see it, we face two dangers," I said. "The rebellion is in such a state of chaos and the Simbas are so volatile that anything and everything could happen that would result in us being injured or killed. A drunken Simba, one of the leaders in a rage, a mob incited to blood, all could happen at a moment's notice. The real danger comes at the liberation of the city. Unprotected, we are at the mercy of desperate Simbas. In the confusion of the fighting, we could well be cut down. At the same time, that very confusion could be our only hope of survival."

"We discussed some of this at the Hôtel des Chutes," Patrick said. "We even talked to Opepe about the possibility of action on his part in the eventual takeover of the city. He made a cautiously positive response, but he would not make a specific commitment to protect the Europeans in exchange for protection from the ANC."

"It's amazing you got that much out of him," I said. "I wish I

183

could believe he would do it. What I don't even want to think about is the hostages' worst fear. That would be if they decided to execute us one at a time until their terms are met. It would put enormous pressure on our governments and even on Tshombé. Let us hope they don't think of it."

Patrick and I swung into an easy and close partnership to face our problems. He told me the word *mateka*, which I had heard used before, literally meant butter in Swahili, or dead flesh, which is what you are when dead. He said he used it jokingly as a greeting with Simbas. We tried to put as good a face on our situation as possible, breaking into a few choruses of *"pas de problème, pas de problème,"* whenever faced with a problem that was obviously intractable. It was like whistling in the dark.

Soumialot came to the prison twice on Saturday, 31 October. He released many Congolese prisoners, including former President Aradjabu, but ignored us.

The Greek, Indian, and other non-Belgian foreign communities organized the feeding of the European prisoners. They cooked rice in large kettles, threw in fish or meat, added a sauce, and carried the result around town, ladling out servings at every location where hostages were kept. We continued to receive our basket of food from LECO.

The next day, without explanation, Makaroff was moved to solitary confinement in the *cachot*. Nothomb was taken to the Belgian consulate to do some unspecified searching of the premises. When he returned, he was taken alone to the same cell across from us where David and I had stayed when Kinghis put us in prison 12 August. The trusties told us Patrick was lonely and unhappy there. They also said many Simbas had been moved to Kindu, which was being threatened by central government forces.

184

Duqué was taken to the Belgian consulate, where the Simbas confiscated a trunk full of Congolese francs left by a Belgian company. A Simba major with the title of *Commisaire du Peuple* took David and me "to search the vice consul's house for food for the Popular Army." We found the house guarded by five Simbas left there by Oscar Sengha, whose wife and child were there. We had thought

Sengha was still in prison. Nothing was found that interested the major, so we were returned to the prison. The major next took Ernie, Jim, and Don to their apartments at the Immoquateur and confiscated Ernie's air pistol.

During the night, our door was opened three times for a body count. We were told some Simbas had attempted to escape.

We saw Dr. Barlovatz when he came to see Nothomb on Tuesday, 3 November. Later, a silence fell over the prison yard, similar to when the RADECO group was taken to be thrown into the Tshopo. A group of guards we had not seen before appeared. They carried hippo tail whips, the infamous *chicotte* supposedly outlawed after Léopold II was bought out of the Congo, which they swished in the air as they swaggered down the courtyard. David said they were from Osio prison, on the Left Bank, known for its harsh conditions, a place from which one rarely returned. I remembered that Kinghis had been kept there.

The guards took Bonaventure Zambiti, former editor of *Le Martyre*, Stanleyville's newspaper, and a nephew of Victor Nendaka, the central government security head. I had talked to Zambiti briefly when he asked for a can of sardines to go with his dry prison rice. I had hesitated to give anyone anything, fearing we would be deluged with such requests. I regretted refusing him now as I saw him being led away. When they passed our cell, the Osio guards patted their whips and said, "We're waiting for you at Osio."

Wednesday, 4 November, and the next two days passed without incident. Radio Léopoldville reported, relayed by some trusty friends with a radio, on military clashes between the ANC and the Popular Army. The reports said Léopoldville came out badly for the rebels. The rumor spread that the ANC had surrounded Stanleyville. Another rumor said that we were to be released the next day.

The trusties told us Lyndon Johnson had won the American presidential election. We had been cut off since before the conventions, and I had not followed the campaign. I was aware that Barry Goldwater was running against Johnson. In our discussions of how the U.S. government was reacting to our hostage situation, David and I were convinced that nothing drastic, like the mounting of a rescue operation, could be expected until after the elections.[10]

185

Carlson told us he had overheard Radio Stanleyville talking, in the Lingala language, about his impending trial as a mercenary. "I feel that the only outcome of such a trial would be my conviction and execution," he said.

"It is unlikely Gbenye would play that card this soon," I said.

The trusties said Carlson's plight was getting a big play in the international media.

The prison director came by to check Congolese identity cards. "We need to establish a register of all Belgian and American prisoners," he said. When I pointed out that as diplomats we did not carry local IDs, he exempted us from the census. This was the first time I was aware that they knew or cared about knowing our names. "We will be establishing dossiers on you," he said.

On 6 November our friends with the radio said Kindu and Paulis had been taken. We thought it was unlikely Paulis was taken because it was deep in rebel territory to the north. Kindu, to the south, was closer to central government–held territory and an important way station for the retaking of Stanleyville. They said the ANC or mercenaries had attacked early in the morning, and all European hostages had been found safe in the prisons. Olenga was said to have barely escaped capture. His damaged car had been found abandoned. A group of Simba prisoners the next day warned us that if they left Stanleyville, "no Americans would be left behind."[11]

Dr. Barlovatz visited us on Sunday, 8 November. He had bribed the prison director, who was an old friend. He brought books and playing cards and gave me some medicine for my cough, which had improved despite my continued smoking. "The military situation is deteriorating for the Popular Army," he said. "I have heard you might be freed within a few days."

A ragged group of Simbas, from the fighting in Boende, to the east, arrived in prison. We heard Commandant Sengha had been released and that Olenga had returned to Stanleyville, claiming that Soviet arms and ammunition would soon be arriving by air.

THE FOLLOWING DAY Radio Léopoldville announced that soldiers of the Popular Army were to lay down their arms or be massacred by the ANC when they arrived in Stanleyville. We saw Martin Kasongo come into the prison briefly, but not as a prisoner this time. Late in the day, a group of thirty-five Belgian men was led into the prison and put into a cell down the line from us. "More numbers, more safety," I said to myself.

This group consisted of the men who had been kept at the Hôtel des Chutes and the Sabena Guest House cottages. Most were released during the day so they could keep their business concerns running. This included the brewery that had kept turning out beer made with U.S. malt and hops. The director of SEDEC found a chance to tell me that the Simbas had cooperated with his firm by using bulldozers to bury potentially spoiled cans of chicken called *Poulet Pili-Pili*. The U.S.-supplied chicken was a concern I was handling when I first arrived in Stanleyville in July. I was relieved to hear this news because I had worried the rebels might have used the occasion to accuse the United States of sending poison to Africa.

General Olenga came the next day to judge prisoners and had Nothomb and Makaroff released from solitary confinement. We welcomed them back joyously. They were very happy to rejoin the fold. Patrick said the Simbas had told him he was in the same cell Lumumba had occupied.

That day, food coming to us from LECO was cut off. We were told we now would share the provisions of the other European prisoners. It was monotonous stuff, but it was a small price to pay for the added company. In the evening, Olenga brought Raoul Massachesi, the Italian honorary consul, to the cell. His company was building the new road to Lubutu; I hoped this route would bring the forces to retake the city. His company was also building a nearly completed new airport some distance from the city. "We found an Italian-made small tank in the forces attacking us at Kindu," Olenga said. "The Italians must suffer along with the Belgians and Americans."

On Wednesday, 11 November, Simba prisoners forced all the European prisoners to clean the courtyard and the latrines. The Simbas were rough, beating those who hesitated. Massachesi was beaten several times with sticks. One Belgian was put in the *cachot* because, it was said, he was heard muttering something like "there isn't much

187

time left for the Simbas, because the ANC is coming." Kasongo came into the courtyard later in the day and motioned for someone to close our door.

Barlovatz came the next day. He treated a Belgian with a bad heart and someone suffering from dysentery and malaria. Guards from Osio came again and took more prisoners. Gbenye, we heard, had ordered them not to take political prisoners, only Simbas. On Friday, the Belgian prisoners were forced to clean up the yard again, but this time the consular cell was exempt. "You are persons of importance and will not be required to work," a Simba said.

"Yes, we have set up our consular offices in our cell," Patrick said. "Please form the line to the right for visas."

"We should put a sign over the door," I said. "Cell Number 8, Consulates of Belgium, the United States, and Italy."

Dr. Barlovatz came again and told us Jomo Kenyatta, president of Kenya, had proclaimed over the radio that "no European would be harmed in Stanleyville." The doctor said Gbenye and Soumialot were about to hold a press conference to announce the release of the Belgian prisoners and the placing of the American consulate under "comfortable house arrest."

That evening, a Simba prisoner charged into the cell with a guard. "They have beer in here," he shouted. "That is not permitted." When a search revealed no beer, the Simba was hauled off to the *cachot*.

To pass time and keep fit, I walked briskly up and down the length of the cell a hundred times a day, the only one of us to exercise regularly. I read during the day for as long as I could keep my mind on it. My mind kept going back to the near impossibility of a peaceful end to our ordeal. We would be easy targets in prison if the ANC attacked the city.

Massachesi was the only one now allowed to have his own food brought to him. His servants brought a fully laden tray each day that he shared generously with the rest of us. Sent, among other goodies, was a measure of whiskey in a small medicine bottle. Each day Massachesi insisted I have it as a cocktail before dinner. After dinner, Makaroff, Nothomb, Massachesi, and I played one rubber of bridge. We then turned in, sleeping under the bright single light bulb.

188

On Saturday, 14 November, a trusty told us Radio Léopoldville had announced the presence of ANC troops only ten miles from the city. At first, we dismissed this. Then we heard an unusual amount of activity outside the prison, the roar of vehicle motors revved at full speed and the sounds of rifle and canon fire. The mentally disturbed section became excited and was noisier than ever. "They're saying most unpleasant things in Lingala about the Americans in prison," Paul said.

That evening, after we were settled in for the night, our door was shoved brusquely open by an angry and drunken Martin Kasongo, accompanied by three Simbas. "I am going to be hitting each of you," he shouted, weaving unsteadily. "Sit up on your beds and wait your turn." He began with David in front of him. He swung and struck him a glancing blow on the side of the head. David slumped flat on the plank. Kasongo moved to me. "Who are you?" he asked.

"I'm the American consul," I replied. I saw the hand coming and timed his blow with my fall to make him think he had knocked me down. He continued down the line, everyone submitting silently until he reached Paul Duqué. Paul slid to the ground before he was hit. Kasongo went after him, slapping and kicking him several times. After he completed the round of the room, Kasongo staggered out without a word. We were more stunned than hurt.

About a quarter hour passed before there was a noise at the door as it was unlocked again. Gbenye strode in. "Have you been mistreated?" he asked. Patrick explained what had happened. Gbenye left, muttering something about putting us in a hotel. The prison director stayed behind to tell us he had informed Gbenye of Kasongo's behavior. Sunday morning, we saw Kasongo being led into prison and put in the *cachot*.

Later that day the trusties told us Radio Léopoldville had announced that Col. Leonard Mulamba of the ANC would arrive soon in Stanleyville to negotiate the surrender of the Popular Army.

189

Monday morning, Kasongo was released. The trusties said that Gbenye had made a speech over Radio Stanleyville. Gbenye stated that all Europeans and Americans in Stanleyville would be killed if the ANC attacked the city.[12] Paris radio, we were told, said the ANC was attacking Stanleyville from three sides, and Radio Léopoldville said Stan would be liberated "within a few hours." In the afternoon, Kasongo was brought back to prison and once again put in the *cachot*.

In the afternoon, a tray of food from the LECO bookstore arrived, the first delivery in over a week. I pulled back the cloth and saw two birthday cakes with candles. There were two notes, one from the Jenkinsons and the other from Barlovatz. They had sent happy birthday greetings to me. I had forgotten it was 16 November, my thirty-fifth birthday. Tears filled my eyes as we ate the cakes.

The Horror

Days 105 through 112: Tuesday, 17 November,
through Tuesday morning, 24 November 1964

Tuesday, 17 November 1964

THE GREEK HONORARY CONSUL, DR. HAGIS, STOPPED BY OUR CELL
to give us the latest news. "Olenga got back yesterday from the fighting at Kindu," he said. "Radio Léo reports the Belgian and American
embassies in Léopoldville have sent word to Tshombé to return immediately from a trip to Matadi in view of the grave situation in the
eastern Congo."

In the afternoon, we heard explosions close to the prison. The
trusties told us the Simbas were trying out newly acquired explosives.

Wednesday, 18 November 1964

Early in the morning, we learned fifty Belgians had been released from
detention at Camp Ketele. Our trusties told us Radio Stanleyville and
Le Martyre, Stanleyville's newspaper, were increasingly virulent in their

attacks on Americans. Christophe Gbenye was quoted as repeating charges that Dr. Paul Carlson was a major in the American Army, a mercenary, and a spy.[1] The paper suggested that Carlson and his cohorts would be exhibited in cages at the Stanleyville Zoo. I remembered visiting the dirty cages, with the scrawny monkeys that had survived Stanleyville's troubles, in July with my wife Jo and my son Evans and shuddered at the prospect of joining them.

A little later, I became aware of a humming noise coming from the streets outside the prison. "It sounds like crowd noise," I said. I had a chilly feeling in my stomach. The old pain was coming back.

A silence settled over the prison, signaling again that something ominous was about to happen. The noise outside became distinguishable as the buzz of a crowd; I could hear talking and shouting. It became louder and closer.

Through the open door of our cell, I saw a Simba officer running toward us. He shoved his head in the door. "All Americans, outside!" he shouted. "Quick! Don't bring anything. Come as you are."

We were eight Americans—the five consular staff members, the PAX boys Jon Snyder and Gene Bergman, and Dr. Carlson. We followed the officer across the courtyard and into the entryway. "Write your names here," barked a guard seated behind the desk. He shoved a blank sheet of paper toward us. I printed my name at the head of the paper, knowing my signature would be undecipherable. The others followed. This was the first time I was aware that a record had been made of the names of the American or other expatriate prisoners. It was obvious something serious was about to happen.

They led us outside. As we emerged, a howl went up from the crowd gathered before the prison. A hunchback midget without legs pushed himself up to us on a wheeled cart. Dressed in rags, he rose to his two-foot height and screeched curses at us in a high-pitched voice, shaking a stick clutched in his tiny arms.

Simbas pushed us into two vehicles, four with me in a canvas-covered jeep, the others in a vw Bug. Our driver was a rebel security officer I remembered seeing before at some minor incident. "You are going to the Lumumba monument to be executed," he said in a tone that one would use to say we were going shopping. When the cars started moving, a roar rose from the crowd packed densely along both sides of the street as if gathered for a parade, except for the ominous *mateka* that I could hear among their shouts.

David, Carlson, and the two PAX men were with me in the jeep. "Guess this is it," David said. The others murmured something similar. I heard the phrase "last ride."

"Somehow I don't believe it," I said. "We've been through this before, boys. Something's always happened." There was no response. I doubt I was convincing. Whistling in the dark again? The ache in my stomach belied my words.

We arrived at the monument before we could dwell further on our fate. People were everywhere, filling the square and the surrounding buildings. Spectators were at the windows and lined the parapet of the roof of the large PTT building. They clung to trees and light poles. The shouting became louder as the vehicles stopped. A few dozen yards away was the rectangular concrete frame holding the photograph of Patrice Lumumba.

"You are about to be killed," our driver said and left. Don Parkes, Jim Stauffer, and Ernie Houle were taken out of the VW and stuffed into the back of our jeep. Several armed Simbas formed a guard around the vehicle as other Simbas surged against it. They reached through the canvas top and pulled at our beards. Others struck at us with sticks and bayonets. Luckily, they had difficulty getting through the canvas cover.

"They are mercenaries captured in Kindu," someone said. "It's Major Carlson and his men," another barked. "We will chop off their ears first. Then we'll cut off parts of their bodies." They gestured to show how they would do it and which parts they would eat. A Simba grabbed between his legs and waved a machete to show where he would cut.

Someone succeeded in getting a knife into the jeep and cut Don over the eye. Blood spilled down his face. Hands reached in to scratch our faces. Lighted cigarettes were pressed against us. Among the faces surrounding the jeep, I recognized Commandant Oscar Sengha, who had befriended us in August. I looked him straight in the eye. He stared back, then turned away. I saw Martin Kasongo flit by.

193

"Which one is the general?" the Simbas asked. "Is there a colonel? The major? That one should be an adjutant."

The noise of the crowd surrounded us. Simbas pounded on the jeep in frustration at not being able to get at us.

If the end has to come, I said to myself, let it come quickly.

A Simba officer opened the back flap of the jeep and ordered us out. The crowd roared when they saw us. The Simba tormentors were kept back by our guards. The line formed behind me as I followed the officer. We headed for the monument. I saw Lumumba's upraised hand in the photo. Our guards crowded close, fending off Simbas. The noise rose to a frenzy. I recalled Dr. Barlovatz's description of the slaughter and cannibalism orchestrated by Alphonse Kinghis in front of this monument in August. Looking around, I tried to see someone or something to indicate what would happen to us. Olenga, Gbenye, and Soumialot were not in sight. I expected one of the rebel triumvirate would surely have to be there if anything was to happen.

Then I saw General Olenga, standing with a group of Simba officers about twenty yards away. He was shouting and waving his hands. I saw somebody slump to the ground; Olenga either struck or shot him. Everyone—Simbas, the crowd—was shouting, shoving, and milling about. The noise of the mob reached fever pitch. We stood motionless. Olenga was the only leader I could see present, but he was the most powerful of the three. I knew our execution could only take place if he ordered it. Only he could prevent it. Would he be our executioner or our savior? Olenga pointed our way and shouted something.

The Simba officer motioned for me to turn around. "Go to jeep," he shouted above the noise. "Quick. Quick." I turned to the others, urging them to move. They needed no encouragement. We trotted back to the jeep as the Simbas parted to give us room. We scrambled into the jeep. The crowd's roar changed tone, evidencing their disappointment as the realization dawned that they would not see us killed.

From the bottom of the pile of eight bodies, I managed to see outside. Our guards did not seem to know what to do. The driver was not in sight. The crowd continued to roar. "Olenga saved you," the Simba guard squad leader said. "We take you back to prison."

194

Still no driver appeared and no key materialized. He must have taken it with him when he left. It was the driver's jeep, and I imagined he did not want it stolen during our execution. The guards slung guns on their shoulders and started pushing. There were only five of them, and the jeep with its heavy load moved slowly. The crowd followed along, yelling "*mateka, mateka,*" the dead meat they thought we should become.

The guards pushed for a few blocks, with the crowd following closely. We stopped in front of the *sûreté* office. Our driver came out. "Consider yourselves lucky to be alive," he said as he jumped into the driver's seat and put the key in the ignition. Nothing happened. Maintenance was not a strong point with the Simbas. Our faithful guards and some hardy bystanders put their backs into giving us a push-start. The engine started after a few tries. "We will be going to the Palace to see Gbenye," the driver said. "You were saved at the last minute by his intervention."

I was now going through a horror of my own. The bodies on top of me jammed me against a sharp object on the floor of the jeep. I could not move. Terror and panic seized me. Crushed into immobility against the object poking me, I felt I would burst with claustrophobic panic. We could not stop and get out of the jeep in front of the disappointed crowd. "Guys, do something," I said in desperation. "I have got to move, or I'll die."

Everyone made a concerted effort to lift their weight from me. As they rose, the pressure shifted and I moved away from the sharp object. The bodies settled back. My wave of panic subsided. "I'm okay now," I said. "Thanks, fellows."

We swept by the PTT building and headed toward the airport and the Palace. "What will happen, now?" I said idly. No one knew, and no one replied.

"It was thanks to President Gbenye that you are alive," the driver said again. Olenga had been at the monument, but I had not seen the other leaders. I thought only the general could have ordered us back to the jeep in front of the angry crowd.

We pulled into the Palace grounds. Another crowd was gathered, at least as large as the one downtown. Had we been saved from one

195

mob to go before another? The jeep stopped. We were told to get out. My cramped legs unwound, and I stumbled forward. Several hands stopped our progress.

"Stop, stand there," someone said. We lined up again. This time, we were to pose for our photograph. A man, probably Greek, peered into a Roloflex-type camera, trying to get us all in. He snapped a few pictures and signaled he was through.

Simba guards urged us forward, gently, through the crowd, up to a balcony where Gbenye stood before a microphone, dressed in a white shirt and tight jeans. We formed two rows in front of him, our guards standing behind. The people filling the vast lawn appeared more organized than at the monument. Simbas with MP written on their helmets kept people in place behind placards proclaiming affiliation with local *Mouvement Nationale Congolaise–Lumumba* (MNC-L) parties. Gbenye was speaking, and the crowd was responding on cue, applauding, booing, and yelling in response to his gestures and words.

He was speaking in Lingala, waving his arms, his lips moving wildly behind his thick beard. I looked to Paul. He looked ghastly. His face was drawn, his jaw sagged under his open mouth as he listened to Gbenye. The photographer took more pictures.

Gbenye changed to French. He said Major Carlson and his mercenary troops, pointing to us, had been tried by a military court and condemned to death; the crowd applauded. The executions had been put off at the request of Kenya's President Jomo Kenyatta, who had made an appeal for our lives; much booing came from the crowd. Kenyatta was undertaking negotiations in Nairobi to halt the fighting in the Congo; scattered sounds of approval rose from the crowd. Gbenye talked about Lumumba and claimed the present revolutionary government was following his program. At the sound of Lumumba's name, the crowd burst into high-pitched cries.

196

Gbenye shifted to Lingala again. I heard the words Lumumba, Carlson, and Kenyatta. He spoke longer than he had in French. In the rhythm of his speech and the responses of the crowd, I sensed he was having difficulty getting the crowd to accept that the executions would not take place today. He led the crowd to peaks of excitement, then tried to calm them. I hoped he could maintain control of the crowd's mood. We were in the midst of a hostile crowd, guarded by only a few Simbas.

I heard the word "major" whispered close by, but neither Gbenye nor anyone else pointed to or otherwise singled Carlson out from the eight Americans. I looked at Paul, who understood some Lingala. I could see the terror in his eyes. He showed such agitation over what Gbenye was saying that I worried he might make some move that would identify him. As long as we were an undifferentiated group, we were protected. "Safety in numbers," I thought.

I saw the Simba mayor of Stanleyville, standing directly behind Ernie, move the barrel of his automatic weapon alongside Ernie's head. Slowly, the mayor reached up with a knife in his other hand toward Ernie's ear. Ernie did not appear aware of this. Gbenye saw it and made a sharp downward motion with his hand. The knife disappeared, and Gbenye continued. He switched to French again. "The execution of the eight American mercenaries will take place Monday, a delay of four days, if negotiations do not succeed," he promised the crowd.[2]

Gbenye motioned for us to be led away. For the first time, I noticed it was raining, a heavy downpour, which was always a calming influence. We were led to the jeep, loaded in, and driven hurriedly back to the prison. The prison director was in the entryway and stopped us. "I must compliment you on your dignified bearing at the monument," he said.

Once in the cell, Carlson knelt and said, "We should pray." Shaken by the events of the past hour, I welcomed a moment of quiet. Paul said a few words, and we bowed our heads in silent thanks. Paul got up and looked at the cut on Don's head. "It's deep," he said, "but not serious." Our cellmates greeted us quietly; they were as awed as we were by the close presence of death.

I could see Paul was most visibly troubled by the events that had centered on him. "They have sentenced us to death," he said. "How can we get out of that?"

"It's part of the game they're playing," I said. "I'm not saying it isn't serious, but so far it's being played only in words."

"But our execution is set in four days," Paul said.

"That's a long way off," I said. "A lot can happen before then. We would no longer be valuable to Gbenye if we were executed. He'll hesitate to play that card." I knew the real danger lay in the denouement, but I did not mention that.

I knew I had not convinced him. We went to our planks and gathered our thoughts and wits, each in his own way. I had been proven right, we were too valuable as hostages to be executed. However, our future was not assured. There still seemed to be no way out, no end game in sight in which we survived.

Not long afterward, Gbenye came to our cell. "You will move to the Victoria Residence tomorrow," he said. "I hope the negotiations will be successful." I stared at him and said nothing.

Thursday, 19 November 1964

Dr. Hagis told us in the morning that yesterday's demonstration and execution scene before the monument had been advertised days in advance. Notices had been sent to the interior for people to gather in Stanleyville. "I don't believe it was ever planned to have you executed," he said. "It was all staged."

"I'm sure it was intended to get the attention of the outside world and to get negotiations started," Patrick Nothomb said.

"Well, it sure got my attention," I said. "But, I don't see negotiations going anywhere. Neither side is willing to give what the other wants. There is no way Tshombé will recognize the rebels, not now that forces are closing in on Stan."

"At any rate," David chimed in, "it might get us out of this hole."

We were encouraged to think this would happen soon when a guard told us in the early afternoon to pack *"vos choses"* ("our things") in preparation for a move to the Victoria, an apartment hotel close by. We sat on our planks with our belongings packed. At eight in the evening, guards came and told Nothomb, Paul Duqué, Gleb Makaroff, and a Belgian lawyer from the cell next door to follow them. We were told they were being taken to the Victoria. The rest of us remained in our cells.

Friday, 20 November 1964

Midmorning, a guard came to the cell. "I want the American consul," he said. When I stood, he said, acting nervous, "Follow me, quickly." We went through the portal and stopped at a vw parked outside.

Alone in the driver's seat was the security man who had been our driver to the monument and Palace two days before. "Get in, quickly," he said.

The driver said nothing as he drove off at great speed, looking around as if it were dangerous to be on the streets. We went past the deserted PTT building and out to the grounds of the Palace. A group of Simba MPs, armed with rifles and spears, crowded around the car when it stopped. They waved their weapons at me. The driver came around to my side, opened the door, and motioned me out. The MPS rushed toward us. The driver bundled me up the steps, appearing to fend off the closely following Simbas. He led me into an office where Gbenye was standing behind a desk. Outside the window, the Simbas waved and gestured; it seemed to me that only the glass and Gbenye kept them from venting their ire on me. There was no exchange of greetings, and I remained silent. Gbenye walked over to me, waving toward the group as if to show me the angry mood of the masses.

"I have been in touch with Ambassador Godley about negotiations in Nairobi," he said. "I am authorizing [Thomas] Kanza to handle the negotiations in Nairobi about the Americans in Stanleyville. I have a message here for you to send to Léopoldville." He handed it to me. I read it quickly. It was in French, and it conveyed the familiar message that American citizens in the area controlled by the Popular Army would lose their lives if military operations against it did not cease.

"Translate it into English," Gbenye said.

"Let me have a typewriter," I said.   199

Gbenye left the room and a typewriter was found. I typed out a quick and rough translation, hunt and peck fashion, on the unfamiliar European keyboard. The Simbas outside continued their antics, trying dutifully to intimidate. My translation sounded stilted because

I wanted it to be obvious these were not my words. And the pressure did not improve my writing.

When I signaled I had finished, François Sabiti, the former rebel commissioner, came in and took my text with him. Whoever he showed it to was close by because he returned almost immediately. "It's been approved," he said. It was retyped, this time with carbons. "Sign it," Sabiti said. I signed and was given a copy. It read:

AMEMBASSY LEOPOLDVILLE

Inform you that US responsibility interference in internal affaires well established STOP Material and other aid furnished Tshombe pro-vokes very serious consequences STOP Considerable human losses seen in areas in which American aid has been used STOP Arms seized by revolutionary government such as armoured car and other confirm US responsibility STOP Confirm Paul Carlson captured and condemned to death STOP All American citizens are in danger STOP Any arrangement other than negotiation with revolutionary gov-ernment can only cause elimination of American citizens gathered in several regions other than Stan STOP Witnessed population of esti-mated ten thousand gathered in demonstration confirm insistently execution Paul Carlson and even all American citizens STOP Revolu-tionary government authorities sincerely desire initiate negotiations before it too late STOP During negotiations must prohibit use by Tshombe of US aid furnished him to attack regions controlled by revolutionary government STOP Ask you particularly intervene effectively with Tshombe obtain cease fire during these negotiations or risk compromise desired results STOP Confirm with certainty that only way save Carlson and other American subjects STOP After inter-views with revolutionary government convinced negotiations can achieve desired objectives STOP In name all American citizens in popular Congolese republic and for prestige of USA request initia-tion negotiations which constitute our last chance STOP In case of delay I say for myself and for my companions goodbye STOP

HOYT AMCONSUL STANLEYVILLE
NOVEMBER 20, 1964

In my haste, I had translated the last word, "*adieu*," as "good-bye" instead of the more final "farewell."[3]

Gbenye came in several times during this process. The Simbas outside the window eventually went away. They were probably tired of their tricks, which, in any case, were no longer needed. As I was leaving, I turned to Gbenye. "Do you know the Americans are still in prison?" I asked, breaking my resolve not to ask anything of the rebels.

"Really? I didn't know that. I will arrange your transfer to the Victoria," he said and waved to indicate my presence was no longer required.

The same driver took me back to prison. He was friendly and relaxed in contrast with his nervous behavior on the outward trip. "We look forward very much to negotiations," he said. "You are doing us a good service by supporting them."

When I showed the message to David, he said, "Note that the word negotiation is repeated six times. I think this means Gbenye thinks this is the best way out of their desperate military situation."

"With the ANC advancing on Stan," I said, "the smart rebels must see a cease-fire and negotiations as the ways to prevent total collapse and defeat. Only then could they salvage something for themselves. I don't think they can defend Stanleyville any more than the ANC did. As far as we are concerned, negotiations would immensely improve our chances of survival. As long as they are possible, we are very valuable to the rebels." On the other hand, I thought, when they're no longer possible, we're dead meat.

At seven in the evening, guards ordered all the Belgians and Americans left in the prison to come outside with their belongings. David and I were led to the prison director's office just outside the prison entryway. "Here are the cases you left with us," the director said, pointing to our briefcases on his desk. "See, nothing has been disturbed. Open them and see." I unlocked mine and saw my unfinished airgram on economic conditions in Stanleyville that Jo had been typing when we heard the rebels were coming in early August. My continuing letter to my wife and my *Economist* desk diary were also there.

201

David opened his. It still contained our journal notes up to the time of entering the prison forty-two days before and the large remaining sum in Congolese francs that David had salvaged from his house the day before the rebels took Stanleyville.

"Count it to see that it's all there," the director said.

David counted the money. "It's all here," he said. He put a hefty number of bills in a pile and shoved it toward the director. "Here are some for you."

"Thank you very much," he said as he pocketed the money. "I hope you had an enjoyable stay." I was sure he thought we might be back. The money was our insurance. I thought he had been decent to us and deserved the reward David gave him.

David put the rest of the money back in the briefcase, and we went outside to join the others, who were lined up and waiting for us. The deformed midget again spouted obscenities. There was hesitancy about where, when, or how to go. Then we were ordered to start marching. Lugging our belongings, I thought we looked like a bunch of recruits headed for basic training. After a few blocks, we halted in front of a multistory building with a sign reading "Résidence Victoria."

We entered the small lobby, which was filled with Belgian and American men. A Simba colonel I had not seen before was shouting at them. "We want to place you at places around the city to protect us from the bombing," he said. "But what we really should do is kill everyone, right now."

After some more haranguing, the colonel left, leaving a contingent of Simbas who continued to taunt us. They told us to sit and be still. Some of us sat quietly, while others milled around.

I found Patrick Nothomb in a little alcove under the stairway. "Welcome to our new home," he said. "We were called down about an hour ago. That colonel was quite agitated. He thinks an attack is imminent and is looking for some way for the hostages to protect them. We must do something to stave them off. I'm particularly worried about the *jeunesse*. I'm not sure the Simbas can control them if there is an attack. It's time to send another message."

202

"I just did one, at the Palace, for Gbenye," I said. "Might as well do another."

"It has always worked before."

He found some paper and a typewriter. David and I helped him draft a message. I typed in English what Patrick had written in French.

The Horror

The American and Belgian Consuls at Stanleyville, Michael Hoyt and Patrick Nothomb, solemnly affirm that all American and Belgian citizens residing in territory controlled by the Popular Government of Stanleyville are alive as of November 21 [it was after midnight], 1964, and they will so remain if an immediate end is put to Belgian and American military aid to the Leopoldville Government.

The Consuls with the greatest insistence request their respective governments not only to cease immediately this military aid, but also to obtain without delay a general cease fire from the Tshombe Government. This request particularly, and above all, implies a cessation of the bombardments, which have recently multiplied. This cease fire is in fact a condition for the opening of negotiations through the good offices of President Jomo Kenyatta, which the Revolutionary Government is ready to initiate immediately with the American and Belgian Governments concerning the fate of their citizens.

In the name of all American citizens—men, women, and children, and in their own names, the American and Belgian Consuls respectfully beg their Governments to adopt immediately a policy of absolute neutrality, the only policy in fact capable of safeguarding the lives of their citizens. This message represents a genuine plea from the Belgian and American communities residing in the liberated territory, that they now make to their Governments through their respective Consuls.

s/s Nothomb s/s MPHoyt

"That certainly gets the word out," I said. "I'm not sure what our people can do about it. It's tough decision time for them."[4]

"It just might buy time once again," Patrick said.

We typed several copies in both English and French and gave them to the guard commander. He said he would deliver them. We remained in the lobby all night.

203

Saturday, 21 November 1964

A Simba officer arrived at dawn and ordered us to go upstairs to our rooms. David and I were assigned to Makaroff's apartment. The others were distributed among other rooms.

We had barely settled in our rooms when Simbas came to take Patrick and me to the radio station, where we recorded the message we had written during the night. Then we were driven to the airport and taken up into the control tower. Into the same microphone through which I had said good-bye to my wife Jo more than three months before, we read the messages again, addressing our embassies in Bujumbura. The colonel of the night before nodded his head in approval when he heard the word "cease-fire." "That is exactly what we want," he said.

Out of the windows, I saw raggedly dressed recruits, with branches stuck in their clothing, lined up and undergoing drill. It meant the rebels were still training to continue the fighting.

We returned to the hotel, and I slept for a few hours, on a bed, between sheets, for the first time in weeks. I awoke hungry and thirsty. Gleb prepared a lunch of cheese, salami, and bread, washed down with a couple of big bottles of STANOR beer. I enjoyed sitting on a chair at a table, eating in a relaxed and civilized manner. In prison we had eaten hunched on the low wall that braced our plank beds.

I hacked at my month-and-a-half growth of beard, a tricolor mixture of black, red, and white. Afterwards, I heard the Simbas had passed the word that all the men were to shave their beards. "Your white faces will show better without beards," they said. "We can then identify you when your brothers come." A Portuguese barber making the rounds of the rooms gave me a quick and sloppy haircut. After a long shower, I felt cleaner and more relaxed than I had in months.

I was convinced we were much safer here than in the Stanley-ville Central Prison, where we had been readily available to the Simbas if the city was attacked. Here we were with a large number of other hostages. Between two and three hundred people were in the hotel. There were men, women, and children, mostly Belgians, with perhaps a dozen Americans, crammed eight to a room.

I saw Al Larson and Del Carper, who had been brought from the missionary station at Kilometer Eight in the general roundup of Americans and Belgians. Initially, they had been kept at the Hôtel des Chutes. Chuck Davis was also there, but his family was still at Kilometer Eight. Phyllis Rine, the missionary teacher and nurse who had babysat Evans, was here with the Schaub family.

Guy Humphreys, the former American missionary and plantation owner, came up to me. "Compared to the interior, Stanleyville is a safe haven," he said. "I was lucky to survive. The interior is a real mess. I barely made it here, bribing and bluffing my way through Simba roadblocks. Now all we can do is wait for the next move."

We did not have long to wait. In the middle of the afternoon, a squad of Simba soldiers, well armed and dressed in fresh uniforms, came bounding up the steps, banging on doors. "All men, come down," they shouted. "No baggage. Just come."

Approximately one hundred of us went down to the street. Some were loaded on an old yellow school bus. When that filled up, another group was put in the back of a dump truck bearing a USAID handclasp emblem. Those left were told to go back upstairs. The Simbas came aboard the bus, crushing those already there to make room. David and I, with Nothomb and Duqué, were in middle seats. I could see Carlson, Larson, and Carper.

We started moving. Someone speculated that we were going to the Tshopo bridge to be thrown into the falls below. We passed over the bridge but did not stop. We followed the road north, past Kilometer Eight. "You are going to Banalia," the Simbas said, a city approximately eighty miles away. "Then if they take Stan, you will not be freed. We will keep you with us in the bush forever." I had visions of us being dragged through the country, moved continually, forced to live and survive with the Simbas. We had brought nothing with us from the Victoria except what we wore.

After a few miles, the bus motor quit. The Congolese driver got out and fiddled with it. He got the motor started, and the bus ran for a few yards before it stopped again. A Simba asked if anyone in the bus was a mechanic. Nothomb said something to a man who then volunteered. I believe Patrick told him to make sure the bus would not move. While he was working on the motor, the Simbas lounged around outside the bus, smoking what looked like hemp. This was the first time I had actually seen them taking drugs. They carried new

205

automatic weapons, AK assault rifles, with boxes of ammunition. The rebels had evidently received a fresh supply of arms.[5]

We had stopped by a small village. The residents offered to sell us papayas and brought water. I did not drink, fearing it was not safe. A jeep drove up with three Simbas and a Belgian man tied up in the back. He bore signs of having been brutally beaten. Huge lumps stood out on his bare, bloodied head. The Simbas told us he had been found in Aketi with a military service card in his possession, leading them to assume he was a mercenary. They were taking him to Stanleyville.

It became obvious to our Simbas that the bus was going nowhere for now. It was now dusk. They herded us into a mud wattle hut that had been cleared of inhabitants and furnishings. We sat on the bare dirt floor, hunched in rows, pressed against one another. "Here, Mr. Consul," said the man behind me. "Just lean back and relax. We have nowhere to go." Grateful for the support, I leaned back against his knees. I settled in for what I anticipated would be a long and uncomfortable night.

After a few minutes, we heard a Simba shouting, "The consuls, we want the consuls. Have the consuls come out."

David, Patrick, Paul Duqué, and I were passed over the heads of the crowd of bodies through the doorway, not knowing what was to come. The colonel from the Victoria Hotel was standing there. "Are you all right?" he asked. When we nodded, he continued, "It's all been a mistake. The move was premature, before all the arrangements could be made. You are all to return to Stan. It is important that the consuls return immediately." They told us to climb into the back of the dump truck. We clung to the front of the steel bed, the fresh wind streaming through our hair, as we raced down the road back to Stanleyville.

We reached the city after dark. No one was stirring. Men stood at regular intervals along the street. They were silent, holding spears at their sides.

"*Jeunesse,*" whispered Duqué.

When we pulled up at the Victoria, we were told to return to our rooms. The rest of the group returned a few hours later in other vehicles that were sent for them. We had survived once more.

206

The Horror

Sunday, 22 November 1964

Nothomb and I were taken to the Palace early in the morning. Gbenye handed me a telex message addressed to him from Ambassador Godley, dated some days earlier. In it the ambassador said he appointed me his representative in Stanleyville to negotiate with the rebels. To facilitate that, he requested I be given "independent means of communication."[6]

"That cannot be permitted," Gbenye said. "It would not be understood by the people. They would regard it as a measure of favoritism. I want you to cable back to the ambassador and tell him messages can be sent through Kanza, our comrade in Nairobi. The Belgians can do the same. Tell them that all your citizens are well and protected by the local authorities."

I typed out a message in English. It read:

AMEMBASSY LEOPOLDVILLE
Your message through President Gbenye received November 22. Estimate situation prohibits SSB contact for now and will send written and oral reports to embassy Nairobi through Kanza. American citizens in area well and protected by local authorities.

Pass to Belgian embassy from Nothomb. Will also send reports through Kanza to Belgian embassy Nairobi through Kanza. Belgian citizens also well and protected.

HOYT (Nov. 22, 1964)
s/s Vu OK Nbs/s H

Gbenye left the room with my message. As had been the case with Sabiti, he returned quickly and said it was okay. Patrick and I initialed it. They made copies and handed one to me.[7]

"I want to admit to you that I do not want to execute Carlson," Gbenye said. "It would set off a chain reaction that could result in the death of all Europeans. I can tell you that Kanza will be coming to Stan soon." We had heard a rumor that Kanza, who was American educated and had been a member of Lumumba's government, had been in Stanleyville last month. The rumor indicated that he had soon left in disgust when he saw the chaos created by the rebel regime.[8]

207

Gbenye introduced us to a black man in a rumpled safari suit. He said he was a journalist who had come from Uganda. Patrick and I shook hands hurriedly as we were taken to a vehicle to be driven back to the Victoria.

At the hotel, Patrick, David, and I discussed the situation. Radio Léo reported that ANC and mercenary forces were advancing on Stanleyville. International radio reports said Belgian paratroopers were poised on Ascension Island in the South Atlantic. While we could not be sure they were accurate, we knew these reports would make the rebel leadership desperate to do something to halt the advance. They were trying to obtain a cease-fire and initiate negotiations, using the hostages as leverage.

"It is obvious that if a cease-fire fails to materialize, and it comes to an attack," I said, "they intend to use us in some fashion to protect them. What can we do to survive when the attack comes? Do you think we could approach our guards and try to make some sort of deal? They're here on a regular basis and seem friendly enough."

"I told you we had talked to Opepe along these lines at the Hôtel des Chutes," Patrick said, "He seemed interested but would not make a commitment. I discussed this here with our old Congo hands like Romnée and Faeles. We came to the conclusion it is just too risky to raise the question of protection with any Simba at this point. They might react violently. We think it better to wait on events. When the time comes, we will try to make a quick deal with whoever is guarding us."

"We have to do something," David said. "Otherwise, we don't have much chance to survive. The prospects are not good."

"About the only way we could survive is in the chaos and confusion of an attack," I said. "The leadership may not be able to organize our execution. Then again, we could be killed at any time by panicky troops."

208

Monday, 23 November 1964

The morning passed quietly. Rumors flew. One said Opepe had fled to the Sudan. We had not seen him for some time. It was rumored he was out of favor with the leadership for his sympathetic treatment of Europeans. Someone said the leaders had their cars loaded and ready to flee at a moment's notice with their share of the Kilo-Moto gold. Our guards appeared relaxed and unconcerned.

I looked in on Carlson on the upper floor. He had been tending to the ill among the hostages. He seemed in good spirits. His work helped keep his mind off his troubles. "In case things get too bad for me," he told me, "I do have some drugs to help."

"Just think," said a Belgian in the room. "Soon you will be shaking President Johnson's hand."

We had a relaxed lunch, with cold Stanor beer and the inevitable sardines, tinned beef, and rice. David and I worked at getting our journal up to date after the hiatus of forty-two days in jail. We avoided thinking about Carlson's postponed execution. Gbenye had talked of a four-day reprieve, which would have made it yesterday, but he had also mentioned Monday. Numbers and days meant little in the chaotic situation. I suspected the date of our execution was being kept vague and did not expect it to take place while negotiations were still a hoped-for possibility.

I picked up the continuing letter to Jo that I had not seen since going to prison the last time. I read what I had last written:

> Jo, all through these times I have been thinking constantly of you and my sole wish has been that I would survive to see you and the children. I have looked death in the face many times since seeing you and each time I have fought to stay alive in order that you would not have the pain of my death. I hope that the news you have been getting does not reflect the very real danger to our lives that we have been under.[9]

I could write no more and put it aside.

At four in the afternoon, Simbas came and told Nothomb, Massachesi, and me to go with them. "You are going to a reception at the Palace," they said. When we arrived, we were shown into the large reception room filled with civilians and rebel officials. Women and men, well dressed and relaxed, milled around while a band played in the background. Drinks were served. Peter Rombaut was there. I had not seen him since his visit to the Sabena Guest House cottages in early September and welcomed him warmly. He told us he had been spending his time lately at the tobacco factory. I identified Kinghis and Sabiti. The only Simba officer I knew was the *Commisaire du Peuple*, the man who had supervised the search of the apartments at the Immoquateur in early November. The band played African high life music while we sipped our drinks.

We were told we had been summoned for a reception held in honor of a British subject from Trinidad, named Hugh Scotland. Gbenye brought him to where the consuls were standing. He was the Indian-looking man we had met the previous day. He had on a fresh safari suit, with his black wavy hair plastered to his head. "I would like you to meet Mr. Scotland," Gbenye said. "He is a journalist, a friend of our foreign minister, Mr. Kanza, and has been touring the area held by the Popular Army for the past few weeks. He will be leaving tomorrow for Nairobi, where he will report to Mr. Kanza. He will be writing on his visit to the Popular Republic."

"Pleased to meet you," Scotland said. "I would like to interview each of you to show that you are being treated well." He took us aside one by one to record an interview on a small tape recorder.

I could not hear what the others told him, but when it came my turn, I kept my answers terse and tried to act grim. I refused to reply to the question of what I thought about U.S. interference in Congolese affairs.

When I finished, I was handed a copy of a telex just received from Ambassador Godley.

FROM: LEOPOLDVILLE, NOVEMBER 23, 1964 URGENT

TO: PRESIDENT GBENYE STANLEYVILLE

mon gourvernement ma charge de transmettre a Stan le message suivant pour le consul des etats unis Michael Hoyt

Commencement text for U.S. Consul Hoyt STOP You should inform Mr. Gbenye that Ambassador [William] Attwood is scheduled to meet with President Kenyatta and Mr. Kanza at 0800Z November 23 in Nairobi to discuss the matter of U.S. missionary Carlson and other Americans in the Stan area

SIGNED GODLEY FIN TEXTE SIGNE GODLEY[10]

Mac was trying to stave off Carlson's execution, as well as ours, with the prospect of negotiations in Nairobi. I hoped this would ease things for us with the rebels.

Pocketing the message, I tried to maneuver into a position to say something to Scotland out of hearing of the rebels and his tape recorder. I came up beside him on the dance floor. "It is extremely dangerous here for us and for you," I whispered in English. "Be extremely careful." He looked startled, but said nothing and walked away.

Arrangements were made for Scotland to come to the Victoria in the morning "to take pictures of how well the hostages were housed." The party wound down. We were driven back to the Victoria Hotel.

Patrick, David, and I reviewed events. "This friendly attitude of the rebels is certainly welcome," I said. "But that doesn't ease the threat against us. We are still in a very precarious position."

"The radio reports the ANC advancing on all sides," Patrick said. "We are hearing about the arrival of Belgian paratroops at Kamina." Kamina was the large Belgian base on the northern edge of the Katanga.

"The latest report is that the ANC is at or near Lubutu," David said. "That is where the new road starts, a little more than a hundred miles from Stanleyville. We have no way of knowing if these reports are true, but they are sure to agitate the rebels."

"Even with this talk of negotiations and cease-fires," I said, "I doubt the military advance on Stan will or can be stopped."

"That's right," Patrick said. "In the Congo, once something gets started, it just goes on and on. Nobody has that much control in this vast country."

"I'm convinced the city will be retaken," I said. "We're going to be sitting ducks."

We agreed we could do nothing for now and Patrick left to return to his room.

211

David called Alex Barlovatz. "Lucy said she would be cooking 'pygmy turkeys' for us for Thanksgiving on Thursday." It took me a few seconds to realize she meant chicken. I knew Alex would find some way of getting the meal to us.

Tuesday, 24 November 1964

I awoke to the sound of aircraft flying overhead. It was first light, six o'clock. We had heard that noise only a few times since the rebel takeover, once during the Red Cross mission in late September and several times in the distance.

"Whatever these planes are doing, they mean trouble for us," I said to David and Gleb.

We looked out our window but could see nothing in the sky. The streets were deserted. I shaved and showered, not wanting to pass up this luxury after weeks in prison. I put on a clean white shirt, slipped my diplomatic passport and health card in my shirt pocket, and joined the others for a breakfast of beer and sausage, the Belgian working-man's fare.

There was still no movement on the street below. We telephoned around town to see if anyone knew what was happening. Someone said B-26s and other aircraft had flown over the city, heading toward the airport. Someone from the top floor called to say they had seen parachutes dropping near the airport.

"These could be the Belgian troops reported to have been at Ascension and then at Kamina," David said.

Several bands of heavily armed Simbas came down the street below us, going in the opposite direction from the airport. We drew back from the windows so they would not notice us. They must have known we were there because some of them shook their fists in our direction. They passed by. Our regular Simba guards had not yet come.

"There's nothing to do but wait," I said.

"I don't think it will be long," Makaroff commented.

He was right. At seven, the clump of heavy boots sounded in the staircase. A motley group of Simbas came down the halls, throwing open doors and shouting for everybody to come down to the street. We streamed out, women and children along with the men. "Line up! Line up!" shouted the Simbas. We formed a column of approximately two hundred people, I guessed, mostly Belgians, with a sprinkling of Americans. Nothomb and Duqué led, with David and me directly behind them. I sensed the denouement of all our tribulations was coming.

Colonel Opepe, his shirt hastily tucked around his fat belly, strode along the side of the column. He appeared to be in charge of eight or ten variously armed and dressed Simbas. I assumed the Simbas were a group scratched together from those at headquarters. They carried pistols, rifles, and automatic weapons. The oldest Simba was about Opepe's age and the youngest was barely a teenager with a rifle almost bigger than he was. One lugged a light machine gun with a tripod attached to the barrel. Among the others, I recognized the security-type Simba; he had been our driver to the Lumumba monument.

They barked the order for us to start moving. Then someone said to stop. The Simbas spoke in mixed French, Lingala, and Swahili.

"They say we are going to be killed," a Belgian behind us said.

"Opepe says they're taking us to the airport to use as shields against the enemy," another said. "Now, he's saying he will protect us."

It had taken the rebel leadership an hour to react to the airplanes and send this squad to get us. That had gained us valuable time. The question now was how much time would it take for the troops, of whatever composition and nationality they were, to get to us from the airport? If Opepe had truly wanted to protect us, I thought, he could have left us in the hotel. But that would have meant defying the orders undoubtedly given to bring us out. The rebels had sworn to use us as hostages and shields against attack. They were now playing that out.

The column was ordered to start moving again down the street. I saw Paul Carlson trotting up to join the rear of the file, encouraged by a Simba. David was at my side. I did not see the other consulate staff members.

"It was you who was negotiating for us." I realized it was the security-type Simba walking alongside me who was shouting angrily at me. "And now, see where we are." I had been identified and was no longer just someone in the crowd. I turned my head away and plodded on, trying to look as inconspicuous as possible.

A pickup truck drove up and stopped. A Simba pointed a heavy machine gun mounted on the bed in our direction. Out of the cab

213

jumped Major Babu, a huge, black-bearded deaf mute, whom I had seen before in Soumialot's entourage. He waved his hands wildly toward us. The column stopped, and Babu and one of his men argued with Opepe. It was clear Babu wanted to start shooting then and there. Opepe appeared to prevail. I was relieved to see Babu get back in the truck in disgust and drive off with a roar.

The column was started again and arrived at a T-junction in the street. We were ordered to turn right. The street sign showed we were turning off "Rue Sergeant Ketele." About half the column was still on Ketele Avenue, and we were ordered to halt. With more palaver and indecision, I could see that some of our guards wanted the killing to start. I hoped our luck would continue during this delay.

Two Simba officers drove up in a jeep. "Shoot them all," they shouted.

"We are taking them to the airport as shields against our enemies," Opepe said.

"But they're already there," the officers said. Opepe appeared to tell them to leave. In too much of a hurry to argue any longer, they cursed and drove off at high speed. Another danger passed!

"Sit! Sit down!" our guards ordered. We did. The Simbas positioned themselves on the inside of the L-shape formed by the column. Opepe stood behind them. Up to now the Simbas had carried their weapons pointed ahead, away from us, as if to protect us. Now, all guns were aimed in our direction. The light machine gun was now set on its tripod and pointed at the column. Not a good sign, I thought.

I heard a burst of fire close by. Overhead I saw a block of masonry shatter and fall from the corner of the building. I watched, motionless, as the youngest Simba, with his rifle at his hip, slowly and casually begin firing into the crowd. As the other Simbas joined in, the machine gun spurted fire. Startled, I just stared at the scene unfolding. Before I had a chance to react, I heard David's voice.

"Let's go! Let's get out of here!" David shouted as he pulled me by the arm. I started to run with him.

I felt energized and exhilarated. After all the time cooped up, constrained, frustrated at every turn, I was suddenly able to act. No more

214

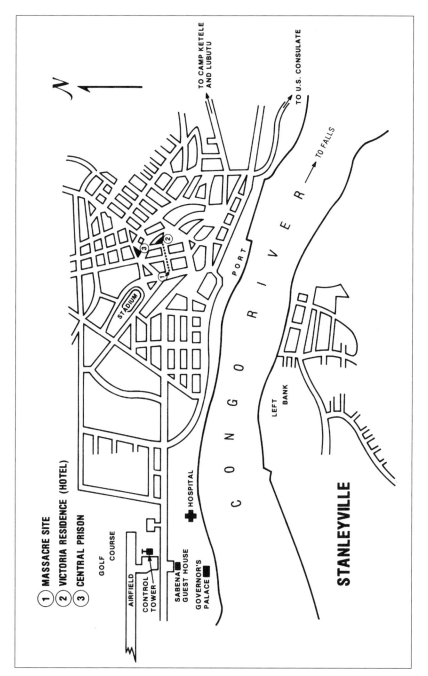

Stanleyville, detailing the location of the 24 November 1964 massacre site,
the Victoria Residence hotel, and the prison.
National Defense University, Washington, D.C.

215

waiting for events, no more indecision! We were committed, irrevocably, to risk all. Making it or not, soon it would all be over. What a glorious feeling! Free at last!

We ran for our lives. An alley appeared on the left, an avenue of escape from the shooting Simbas. I headed for it, David at my side. Several people running with us dropped to the ground. I had to keep running! I heard, or imagined, bullets whistling by me. Screams of women, men, and children mixed with the guttural shouts of the Simbas.

We reached the gravel driveway leading to the back of a building. My body leaned forward, faster than my feet could go. They slid on the loose stone, and I fell heavily.

"Get up! Get up, Mike!" David screamed, reaching to help me. I was already up and running again. David fell and jumped up. I fell again and leapt to my feet to continue running.

We passed a pile of lumber and I lost sight of David. Alone, still running, I looked for protection from the bullets. In front of me was a small staircase leading to a closed door. Rather than trying to reach the door, I dove behind the low wall that formed the far side of the staircase. I huddled down, hoping to be shielded from the Simbas.

The wall was about two feet high and not long enough for me to lie behind. Crouched on my hands and knees, my feet against the building, I tried to keep low and small. Looking ahead, while keeping my head and my rear below the level of the wall, I could see I was clearly visible to anyone on the next street. Nobody appeared. I waited. The noise of firing continued from the direction I had come. People were still screaming, and Simbas shouted angrily. It seemed to continue for a long, long time.

Gradually the sound of the firing and shouting grew distant. I peered cautiously over the wall. No one was there. To my right, across an empty lot, I saw an Indian couple on a second floor balcony. They were looking down on the street below. If they were exposing themselves to whoever was on the street, I thought, it should be safe for me to do the same. I rose cautiously.

A lone soldier in camouflage uniform stood on the other side of the fence enclosing the lot. He wore a red beret and was white, possibly a European; this was all I could see without my glasses. It was conceivable white soldiers could come to the aid of the rebels, but I dismissed this as unlikely. I raised my hands in the air as I rose to draw the soldier's attention to show him I was unarmed. When he saw me, he raised his weapon in my direction and motioned for me to come toward him. I climbed through the wire fence. He continued pointing his weapon at me, and I continued to keep my hands high and visibly showing I had no weapons.

"I am the American consul," I said in French when I got close to him, hands still high. "Take me to your commander."

"Come, come this way," he replied in French. He was a Belgian paratrooper. I knew I was safe. My ordeal was at an end.

The trooper led me down the street to a jeep, where officers huddled around a map. There was no firing now. I identified myself again. One of the officers said he was Colonel [Charles] Laurent, the commander of the Belgian paratroop operation. "I am very glad to see you safe," he said. "We have not yet heard about the others in your staff."

I mumbled something about being happy to see him. "There are American missionaries out at Kilometer Eight," I said. "We need to get out to them immediately."

"My orders are to secure this area of the city," he said.

"Can't you spare some troops or transport to go out there?" I pleaded. "I am willing to go."

"We cannot move from our assigned area," he said. "All the hostages are to go directly to the airport."

A three-wheeled vehicle rolled up and stopped. A man dressed in a military uniform, a pistol strapped to his side, got out and came up to me. When he got close, I recognized him as John Clingerman, whom I had replaced as Stanleyville consul. He did not recognize me at first, apparently put off by my weight loss and wild haircut. "Mike," he said. "It's you. You're safe. Thank God." We embraced roughly and happily.

217

"I'm having some trouble persuading them to take me out to Kilometer Eight," I said. "Our people are still out there."

"Don't you worry about that," he said. "Your orders from Washington are to go immediately to the airport for evacuation. We've spent $4 million rescuing you, and I don't want you getting killed now."

David walked up and joined us. "I've been hiding in a toilet," he said. We embraced silently, not needing to say anything.

"Now, you two go out to the airport," John said. "Right now. I'll take care of the missionaries."

"Do you know anything about the others?" I asked John. "Ernie, Don, and Jim were in the same column we were in. I haven't seen them."

"The Belgian consuls are safe, but we still don't know about the rest of our people," John said. "We just found Paul Carlson's body. He was shot just as he was about to climb over a wall. Phyllis Rine was found in the street, having bled to death. Her leg was shot off."

John and the colonel urged us again to start walking toward the airport.

"Guess that's all we can do," David said. I looked at him, too numbed to talk, shrugged my shoulders, and started walking with him.

People were on the streets, wandering around, moving in the direction of the airport. Bodies were strewn about haphazardly, Simbas mixed with Europeans. A woman was clutching a bloody bundle that was her dead baby. Someone persuaded her to lay it on the ground, to leave it and walk with us. A solemn, straggling column formed, leaving the carnage behind. Blood was on David's clothing and some was on mine. We both had torn our clothing when we fell but were unharmed. I put my hand on the now childless mother's shoulder to show sympathy with her suffering. She stared ahead, putting one reluctant foot ahead of the other. We walked heavily, in sorrow but in freedom. We were no longer hostages.

"What a terrible massacre," David said, feeling undoubtedly the urge to break our silence and talk about the horror we had been through. "It will go down in history as a horrendous tragedy. The Simbas lost any credibility they may have had as true nationalists because of it."

"I can't believe it," I said. "All those people dead, and here we are alive. It's so sad. And Paul . . . after all he had been through . . . it was tough on him. He did not understand it. He came to the Congo to practice medicine. And he had to be the one not to make it. Poor Phyllis. . . ."

We continued the long walk to the airport. A few vehicles, carrying the wounded, passed us. The refugees strung out ahead and behind. We walked in silence until we reached the terminal buildings. We heard an occasional shot ring out. We saw Belgian paratroopers dug in around the airport buildings. They had set up their operations center in the baggage room I knew so well.

David and I stood in the baggage room and talked to an American crewman from one of the American airplanes that had carried the Belgian paracommandos. A Belgian officer came up to us with a black civilian. I recognized him as Hugh Scotland; his otherwise slicked-down hair was in a wild tangle. "We found this guy with rebels at the Palace," the officer said. "He held up his passport, saying he was a British national."

"Yes, he's a Trinidadian journalist and not a rebel," I said.

"He should be put on an airplane and taken to Léopoldville," David said. "He'll be killed if left here. The British embassy might be able to get something out of him about the rebellion."

"See if you can get him to Léopoldville," I told the officer, who led Scotland away.[11]

An armed U.S. combat soldier was directing refugees to two aircraft standing by with engines running. They were C-130 Hercules, the aircraft the United States flew to the Congo whenever there was trouble. One slowly rolled away. We left the protection of the terminal and ran toward the other. I ducked as I heard shooting nearby. David and I entered the aircraft through the door below the flight deck.

As we climbed the ladder inside, I saw the airplane's cargo hold was filled with rescued hostages. Blood stood in pools on the floor. Medical personnel were working on the wounded. Others lay about in shock. The rear ramp closed as we stepped onto the flight deck. The door behind us closed on the bloody scene. We buckled into our seats on a bench behind the pilots and crew.

219

The aircraft taxied, and in an instant we were roaring down the runway. It cleared the trees, crossed the silvery Congo River, and headed over the blanket of trees toward Léopoldville. We had been whisked away from the horror in a matter of minutes by this wonder of modern technology.

After we reached altitude, the aircraft commander left his seat and came back to us. "Welcome back," he shouted over the roar of the engines. "Your staff people are okay. I just heard over the radio that the other three are on the flight ahead of us. We are going as fast as we can. There are many seriously wounded in the back who will not make it if we don't get there soon."

I mumbled something about being grateful to him for the operation, which we now knew was designated Dragon Rouge.

The few hours' flight did not seem long. Soon we would be back to the comforts of the "real world." Time and the forest below passed quickly. I looked at David, and he looked back. We said nothing—too exhausted, too saddened, too happy to be alive. Soon we spotted the great silver patch of wide river forming Stanley Pool as we banked for the landing. When we rolled to a stop, David and I climbed down the ladder and out through the side door. As we went past the rear ramp, I could see blood pouring out, spreading out over the tarmac. The horror had followed us to Léopoldville.[12]

> I have wrestled with death. It is the most unexciting contest you can imagine. It takes place in an impalpable greyness, with nothing under-foot, with nothing around, without spectators, without clamour, without glory, without the great desire of victory, without the great fear of defeat, in a sickly atmosphere of tepid scepticism, without much belief in your own right, and still less in that of your adversary. If such is the form of ultimate wisdom, then life is a greater riddle than some of us think it to be. I was within a hair's breadth of the last opportunity for pronouncement, and I found with humiliation that probably I would have nothing to say. (Conrad, *Heart of Darkness*)

Return

AT THE TAIL OF THE AIRPLANE, I SAW THE BIG RUFFLED SHAPE OF Ambassador Godley. He enveloped me in his bear-sized arms. "It's great to see you, Mike," he said. "It's been a long haul."

I felt his joy in seeing us was genuine. Friends from Léopoldville and Stanleyville crowded around to greet us, slapping us on the back, congratulating us for having survived. Max Kraus was his usual cheerful self, trying to push back the surging press people.

David told someone to inform the British embassy of Scotland's presence as a U.K. subject and a potential source of information. David was taken away by his fellow CIA comrades.

I went with Mac to his car waiting on the tarmac. With flag flying, we sped into town to the ambassador's residence. Mac said little, but I could tell he was bubbling over with the success of the paradrop. I was too drained by the shock of the killings to make more than perfunctory conversation.

We drove into the residence grounds. The last time I had been there was at the Fourth of July reception I had organized, almost five months before. Moïse Tshombé had visited here, just before he became prime minister.

I had no time to change clothes—I had none to change into anyway—and was ushered into a luncheon already in progress for local businessmen, mostly heads of the big Belgian concerns in the Congo. I knew most of them from my time as the embassy commercial officer. I was the center of attention. They questioned me gently on my experiences and listened in quiet awe. I said it would be a hard, long struggle to reestablish any sort of normal commercial and economic life in the area devastated by the rebels. Political and social reorganization, I told them, after the ravages of the rebels and what would inevitably come from the ANC, would be difficult.

I found it hard to focus on the present. I was sitting down at a table with the finest china and silver, drinking good wine, and picking at an excellent meal. I was now with the leaders of the business community, while less than five hours ago I had been a frightened hostage of the Simbas.

When the guests left, Mac told me Max Kraus had organized a press conference. I was still in my dirty bloodstained shirt. David arrived, and I noticed that he had changed into clean clothes. A microphone was set up on the coffee table on the porch about three in the afternoon, and Mac, David, and I fielded questions from the assembled reporters. I recognized Jon Randal, the *Time-Life* correspondent, hobbling around on crutches after having been wounded when the mercenaries blew up the Lumumba monument in Kindu. I noticed that Lloyd Garrison had replaced Tony Lukas for the *New York Times.*

Most of the questions concerned the massacre scene and the "flag-eating" incident, which somehow was well known even before the rescue operation. There were also questions about the communist nature and affiliations of the rebels. Godley tried to answer those. I was quoted in Garrison's story as saying the rebels claimed to be socialists "but not Communists, although they expressed sympathies with other Socialist countries." On the flag incident, David said we had chewed on the flags but had been unable to eat them.[1] There were questions on how we were fed. "That was not a problem," I said. "We worried about lots of things, but not food."

Mac ended the press conference and took me into town to his office. Prime Minister Tshombé arrived just then to be briefed on the day's events. He started by telling us that on his way to the airport that morning to greet the hostages, he had identified Hugh Scotland in a car going into town. "I knew him from Madrid," he said, "where he was a member of the leftist press. I turned around and gave chase. He is now in prison. He is definitely not on our side."[2]

Tshombé was interested in what had happened to the consulate staff during the rebel occupation. I told him briefly about how we had been the only consuls detained at first and had been mistreated; only toward the end were virtually all the Europeans rounded up and made hostages. Mac and Monty Stearns filled him in on Operation Dragon Rouge, the code name for the rescue operation. They seemed relieved when Tshombé signed some paper they had prepared for him. Tshombé expressed himself pleased with the whole business.

"Mr. Prime Minister," I put in as he was about to leave. "May I make just one suggestion to you from my experience in Stan?" When he indicated I should proceed, I said, "The best leader, in my view, to lead the population of Stan into any sort of normalcy would be Aradjabu. I urge you to save him."

"I will look into it," Tshombé said.

"The Secretary is on the phone for you," Maggie Conrad, the ambassador's secretary, told me. I took the phone and talked to Dean Rusk. He was most laudatory of our behavior while we were held hostage. He said my wife had been superb. I thanked him for all his efforts to save us.

The next call was from Jo in Tucson. It was a radio patch call and the connection was not clear. Jo told me she had gone first to Jerome in Arizona when she left the Congo after our last radio contact, then to Tucson to put the kids in school. She said she would meet me in New York. I could think of nothing to say except that I loved her very much, missed her, and couldn't wait to see her.

223

A call came in from Tony Ross, our ambassador in Bangui in the Central African Republic, where Paul Carlson said his family had gone when they fled the Congo. "Would you talk to Mrs. Carlson?" he asked. "She knows that her husband was killed."

"I want you to know that Paul had been holding up well," I told her. "He was doing his work, tending to the hostages, making the rounds of the sick and comforting them. I am so sorry that after all he had been through, he was the one not to survive the ending." I could not say anything more. Jo had gotten the good news, Lois the bad.

I was then driven to the ambassador's residence so I could take a bath and lie down for a rest. I talked to Martin Beek, who had been my Belgian assistant in Léopoldville. I remembered the mini-standoff between Mac and me over his status. I had met Beek in Lodja, almost in the exact center of the Congo, on one of my visits to the interior. He had lost his business in the troubles. Impressed with his talents, I offered him a job as the head of my commercial library. When Mac arrived as a bachelor ambassador, he wanted Martin, together with his wife, to run the residence as his housekeepers. I maintained he was more valuable where he was and was permitted to keep him. I knew Mac had brought him to the residence as soon as I left for Stanleyville.

The Beeks were in tears. "We were so worried about you," he said. "And we have you to thank for getting us out of Lodja before the rebels took it."

There was a quiet dinner, more wine, more talk, whiskey, and the day finally came to an end. It was the end of an ordeal that had begun 112 days before. Bob Blake, the deputy chief of mission, Mac, and I were in the living room, having a last drink. Feeling the alcohol after so much time without it and feeling good in general, I could not resist a poke at Mac. "You know, Mac, there was one thing that kept David and me going."

"What was that?" Mac asked.

"It was the thought that if we didn't make it, you wouldn't either."

Bob choked on his drink and sank down, trying to disappear into the couch. Mac did not respond. He was probably as far gone on the liquor as I was, or he chose to ignore my jibe.

Bob took me to spend the night at his house, on the ridge in Binza, overlooking the house where Jo and I and our four kids had spent almost two years. In the distance, the moon shone on the Congo River descending to the cataracts below Stanley Pool.

I AWOKE WEDNESDAY morning, 25 November, to the first day of the rest of my life. I began shedding the 112 days of terror with a swim in the large pool on the back patio. Floating in the water, face down, motionless, I felt completely free. I held my breath to preserve the feeling of no constraints on body or mind. I repeated this several times, then swam several laps to get going again. Happiness would be complete when I saw Jo. Meanwhile, I looked forward to being useful again.

Sylvia Blake lent me some of Bob's clothes, and I threw away the bloodstained ones. After the first real breakfast I had in months—incomparably better than the previous day's beer and sausage—Sylvia drove me to the embassy. I was told the five of us were to take the evening plane from Léopoldville to Rome, make a connection to Paris, and then on to New York. We would arrive on Thursday, Thanksgiving Day.

I learned how the others had survived the massacre in Stanleyville. Ernie Houle had remained in the street when the firing began and was untouched when the paratroopers arrived and chased the Simbas away. Jim Stauffer and Don Parkes had run directly into the arms of the paras. Gene Bergman and Jon Snyder emerged unscathed. Carlson had followed them but was shot before he could climb the wall after them. It was confirmed that Patrick Nothomb and Paul Duqué had escaped unharmed, as had José Romnée and Michel Faeles.

Almost all the other Americans, Belgians, and other civilians I had known and worked with had survived except Phyllis Rine. It was confirmed that she had been shot in the leg and bled to death on the street. Twenty Belgian civilians were killed in the massacre on Rue Sergeant Ketele and in adjacent alleyways and houses. Another forty had been wounded, with five more dying during the flights to Léopoldville.

Embassy personnel were dealing with the aftermath of the rescue

225

operation, cleaning up loose ends and preparing for another jump on Paulis to save hostages there. There was a vicious international campaign against the rescue operation mounted by the Soviet-bloc and radical African states. My former colleagues and others in the mission took the time to give me a joyous welcome.

Monty Stearns, David, and I conferred and drafted a cable giving a rundown on the events from Friday until the paradrop on Tuesday. It described how the rebels used the hostages to stave off an attack. "Rebels' intention was evidently hold hostages in reserve for deployment around military targets to prevent their being attacked or bombed." It told about the message Nothomb and I broadcast, "saying that their lives would be forfeit if negotiations were not opened and an attack were launched on the city." The aborted attempt to disperse us to the bush on Saturday and the reception to meet journalist Hugh Scotland on Sunday were described. The cable related what we had seen of the massacre in the streets, with the paras chasing the Simbas away after the slaughter. The last paragraph read:

> Not clear whether Opepe ordered the firing on hostages, did not order it, or at last minute tried to prevent it. It is clear that Simba troops, just as entire population Stanleyville, impregnated through long repetition by rebels with idea that Belgians and Americans were hostages to be killed in case of military action against the city. This is known to have been a matter of heavy public propaganda in the city as well as the constantly repeated theme of shouts and threats directed at consular staff during their ordeal.[3]

The news came from Stanleyville that Joseph Opepe had been identified in a pile of dead Simbas. Speculation was that his own men had shot him for not having fired on the hostages sooner. I also learned that Aradjabu had been killed on orders from Joseph Désiré Mobutu and Victor Nendaka because he supposedly let the rebels take the city.[4]

Monty and I drafted a cable to give recognition to those who had helped us and the other hostages in Stanleyville. The cable to the department, with copies to Brussels, New Delhi, Athens, and London, read:

226

Hoyt reports that Honorary British Vice Consul Peter Rombaut, local manager British-American Tobacco Company Stan, during entire period incarceration was tower of strength and friendship, did everything possible, with Belgian Consul Nothomb, until latter's imprisonment, effect release Americans. Also BAT paid all Americans' and local employees, brought food, did laundry, etc., for Americans even while they were in prison. Request Secretary and/or Ambassador [David] Bruce bring Rombaut's action to the attention of high officials HMG [His Majesty's Government] as finest example British-American coordination. Request [Douglas] MacArthur take similar action re Nothomb.

Until incarceration himself Belgian Consul Nothomb also most helpful. Although his hands full doing what he could for Belgian community, he never failed endeavor obtain release Americans and when permitted travel throughout rebel territory he always checked on American's [sic] welfare, whereabouts. Specifically, on August 21 he made demarche with military authorities which in Hoyt's opinion saved lives 5 American consul personnel following receipt Stan inflammatory telegram from Olenga calling for judgement all Americans "without pity" which then resulted in August 21 message from Hoyt.

During latter days of detention, food, clothing and bedding for all detainees began running short. Indian and Greek communities organized themselves and collected through entire community these essential requirements and delivered them at considerable personal risk to places of detention. Recommend this be brought to attention of Greek and Indian govts with expression of appreciation. Hoyt and I calling on Indian ambassador today.

Comment: [portion excised] fact that Indian colony Stan helped American and Belgian detainees we think might be well publicized only rpt only after rest of rebel held areas are liberated lest reprisals against Indians result.[5]

The call on the Indian ambassador was not able to take place as planned. I spoke by phone to the British and Belgian ambassadors, whom I knew, and conveyed my appreciation for what Peter and Patrick had done for us.

227

Mac came back from the airport, where he had gone to meet the plane bringing Paul Carlson's body. "They didn't even have the body wrapped," he said, looking pale. "Marines finally covered it with a flag, and we had a brief ceremony." Then he turned to me. "You know, Mike, I knew it would be bad for you in Stan when the rebels came— but not that bad."

"Well, it all happened so much faster than we anticipated," I said, feeling more placatory than I had the previous night.

In the afternoon, we all attended a debriefing from Lt. Col. Donald V. Rattan. He had been with the land column, led by Belgian Col. Frédérick Vandewalle, that entered Stanleyville at eleven on the twenty-fourth. Rattan and a sergeant were accompanied by a contingent of eighteen CIA-recruited black, anti-Castro Cubans, part of the three-mile-long column, named Ommegang after a Brussels folk procession. The CIA contingent's mission was to rescue the consulate staff and was code-named "Low Beam." The Vandewalle column consisted of ANC units, Katangese *gendarmerie* from Tshombé's secession days, and Belgian military assistance forces, spearheaded by armored vehicles of the mercenary troops under Maj. Mike Hoare. Hoare had taken the consulate as his headquarters and residence.

Rattan said the column was under continuous attack by rebel fire from the bush after leaving Lubutu. Several in the column were killed or wounded. At three-thirty in the morning of 24 November, South African NBC correspondent George Clay was killed, and Vandewalle, urged by Hoare, ordered the column to stop and defend itself. Rattan said his main fear was that the barrels of gasoline they were carrying would have exploded like bombs if they were hit by rebel fire. Ommegang thus was not able to rendezvous with the paradrop.[6]

"The Cubans went to Kilometer Eight at Clingerman's request to rescue the missionaries there," Rattan told me. "They were all okay except for a Canadian man who was killed just before they arrived."

"Here's a cable for you from the Secretary," Maggie Conrad said. I read:

Message to Hoyt from the Secretary
The entire Department joins me in expressing to you and your staff our gratitude and relief at your liberation after three harrowing months. During that time your welfare and safety have been uppermost in our minds. In spite of the humiliations and hardships which you have suffered and the difficult conditions under which you have

lived, you have all discharged your duties in the highest traditions of the Foreign Service and we extend our sincerest congratulations on your fortitude and courage. We all look forward to having you back with us again.

Please extend to Messrs. Grinwis, Houle, Stauffer, and Parks [*sic*] my similar admiration for their devotion to duty.[7]

"Jo's on," Maggie said, handing me the phone. It was on a ham patch, and we could say little but "Love you, over." Jo said she had arranged to fly to New York to meet our plane on Thanksgiving.

I went to the Blakes to dress for the journey home. It was winter in the States, and we found a suit of Bob's that fit me reasonably well. Mac sent his overcoat; it was a few sizes too big for me, but he insisted I take it. I had no watch or glasses; they had long ago been stolen and broken, respectively, at the consulate.

When I returned to the embassy, Col. Knut Raudstein, the army attaché and a close friend, greeted me. "Michael, guess what I have here?" It was my briefcase. "I went to the Victoria Hotel in Stan and got this out of your room. David's was there, too. You gave us quite a time. That was quite a cliffhanger. Shirley and I are sure glad to see you."

"Now I have one piece of luggage to take back to the States," I told Knut, thanking him for the return of our notes and papers.

The city was in the hands of the ANC, he said, and the paras were at the airport preparing for the Dragon Noir jump the next day on Paulis. The rebels were still in force and fighting on the outskirts of Stanleyville. The rebel leaders had apparently made their escape to the east. Knut talked of the terrible toll that was being taken on the Stanleyville population. Suspected rebels were being killed by ANC and security forces.

The five of us from the Stanleyville consulate boarded the evening Air Congo flight to Rome. We took full advantage of the luxuries of first class, toasting our good fortune to be alive and trying to forget the past months of terror and the dead we had left behind. In Rome, we were met by Alan Ford from the embassy. He took us to his house, where we had a sumptuous breakfast. We then took the next flight to Paris.

229

Media people met us at each airport and asked about our experiences. The most frequently asked question was what we did for food. I usually answered, "That was the least of our problems." The articles written said I reported that we were badly treated by the rebels and were saved only by the timely arrival of the paratroopers. I was quoted as making the complaint that David had made about the inedibility of American flags furnished by the U.S. government. A representative of *Readers Digest* urged me not to make any commitments for my story until his office could contact me. I said I assumed there were government regulations about it. In the transit lounge in Paris, I bought a gold watch to replace the one taken by Major Nasor back in August.

The trip over the Atlantic seemed short. All I thought about was seeing Jo. We landed in New York. The plane came to a stop out on the tarmac, a good distance from the terminal. My name and the others were called out over the loudspeaker. Our hostess said we were parked out there because immigration and customs thought we did not have passports and health certificates. We all had them in our pockets, but no one asked for them.

From the door of the plane where a ramp had been drawn up, I recognized Jo, even without my glasses, standing about fifty yards away, next to a military plane. I ran down the steps and across the tarmac to her. Someone said the television coverage showed me sending a woman flying, but I was unaware of anyone but Jo. She was in my arms and nothing else mattered.

We were interrupted by someone who said the news media wanted to talk to me. They were on the other side of a chain link fence that was bulging in from the bodies pressed against it. We were in quarantine because they had not seen our health certificates. I took Jo's arm and went to them. Microphones were stuck at me and questions shouted through the fence. "What was your most anxious moment?"

"When they started firing at us."

"How do you feel?"

"I'm feeling fine," I am reported to have said. "It's wonderful to be back. I'm glad to be reunited with my wife on Thanksgiving." The articles said we looked tired but otherwise bore no physical signs of our ordeal.

Someone jerked me away, apparently deciding I had said enough. Jo and I went up the ramp and boarded a U.S. Air Force Convair, the same type that had flown us to Stanleyville, to join the others and their family members. The parents of David, Don, and Jim were there as was Ernie's brother and sister. I had eyes only for Jo. We snuggled in our seats. Tears of happiness came to my eyes, and I felt a deluge coming. "Not now," Jo said, holding me closer. I recovered.

Two officers from the State Department came to greet us, James O'Sullivan, who had been deputy chief of mission in Léopoldville when I first arrived, and Wayne Fredericks from the Africa Bureau. Dr. Woodward, head of the medical division in the State Department, came up. "How do you feel?" he asked.

"Just great," I said. He looked at me and pronounced me fit, presumably medically cleared to enter the United States.

"Here, you'll need this," O'Sullivan said, offering me a one hundred dollar bill. I was about to say I didn't need it, having picked up money in the embassy in Léopoldville, when Jo nudged me.

"Go ahead, take it, Michael," she said. I did. There were more greetings and congratulations. All I could say or think was that it was great to be home with Jo close beside me.

After an hour's flight, we arrived at Washington National. Jo and I were led to a battery of microphones for more questions. We had the same exchange as in previous encounters. At the end, the question was, "Would you return to Africa?"

"Certainly, after a while," I replied. Parenthetically, I thought it would be a long time before I wanted to return to the Congo.

We were taken to the Mayflower Hotel. Our room was large and had twin beds. "We'll have none of this," Jo said. I called to change rooms. We were moved to a tiny room with a double bed. I ordered martinis, and we watched Huntley-Brinkley on the evening news feature my Thanksgiving dash across the tarmac to embrace Jo.

231

JO AND I were scheduled to report to the State Department Friday morning, but before we did, we had a leisurely breakfast. I stopped for a haircut. "Just who gave you this haircut?" asked the barber. "It's a butcher job like I've never seen."

"An itinerant Greek barber in Stanleyville," I responded, not eager to go into it further. A car was waiting to take us to the department, where we were met by Walker Diamanti.

"Walker talked to me every day after I came to Washington and saw Dean Rusk in October," Jo said. "He has been absolutely fantastic. He even told me about the paradrop when it was supposed to be kept a total secret. He put up with my terrible rantings. He called me minute-by-minute and finally told me you were out and on the way to Léopoldville."

Walker showed me around the Congo Working Group (CWG); dozens of people were working in the Operations Center. "They may have been working on all of the Congo's problems," Walker said, "but in reality they were consumed with the urgency of getting you guys out."

"Sitting in Stanleyville," I said, "we had no idea all this was going on. After the aborted Operation Flagpole, we were aware of absolutely nothing about any concern for us. I felt we had dropped into a dark hole and been forgotten. When those planes came over, I suspected we had not."

David came in, and we went to the large conference room for a classified debriefing. Members of the CWG and all the government agencies involved—White House, Defense, CIA, USIA, USAID, and many State officers from the Africa Bureau—were there.

Bill Brubeck, the African liaison officer at the White House National Security Council staff, led the questioning. He asked about how we had been treated but soon turned to their main concern, the rebel leadership and the influences on them. I said I viewed the rebel leadership as being within the Congolese political spectrum. They were ostensibly followers of Lumumba, Gizenga, and Mulélé; essentially pragmatic; and followed their own interests. However, there was a great deal of anti-American sentiment and rhetoric. David said several communist China–trained Lumumbists he knew had achieved positions of limited power in the rebel structure, but they were not the leaders. He said that some he knew who had been trained in communist China were in jail with us.

We both said the real power in the rebel movement lay with Olenga and his Batetela tribesmen, from officers to noncoms and private Simba soldiers. Recruitment had been widespread among the captured population, but the Batetela were the hard core of the rebellion. We both agreed the success of the rebellion—its rapid spread to nearly a third of the Congo—was due to the worthlessness of the ANC as a fighting force and the lack of organizational effectiveness of the central government.

From the debriefing, which lasted less than an hour, Jo and I were taken to see W. Averell Harriman. Harriman was then undersecretary of state for political affairs, the number-four man in the State Department and the one responsible for managing the Congo crisis among the "principals" of the State Department on the seventh floor. Harriman, the former governor of New York, was gracious, welcoming us to his vast office and inviting us to partake of a cold luncheon buffet of tender prime ribs. He probed me gently concerning the communist influence in the rebel movement. I later learned he held the view, in spite of all CIA evidence and analysis to the contrary, that the Simba rebellion was "a concerted Communist effort to wrest the mineral wealth of the Congo from the West."⁸ "The rescue operation," Harriman said to me, "was essential to demonstrate America will not tolerate its people being taken hostage."

We returned to the Operations Center, where we met Joseph Palmer, in charge of the CWG, and Lewis Hoffacker, director of the center, who had been consul in Elisabethville and a neighbor and friend in Léopoldville. I learned he was to be my new boss when I returned to work in the Operations Center as an editor and watch officer. Also there was the Congo desk officer, Bill Schaufele, a colleague and friend from our tour in Casablanca. We went downstairs to the sixth floor office of G. Mennen "Soapy" Williams, the assistant secretary for African affairs, who was effusive in his welcome. I learned he had been trying to reach a negotiated settlement to the rebel problem and had not been enthusiastic about the paradrop.

233

We read the reports on what had happened in the Congo since we had left. Dragon Noir had been mounted on 26 November, rescuing hostages in Paulis. When Vandewalle's forces reached the Left Bank across from Stanleyville on 26 November, they found twenty-eight Belgian priests, nuns, and missionaries killed by the Simbas.

Terrible retribution by the central government continued in Stanley-ville, but its forces had not yet been able to move against the rebels still on the outskirts of Stanleyville.

David and I were scheduled to meet the press in the large confer-ence room on the ground floor. In Harriman's outer office, Richard Phillips, the assistant secretary for public affairs, gave me a list of brief-ing points. It contained something about the communist China–led rebellion, and I began to say something to indicate I did not agree. "Never mind," Harriman said. "Mike doesn't need this briefing stuff. When questions like that come up, just let David handle them."

At the press conference, I jumped into the question of communist influence in the rebel movement, contrary to Governor Harriman's instruction (see excerpts in the Appendix). Some of my contradictory answers reflected my lack of any clear knowledge of the facts and my belief that there were few outside influences with material bearing on the rebellion. The reporters were interested in our personal reac-tions to events:

> *Question:* Mr. Hoyt, as you look back, is there any one moment that you can think of as being worse than others?
> *Mr. Hoyt:* I think for myself the most difficult time was at first, when they were beating on the door of the vault room in which we had retreated. This was our first contact with the rebels and personally it was very difficult because I was con-vinced if they broke down that door they would just start firing indiscriminately. . . .
> *Vice Consul:* I would agree with the consul. . . . But equally difficult was a week ago Wednesday when we were taken before the Lumumba monument and we assumed we were to be executed there. It was clear from the reaction of the crowd of about eight or nine thousand people that all of us were accused of being American mercenaries.

After the press conference, we went to a reception on the sev-enth floor given by Secretary of State Dean Rusk in our honor along with the Congo Working Group staff. When we gathered for a group picture, I found myself behind Dean Rusk. He thrust his drink in my hands while he posed for the picture. Later Rusk came over to where Jo and I were standing. Jo thanked him for having me rescued and was effusive in her praise for Walker Diamanti's stoicism in helping her deal with her frustration and anger.

"Tell me, Mrs. Hoyt," Rusk said, pulling a half dollar from his pocket and flipping it, "at one point I wasn't worth the flip of a coin in all this business, was I?"⁹

She agreed. I knew that all during the time we were hostages, our lives weren't worth a nickel. At any time our lives could have been forfeited. On several occasions, it had been individual Simbas who had done their duty and protected us. I remembered the lone Simba guard with the rifle who locked us in the women's toilet at the airport in August and told us to be quiet while he went to save us from the mob.

JO AND I spent a quiet weekend, seeing friends, buying clothes, and trying to calm nerves that had been stretched taut for many months. We read the newspaper accounts of the Friday press conference. The *New York Times* carried the banner "U.S. Consul Doubts Rebels Are Reds." In the article it said that although this coincided with administration thinking, the rebels might in time "acquire leftist orientation."¹⁰

On Monday I returned to the State Department, where I was zipped through a medical exam and given a formal medical clearance. I apparently had enough control of my nerves that I was not questioned about my mental state. Walker showed me a full-page ad in the *New York Times*. It showed us bearded at the Governor's Palace in Stanleyville. It was an ad for the issue of *Life* coming out the next day with the full story of Paul Carlson and his death, entitled "Congo Martyr."

I saw Harriman again. The Soviet-bloc press had mounted an international campaign, labeling the rescue operation racist and imperialist. The radical African states joined in attacking the Dragon operations as imperialist moves. Ambassador Adlai Stevenson at the United Nations was having a terrible time countering the attacks against us.

235

"I'll go anywhere, anyplace, anytime," I said to Harriman, "to spread the word on the rebel movement—that they were not authentic nationalists but merely self-seeking murderers."

Harriman gave me a figurative pat on the head. "Go to Tucson and don't even think of returning for at least three months." I learned later that David had gone to New York to help our delegation deal with the vicious campaign.

Jo and I returned to the Mayflower and left the next morning for New York. On checking out of the hotel, I was told the State Department had settled the bill. After a few days in New York, we went to Chicago, where I grew up, and were given a royal welcome. On the late-night Irv Kupcinet guest program, I discovered that some American blacks viewed the rescue operation differently than I did. Eartha Kitt broke into a litany of how it was another example of whites killing blacks. Before I could reply, Malcolm Muggeridge and Bill Mauldin jumped in and defended the operation for me.

Jo and I next went to Tucson. I joyously greeted my children and finally entered our rented house, with its brightly colored "Welcome Home" sign.

IT TOOK ALMOST a year to contain the Simba revolt. The last organized elements, trained for a time by Che Guevera, were finally defeated and confined to an area inland in the Fizi-Baraka area on Lake Tanganyika by mercenary and ANC forces. During this time, the rebels killed a total of 172 missionary and civilian hostages.[11]

Prime Minister Moïse Tshombé was dismissed when the rebels ceased to pose a threat. Joseph Désiré Mobutu took over and, using as an excuse the threat to security that the rebellion represented, set up a repressive regime. He renamed the country Zaire and used his "anti-communist" stance to garner U.S. support for thirty-five years. In 1997 Laurent Kabila, who had taken over the Simba rebellion after Gbenye and Olenga abandoned it in the 1960s, with Rwandan support, chased Mobutu into exile and took over the renamed Democratic Republic of the Congo. Gaston Soumialot had held out in the Fizi-Baraka area for years until, it was thought, his own men killed him. Christophe Gbenye established a prosperous transport company in Uganda, making good use of the Kilo Moto gold. He and Nicholas Olenga took advantage of an amnesty in 1971 urged on Mobutu by the State Department—over my strenuous objections from my posting at Bujumbura, Burundi—to return to Zaire.[12] While Gbenye continues to prosper, albeit under some form of house arrest, Olenga never adjusted to civilian life and disappeared in Mobutu's prison system. Tshombé went into exile after his dismissal. In 1967 he was abducted to Algeria and died in jail there in 1969.

On 9 June 1965, Secretary Dean Rusk presented the State Department's newly designated top honor, the Secretary's Award, to each of the five members of the staff at the American consulate in Stanleyville held hostage in 1964.[13] The inscriptions read:

FOR OUTSTANDING COURAGE AND DIGNITY IN
HIGHEST TRADITIONS OF THE FOREIGN SERVICE
WHILE A PRISONER AND HOSTAGE
OF CONGOLESE REBELS
AUGUST 5–NOVEMBER 24, 1964

Appendix
Press Conference, Washington, D.C.,
27 November 1964

Washington, D.C., Friday, November 27, 1964
4:30 P.M. Department of State Conference Room
(Excerpted from official U.S. Department of State transcript.)

Mr. Richard Phillips: Ladies and gentlemen, may I present Consul Michael P. E. Hoyt, of Chicago, Illinois, age 35; and Vice Consul David K. Grinwis, of Maplewood, New Jersey.

Question: Are you glad to be back, sir?

Mr. Hoyt: Certainly, very glad.

Question: Mr. Hoyt, we are familiar to some extent with some of your experiences during this period, including the fact that you had to eat the American flag. Could you briefly for us go over some of the privations and hardships and other problems that you had during this period?

Mr. Hoyt: I think I will talk about it in a more general way because we get bogged down in a lot of details, but in general there was no recognition of our diplomatic or consular status, and there was no respect for any kind of humanity. We were at times beaten, imprisoned, humiliated, [and] forced to write messages against our will. We actually spent almost half the period in prison treated as common criminals.

Question: Would you say this was a revolt against whites or trying to get back at the United States?

Mr. Hoyt: No, I don't think the movement was primarily against whites or primarily against the United States. The anti-U.S. was more for propaganda purposes. They threatened the non-African communities for specific purposes when it served their purpose, but I don't think this was the purpose of the movement.

239

Question: When did this, as far as the timing is concerned, when did this start in terms of this maltreatment of you and the others?

Mr. Hoyt: Well, when the rebels arrived in Stanleyville, they arrived shooting at the American consulate. There was a specific attack against the American consulate in which the consulate was violated and they beat at the door behind which we were. . . . And when we met [General Nicholas] Olenga the following morning, the meeting with the consular corps, there was a specific diatribe against the U.S. in which he claimed thousands of American soldiers had been seen in battle against him and he captured, he gave me the figure of 108, repeated this same diatribe almost two months later. I attempted to tell him there just weren't any American troops, but this didn't seem to have any effect.

Question: Mr. Hoyt, how did that American flag taste?

Mr. Hoyt: Well, actually, to be absolutely correct, I was not forced to do it, but the four other members of the consulate did.

Vice Consul: We just had to hold the flag in our mouths and made chewing motions but we couldn't actually eat it. It is made of too durable material.

Question: You spoke of beatings. Could you give us some more details on that?

Mr. Hoyt: They beat us primarily with rifle butts. They hit me over the head with the rifle barrel and with sticks and then on another occasion we were beaten with bayonets, forced to dance, and if you didn't skip, you would get hit. On several occasions when we were imprisoned or confined, people would come in and slap us around a bit with their hands.

Question: Did you say you were imprisoned half the period from August until your return to this country?

Mr. Hoyt: Yes, a total of 52 days we spent in the central prison in Stanleyville, a stretch of 42 days which ended a week ago today, and a 10 day period the first part of September. . . . Most of the rest of the time we spent under guard. The five of us were guarded in the consulate until the 21st of August when the authorities in Stanleyville received a telegram from Olenga saying that we should be put before a tribunal and judged without pity. Fortunately, they instead took us out to the women's toilet. . . .

Question: Mr. Hoyt, during this period were you and your colleagues convinced that you would never get out alive?

Mr. Hoyt: No, we couldn't have survived if we weren't convinced, I think that we were—I mean, we could not have mentally survived if we were convinced we were going to be killed. I convinced myself there was a good chance that we would get out alive, although at many times we thought we might be immediately killed.

Question: If the Belgian paratroopers hadn't arrived, do you think most if not all the hostages would have been killed in some way or another?

Mr. Hoyt: Oh yes, I think the pattern had been pretty well established before the arrival of both the ANC [*Armée Nationale Congolaise*] troops and the Belgian paratroopers that they intended to use us as shields, as hostages in the event of military attacks. On November 19, they took us from the Victoria hotel and told us they were going to place us around the outskirts of the city because they had heard a column was advancing. And then again that afternoon, they loaded us on a bus and took us on the road to Banalia, to get us out of the way of advancing troops. In other words, to continue holding us as hostages.

Question: Do you think, Mr. Hoyt, that the paratroop rescue operation was the only way that they could actually save lives?

Mr. Hoyt: Well, that is about the way it looked to me. I really couldn't have seen by that time that they had any real intention of letting us go. It was a matter of timing, getting to us quickly. . . .

Question: How did you and your colleagues escape?

Mr. Hoyt: We ran with the rest of them. It was more just by chance that none of us were killed. . . .

Question: Mr. Hoyt, would you try to describe for us or define the nature of the so-called rebel regime and discuss the relative importance of people like Olenga, [Gaston] Soumialot, and [Christophe] Gbenye?

Mr. Hoyt: Yes. In my mind, effective control of the movement came from the military organization, and General Olenga was pretty much in control of that organization. Soumialot, the Minister of Defense, also was a responsible minister along with Mr. Gbenye.

241

. . . People fighting made use of nationalist and revolutionary slogans, but essentially it was military. . . .

Question: Was there any evidence of Chinese Communist influence or assistance or advisers as far as you saw it?

Mr. Hoyt: We, of course, were in prison, confined most of the time, didn't get around much, but we saw no foreign advisers in the movement. They claimed themselves that there were none, but they said that they felt that those countries were sympathetic with them.

Question: Would you describe this as a Marxist movement?

Mr. Hoyt: Marxist ideology as an economic one was not very much in evidence. There was no attempt to nationalize things, except for trucks. They kept saying they wanted economic life to function normally. But from the very first, they cut off the region from the outside world. The economy was bound to come to a halt and fail. . . .

Question: Was there any evidence of cannibalism?

Mr. Hoyt: I didn't see any personally. But we heard pretty definite stories about it in a number of public executions in the Lumumba Square that there were acts of cannibalism.

Question: Do they consider themselves followers in the tradition of [Patrice] Lumumba?

Mr. Hoyt: They used the figure of Lumumba. Talking further on motivation and techniques, they had a whole ritual procedure which was primarily traditionalist.

Question: The reason I am asking all these questions is that this has been commonly portrayed in the U.S. press as a sort of hangover from Lumumba, a leftist, more or less Marxist, probably communist aided revolution. Some of the things you say imply that this is too simple.

242   *Mr. Hoyt:* Yes, certainly, the Lumumba sentiment was certainly employed. But there are certainly many other elements involved.

Question: You saw no evidence, then, that this was anything but an indigenous revolt, using indigenous tactics, traditional methods of administration and control?

Mr. Hoyt: No, I certainly wouldn't go so far as to say that. There was evidence that a certain number of the leaders had visited Iron

Curtain countries, and they certainly had had contact with the outside world, and it was not strictly an internal movement. I would say it was essentially an internal movement, but not unsupported from the outside. . . .

Question: Mr. Hoyt, you and your colleague speak quite matter of factly on these experiences. How did it seem when you were actually going through them?

Mr. Hoyt: Well, uncomfortable. Not only were the beatings administered physically very uncomfortable, but during the entire period, we were in danger of losing our lives. We never knew when we would be taken out and either beaten or shot. . . .

Question: Mr. Hoyt, as you look back, is there any one moment that you can think of as being worse than others?

Mr. Hoyt: I think for myself the most difficult time was at first when they were beating on the door of the vault room in which we had retreated. This was our first contact with the rebels and personally it was very difficult because I was convinced if they broke down that door they would just start firing indiscriminately. . . .

Vice Consul: I would agree with the consul. . . . But equally difficult was a week ago Wednesday when we were taken before the Lumumba monument, and we assumed we were to be executed there. It was clear from the reaction of the crowd of about eight or nine thousand people that all of us were accused of being American mercenaries. . . .

Question: Why do you think they singled out Dr. [Paul] Carlson for sentence and execution?

Mr. Hoyt: I don't know. I suppose he was handy. He was picked up in Buta by Mr. Gbenye and sent to Stanleyville. . . .

Question: What kind of person is Gbenye?

Mr. Hoyt: I met him under rather trying circumstances in which he forced me to write messages which I ordinarily would never have considered writing, and I can't say that my memories of him are very pleasant. He attempted to be friendly, but this is like somebody smiling as he puts a knife into you. The smile doesn't make him friendly. . . .

Question: What sort of messages did you write under duress?

Mr. Hoyt: Messages saying that—most of them were dictated by Mr.

243

Gbenye himself, the most striking one of them being that he would execute Dr. Carlson and the other Americans if negotiations were not entered into immediately in Nairobi. . . .

Question: Thank you, sir.

(Whereupon, at 5:15 P.M., the press conference was concluded.)

Notes

Chapter 1. At the Bend in the River

1. Joseph Conrad, *Heart of Darkness*, 12.

2. Stanleyville CONTEL 242 to Leopoldville, 22 June 1964, 8:25 A.M.: "Gendarmerie camp attacked by anti GOC [Government of the Congo] rebels night 21 June. Undetermined number arms seized by rebels. Rebels disappeared into communes after capture arms. Second group rebels attacked paracommando camp wounding two unarmed sentinels, capturing no weapons. Commandant Banza states believes rebels arrived from direction Bukavu by truck. Present whereabouts rebels in city unknown. Loyal ANC guarding all strategic locations. Not yet clear how many gendarmes, (who generally unreliable) have gone over to rebels or how many rebels involved. Have requested armed guard for consulate and USIS [U.S. Information Service]. CLINGERMAN." "Messages from Consul [Michael P. E.] Hoyt, American Consulate, Stanleyville, the Congo, July 14 to November 25, 1964 [and other related messages]." Collection of unpublished messages obtained through the Freedom of Information Act. Compiled by Michael P. E. Hoyt. Cataloged and available at Northwestern University Library, Evanston, Ill. (henceforth abbreviated as Hoyt Messages).

3. CONTEL 12, 14 July. Copy of cable not available; wording taken from memory (henceforth abbreviated as Hoyt recollection).

4. See Madeleine G. Kalb, *The Congo Cables*, 248–67.

5. CONTEL 13, 15 July, 10 A.M. Hoyt Messages. CONTEL 14 cable not available. Hoyt recollection.

6. CONTEL 22, 23, or 24 July. Cable not available. Hoyt recollection.

7. G. Jean-Aubry, *Joseph Conrad, Life and Letters*, 135.

8. CONTEL 15, 18 July, 11 A.M.: "Kindu reported threatened by rebels. Belgian CONGEN Vande Brande [*sic*] and Belgian Embassy officer Dedobbeleer spent yesterday (July 17) in Kindu and upon return Stanleyville reported Kindu about to fall to Mulelists. Air Congo sending DC-3 tomorrow Kindu evacuate European women and children Bujumbura. Mulamba in Kindu

July 16 and ANC Stanleyville confirms that he has ordered contingents from Gombari to go by air to Kindu today. Vande Brande reports that of 1500 ANC and 1500 dependents in Congolese, all but 100 disappeared into bush on way to Kindu. None of 100 now in Kindu desire come to Stanleyville. Trains with ANC reported both leaving for and arriving from Kongolo. Vande Brande states that Kindu all but in hands of Mulelists and expects formal takeover in few days. Maniema Provincial President Tshomba reportedly appealed to Mulamba send troops. Vande Brande said someone from American Consulate Bukavu was with Mulamba in Kindu. HOYT." Hoyt Messages.

    9. CONTEL 21, 21 July, Noon. Hoyt Messages.

    10. CIA cable, TDCS-314/00862-64, acquired 14 July, distributed 21 July 1964: "1. On [excised] July 64 [excised] who is responsible for recruiting a 'Popular Army of Liberation' in Stanleyville to support the parent Popular Army currently active in North Katanga Province, confided he is informed by Committee of National Liberation (CNL) leader Gaston Emile Soumialot that a 'delegation' of the CNL will arrive in Stanleyville at the end of July or the first week in August. The arrival of this delegation will be the signal for a general attack by the Popular Army against local Congolese National Army (CNA) troops: after the expected easy dispersal of these troops and the collapse of provincial Congolese authority, a 'Popular govt' will be installed in Stanleyville. [excised] announced he is sending [excised] to Kindu. [excised] to contact Joseph Ramazani, Popular Army representative for Maniema Province, to discuss the details of the delegation's travel to Stanleyville. (Source comment: [portion excised] had intended to personally visit Ramazani on behalf of Haut Congo President François Aradjabu, but decided against this because he no longer has confidence in Aradjabu's profession of support for the CNL and the Popular Army. [excised] characterizes Aradjabu as 'two-faced' and engaged in [portion garbled] those members of the Mouvement National Congolais/Lumumba (MNC/L) who are working in the interests of the Popular Army. [excised] will therefore no longer recruit 'terrorists' to support the Aradjabu govt and, when the Popular Army acts in Stanleyville, will see that Aradjabu himself is overthrown and killed)." "Messages Relating to American Consul [Michael P. E.] Hoyt and his Staff Held Hostage in Stanleyville, The Congo, August 4 to November 24, 1964." Volumes 1 and 2. Collection of unpublished original messages obtained through the Freedom of Information Act and copies of supplemental messages from the Lyndon B. Johnson Library at the University of Texas in Austin. Compiled by Michael P. E. Hoyt. Cataloged and available at Northwestern University Library, Evanston, Ill. (henceforth abbreviated as Hostage Messages).

    11. CONTEL 20, 22 July, 4 P.M. Hoyt Messages.

    12. CONTEL 24, 24 July, 3 P.M. Hoyt Messages.

    13. CONTEL 25, 25 July, 4 P.M. Hoyt Messages.

    14. CONTEL 26, 26 July, 5 P.M. Hoyt Messages.

15. CONTEL 17, 21 July, 11 A.M. Hoyt Messages.

16. CONTEL 29, 28 July, 5 P.M. Hoyt Messages.

17. CONTEL 28, 27 July, 6 P.M. Hoyt Messages.

18. CONTEL 31, 29 July, 4 P.M. Hoyt Messages.

19. Leopoldville EMBTEL 84 to Stanleyville and other consulates, 28 July, 7 A.M.: "1. We are concerned about increasing number of reports that if T-28 or mercenaries used by GOC against rebel-held areas in Eastern Congo, rebels will retaliate by killing whites in areas under their control. British have similar reports and have been considering advising their citizens of danger and suggesting they evacuate. We hesitate to go this far at this time but would like to have your evaluation of danger to American citizens in your consular district and suggestions you might have for action we could take to protect their lives and property. 2. In this regard would appreciate receiving from you detailed list of American citizens known to be in areas now held by or threatened by rebels. GODLEY." Hostage Messages.

20. *Time*, 26 June 1964.

21. CONTEL 33, 30 July, 7 A.M. Hoyt Messages. At times, the rebels later would confuse the word "mercenaries" with the word "missionaries." In this cable, it was either my mistake or the substitution occurred somewhere between my typewriter and the copy eventually distributed in Washington.

22. CONTEL 36, 31 July, 6 P.M. Hoyt Messages.

23. CONTEL 37, 1 August, 1 P.M. Hoyt Messages.

24. CONTELS 38 and 40, 2 August. Hoyt recollection; also from Michael P. E. Hoyt and David Grinwis, "A Journal of the Experiences of the Staff of the American Consulate in Stanleyville from 1 August through 24 November, 1964." Unpublished diary. Cataloged and available at Northwestern University Library, Evanston, Ill. (henceforth abbreviated Hoyt and Grinwis Journal).

25. CONTEL 39, 3 August, 10 A.M. Hoyt Messages.

26. CONTEL 42, 3 August, 4 P.M. Hoyt Messages.

27. CONTEL 43, 3 August, 6 P.M. Hoyt Messages.

28. CONTEL 44, 4 August, 3 A.M. Hoyt Messages.

29. CONTEL 45, 4 August, 8 A.M. Hoyt Messages.

30. Hoyt recollection. The only message on record referring to our staying was an embassy cable early the next morning reporting to Washington on the Stanleyville evacuation the day before. It merely said the three of us "are remaining in Stan for the time being," and nothing about our orders to stay. EMBTEL 332, 5 August, 2 A.M. Hostage Messages.

31. While talking to a member of the Congo Working Group a year later, I was told that on being informed of the fact that we were staying, presumably by the embassy message of early 5 August, the State Department had questioned the embassy about our staying. However, by that time, he said, it was moot.

32. Larson apparently recalled being more positive about their decision

247

not to leave. My recollection was that he had left open the possibility some families might want to go. See Homer E. Dowdy, *Out of the Jaws of the Lion*, 27.

33. CONTEL 46, 4 August, 5:37 P.M. Hoyt Messages.
34. CONTEL 47, 4 August, 6:22 P.M. Hoyt Messages.
35. CONTEL 48, 4 August, 6:30 P.M. Hoyt Messages.
36. CONTEL 49, 4 August, 7:40 P.M. Hoyt Messages. Tony Lukas must have been in close contact with the embassy political section because his articles in the *New York Times* of the next few days carried quotes of my cables.

Chapter 2. Vengeance

1. Stanleyville CONTEL 51 to Leopoldville 51, 5 August, 6:50 A.M. Hoyt Messages.
2. CONTEL 52, 5 August, 6:58 A.M. Hoyt Messages.
3. CONTEL 53, 5 August, 9:15 A.M. Hoyt Messages.
4. CONTEL 55, 5 August, 9:55 A.M.: "1. ANC gen staff advises us ANC has forbidden traffic in city and tells us remain in consulate. Soldiers have been told about consulate. They will advise when we can move to apts. 2. Loewen of Univ. Stan requests emb notify Decker tel 9141 that univ staff ok. Also pass same to German and British embs. HOYT." Hoyt Messages.
5. CONTEL 56, 5 August, 10:18 A.M. Hoyt Messages.
6. EMBTEL LEO 114 to STAN. Hoyt recollection.
7. CONTEL 57, 5 August, 11:14 A.M. Hoyt Messages.
8. The radio contact was reported in EMBTEL 356 to SECSTATE, 5 August, 9:54 P.M. Hoyt Messages: "SSB contact with consulate Stanleyville reestablished 1915Z. Hoyt reports that consulate was attacked by group of rebels mid afternoon. He and two other staff members locked selves in bathroom while rebels ransacked consulate. This was apparently about 1600Z and Hoyt says there was firing going on all around building. Rebels apparently found case of whiskey in consulate and after tentative efforts break into bathroom settled down to drink whiskey. Eventually Hoyt heard rebels withdraw from consulate. He and staff members left bathroom and went to SSB which not damaged. According Hoyt, as of 1915 sporadic firing was audible from direction of airport but nothing visible. He asked us of what happening in city and we told him all contact cut off since early afternoon but that city had apparently fallen. Hoyt states that of five official Americans in Stanleyville, four are at consulate and one is in town. SSB contact broken at 1730Z but we attempting reestablish. GODLEY." I do not know why the embassy reported we locked ourselves in the "bathroom." Maybe it was because I had not wanted to say over the open SSB broadcast that we were in the CIA communications vault.

9. CONTEL STEY 0002, 5 August, relayed directly to SECSTATE by CIA channels at 2352Z, nearly 2 A.M. Stanleyville time. This was number 2 of a series from us. I knew nothing of the previous message, which may have been an operational message from David. Hoyt Messages.

10. STEY 0003, 5 August, relayed in Leo EMBTEL 359 to SECSTATE, 6 August, 7 A.M.: "Preliminary reports indicate: 1. Control airport by rebels confirmed. 2. City calm. No incidents reported. Consulate attacked. All Europeans well. 3. ANC are apparently left retreated towards Cyangambi. Rebel troops appear well disciplined. 4. Authority rebels has not been established or identified. 5. Due attack on consulate will await further developments. But we must reveal ourselves soonest." Hoyt Messages.

11. STEY 0004, 5 August, also relayed in EMBTEL 359. Hoyt Messages.

Chapter 3. Simba! Simba!

1. Leopoldville EMBTEL 358 to SECSTATE, 6 August, 5 A.M.: "LIMDIS: Pursuant Department telegram 165 country team currently planning armed helicopter landing consular lawn Stanleyville to rescue four personnel now at consulate. Plan also includes use T-28 cover. Personnel involved drawn from COMISH [the U.S. Military Mission to the Congo], USIA [U.S. Information Agency] and Marine detachment here. Devlin has coordinated with Mobutu and we hope include ANC officer. Precise timing not yet known but hope achieve release late afternoon August 7. Mobutu concurs and has put his plane, helicopter and two T-28's at our disposition. Plan is well conceived as possible but there are obviously risks involved. One problem remains unresolved is that one man Houle remains as far as we know in apartment in city. Endeavoring get word to Hoyt re plans and get whole group assembled at consulate. One member of rescue team thoroughly familiar Stanleyville terrain and consular layout." Hostage Messages. At the time, the words that the helicopters would be "armed" and the T-28s would provide "cover" somehow had not conveyed to me that they would arrive shooting. That only dawned on me some years later when I had time to read the text of the cable at leisure. The words did not enter into my evaluation of the feasibility of the operation in 1964.

2. EMBTEL 366, 6 August, 2 P.M.: "STANLEYVILLE SITREP. REF EMBTEL 358. Embassy in excellent SSB contact with Stanville at 0700 zulu August 6: 1. Consul reported he had repeat had received reftel and agreed 'in principle' to evacuation project outlined therein. However he emphasized fluidity of situation and wished retain for himself option to halt operation if later circumstances indicated it not feasible. With this objective signal was tentatively arranged whereby green vehicle will be parked in front of consulate if he

249

feels evacuation advisable and feasible at time team arrives. We have told Hoyt that operation can be called back any time before noon August 7 if he believes it advisable. He emphasized riskiness of main operation as well as difficulties bringing Ernest Houle to consulate from latter's apartment downtown, but concurs that preparations should go forward. 2. City calm at time of contact. Army has been driven out beyond airport on northwest side of city. New civil authorities are awaited. Electric current, telephones and water all operating normally. Hoyt is in telephonic contact with Houle and will try to work out method of getting him from apt to consulate. Hoyt states that Stanville radio went on air this morning to announce 'true liberation' had come to Stan, that revolutionary authorities were in control of situation and urged citizens to remain calm and carry on normal activities. According Hoyt, little or no movement of people or vehicles visible from consulate windows. Scattered firing audible from side of city away from airport. No boats in evidence on river. We have advised Hoyt to remain at consulate and will advise him of details re development rescue operation by classified message." Hoyt Messages.

3. There is no record indicating these messages were received.

4. USARMA [Raudstein] Leopoldville 061545Z to SECDEFENSE: "1. Sit rep no. 37, Congo 061500Z Aug 64. . . . 5. 1600Z SSB message from Amconsul Stan: Quote. European community, particularly Belgian and British requests [intends?] appeal leaders of Popular Army at [Stanleyville] fear situation getting out of control, fear local leaders unable to contain. City police effectively in hands of Popular Army—closing station. end quote. Interpret his last two words quote closing station unquote to mean temporarily as something must have occurred that made it unsafe or unwise to continue broadcasting or be near radio." Hostage Messages.

5. The idea that the T-28s would arrive firing still had not occurred to me. However, Prime Minister Moïse Tshombé was aware of the plans and knew that the T-28s would be coming in with guns blazing, as reported in EMBTEL 364, 6 August, 1:55 P.M.: "This morning Tshombé asked me to call. I spoke to him along re EMBTEL 358. Told him we had discussed plan last evening with Mobutu and [Victor] Nendaka [Head of Security] who were in agreement. Tshombé said he had been informed and was particularly concerned that we had to get our people out of Stanleyville. I did not go into detail but said that of course participants would be armed. He elaborated stating he confident one or two passes by T-28's would frighten rebels." Hostage Messages.

6. EMBTEL 390, 7 August, 6:45 A.M.: "Hoyt at 0645 this morning requested evacuation operation be canceled due to presence large number armed men near by. Team had been instructed to stand by and to take no further action without further instructions. This message has been acknowledged by team.

We are now canceling chopper evacuation plan. Hoyt informed." Hoyt Messages. It is still unclear how I was supposed to have been "informed."

7. American Embassy Khartoum interviewed Elbéshir, described as "Sudanese Consul Stanleyville who had arrived Khartoum in company four Congolese rebel representatives." He told the embassy when the "American consul was being held in jail [he was] chained or bound in such manner he constantly bent over with arms under knees. . . . Residents Stanleyville . . . fear greatly for safety Europeans in Stanleyville as rebels see end approaching. They feel prime targets rebel savagery will be American and United Nations personnel and that here is every reason deepest concern for their safety." Elbéshir said he had left Stanleyville about 18 September. See Khartoum EMBTELS 118, 28 September, and 138, 4 October. Hostage Messages.

8. Nothomb, of course, had not been informed of the Operation Flagpole rescue plan. In his memoirs, he wrote: "President Johnson just missed sending a helicopter to Stan to snatch away the five members of the American consulate. I bless the 'lobby' which advised him against the operation. It would have paid off by the loss of the helicopter and its crew, by the immediate massacre of the fifteen Americans in Stan, and by the placement sooner of all other whites in prison." Patrick Nothomb, *Dans Stanleyville*, 96.

9. The embassy's instruction for me to deal with the rebels was undoubtedly prompted by the State Department's preference for negotiation rather than the armed helicopter rescue, as outlined in the following message, which was not sent to Stanleyville. SECSTATE 172 to Leo, 6 August, 12:47 P.M.: "EMBTEL 358. Department appreciates imagination and spirit in which plan evacuate Stanleyville Consulate personnel has been conceived. You should continue operating with clear understanding that it may be called off. . . . Based on Albertville example if rebel troops well disciplined and there is clear authority in city it could be less disturbing negotiate evacuation our personnel and other Europeans as well, perhaps under UN auspices. Appreciate Embassy views this possibility. Use of T-28s and presence US military personnel could have drastic side effects. You also requested give your views on advisability keeping Consulate open. RUSK." Hostage Messages. The Department apparently agreed with my view that the operation, successful or not, would have had "drastic" consequences on those left behind. The last sentence is probably in reply to EMBTEL 332, sent on 5 August, which stated that we were "remaining in Stan for the time being."

10. David later wrote up his notes. I edited them almost a year later, and it was in this form that they were printed and distributed as an informal document by the Department of State with the title "A Journal of the Experiences of the Staff of the American Consulate in Stanleyville from August 1 through November 24, 1964." Hoyt and Grinwis Journal.

11. While David and I were at the Belgian consulate office, it did not

251

occur to me that this might be the safest time to go over to the other building of the Immoquateur and bring Ernie Houle back to the American consulate. Perhaps I assumed he would have nothing to do at the consulate and that he was safer where he was.

12. The embassy reported its contact with me in EMBTEL 410, 8 August, 2 P.M.: "SITREP Stanleyville. Established SSB contact with Hoyt 1100 local August 8. Told Hoyt UN prepared send aircraft on humanitarian basis to Stan ASAP bring doctors and medical supplies for local population and evacuate foreign nationals who wish to leave. Conditions for this mission: 1) Safe landing at airport or at port if boats are to be used. 2) UN staff to have free movement from airfield to city and return. Hoyt speaking freely and apparently without direct rebel supervision, told us that he had not rpt not been able to make contact with local authorities following our request of yesterday but he will continue [trying] to do so today. Hoyt further indicated it might be difficult for UN Rep Rosso in Stan to make representations to local authorities without giving further details. Hoyt assured us that he is well and added in response to inquiry from Greek charge here that Greek consul Stan reports everyone in Greek community alright. Embassy monitoring SSB on continuing basis. Next regular schedule 1600 local." Hoyt Messages.

13. No record of this message was found. Hoyt recollection.

14. No record of this message was found. Hoyt recollection.

Chapter 4. Persona non Grata

1. Relayed to the State Department in Leopoldville EMBTEL 458 on 11 August. Cable not available. Hoyt recollection. The contents were also noted in *New York Times*, 12 and 13 August 1964.

2. "Messages from Consul [Michael P. E.] Hoyt, American Consulate, Stanleyville, the Congo, July 14 to November 25, 1964 [and other related messages]." Volume 2. Collection of copies of unpublished informal messages retained by Consul Hoyt. Compiled by Michael P. E. Hoyt. Cataloged and available at Northwestern University Library, Evanston, Ill. (henceforth abbreviated as Hoyt Collection).

Chapter 5. House Arrest

1. Our consul in Bukavu, Richard (Dick) Matheron, interviewed someone who escaped from Stanleyville on 8 October. Matheron reported that he said: "Together with many other Europeans, observed with own eyes four different public executions at Lumumba monument. Mayor of Stanleyville had trunk cut open with knife by rebel "colonel" (not Olenga) who reached

in and pulled out kidney and ate it while victim dying. At three other executions of more minor Government officials, victims had hands and feet tied. Were made to bend over and heads were cut off at neck with machete." See Bukavu CONTEL 380 to Leopoldville, 26 October. Hostage Messages.

2. Hoyt and Grinwis Journal, 23.

3. The text of the telegram read: "AMBASSADE AMERICAIN LEOPOLDVILLE. TOUT PERSONNEL PORTE BIEN ABRITER ENSEMBLE AU CONSULAT STOP HOYT FULL STOP." Hostage Messages. The message was received, as the *New York Times* reported on 18 August, with a 17 August dateline: "The United States Embassy announced that it had received its first message in more than five days from Michael P. E. Hoyt, the United States consul in Stanleyville, now in rebel hands. The message, received over the commercial Telex, said all personnel were in good health and were sheltered together in the consulate." *New York Times*, 18 August 1964.

Chapter 6. Last Words

1. Text of message appears in Colonel Vandewalle, *L'Ommengang, Odyssée et Reconquête de Stanleyville 1964*, 118: "Obligation d'arrêter tous les Américains se trouvant au Congo et de les traduire devant la cour martiale pour mise en jugement sans pitié ni distinction de religion. Maintenant ce n'est plus un guerre froide, mais un guerre ouverte avec l'Amérique. Cette guerre incombe aux Américains qui s'ingèrent intempestivement dans les affaires intérieures du Congo."

2. The message was picked up by the embassy in Léopoldville and transmitted to Washington in EMBTELS 675 and 677 of 21 August. Hostage Messages. The State Department drafted a reply to the message and instructed the embassy to find any way possible to deliver it to me. The cable, Flash 408 of 21 August, read: "I have received the message from Stanleyville with your signature. It has also been transmitted to Washington. In accordance with normal international practice your consular duties include contact with authorities in control in the localities covered by your consular district. You may so inform General Olenga. You are requested to ask him whether he will arrange safe conduct for the landing of a plane at the Stanleyville airport carrying official American supplies and personnel. They would confirm that you and your present staff as well as other American citizens in the area are in good health and are allowed freely to come and go and that you have free and unrestricted access to communications with me. Please advise promptly whether it would be useful send US official to consult with you further on these matters. You should also repeat to General Olenga and the authorities in Stanleyville my earlier message that I hold them personally responsible for

253

the safety and well being of all Americans in the Stanleyville area." Hostage Messages. No way could be found to deliver the message, and I never saw it. Presumably, the message was to be signed by Ambassador McMurtrie Godley. I know of no previous message holding the rebel authorities "personally" responsible for our safety.

Chapter 7. The General Returns

1. Excerpts in this chapter are from Hoyt and Grinwis Journal, 29–30.

2. The embassy Léopoldville reported on secondhand accounts of Radio Stan broadcasts in EMBTEL 697 to secstate and Brussels, 22 August: "Evacuated from [excised] plantation east of Bumba this week (reached Leo today) told ARMA [U.S. Army Attache office] tonight Belgian planter, considered reliable [excised] reports Radio Stanleyville midmorning August 22 announced all Americans in Soumialot controlled area to be tried by People's Court (Tribunal Populaire). UNOC [United Nations Operations in the Congo] and Belgian embassies state negative info this report. Belgian ambassador confirmed with his radio operator who monitored Radio Stanleyville today until 1600Z, they had not repeat not heard this announcement. Belgian ambassador ordered Radio Stanleyville monitored rest of tonight. Will inform me immediately any such statements. Will appreciate confirmation FBIS [Foreign Broadcast Information Service] monitoring Stanleyville 24 hours daily. GODLEY." Hostage Messages.

3. The State Department regarded our predicament serious enough to suggest hostages be taken to trade for us. See SECSTATE 418 to Leopoldville, info Brussels, 22 August 1964: "STAN CONSULAR STAFF. There follow some suggestions which Emb should explore and comment upon. 1. We need counter hostages. Can GOC (perhaps Nendaka) put under protective surveillance any relatives of rebel leaders such as Olenga (if he is still alive) Soumialot, or any others whom EMB believes may be influential there. It might be possible to grab some important rebel leaders in Leo or Bukavu for this purpose." Hostage Messages. There is no record of any follow-up to this suggestion of taking counterhostages by a midlevel official in the Africa Bureau. On 29 August, a Congo Working Group was formed in the Operations Center in the State Department to deal with the Congo problem on a more organized basis.

4. The Africa Bureau's assessment of our situation follows (Hostage Messages).

CIRCULAR 392 to all African posts, August, 29 1964

AMERICAN PERSONNEL STANLEYVILLE

Dept gravely concerned about present and future welfare Amconsul

Stanleyville Michael Hoyt and four members his staff, as well as about 20 American missionaries and educators, all of whom have been trapped Stanleyville since it fell precipitously to rebels Aug. 5. There are in addition to Americans at Stanleyville Sudanese and Belgian Consuls and UN CIVOPS [civilian operatives]. Probably also many other foreigners, mostly Belgians, Indians and Greeks in private capacities if they have not since escaped.

All communications between Stan and Leo have been cut since Aug. 21, when a telex message was received signed Hoyt but obviously not drafted by him. It stated that continued military assistance to GOC would jeopardize lives all Americans resident Stan, including Consulate staff. Subsequent reports reiterate threats on part rebels to Americans in area, thus giving impression rebels consider Americans as hostages and intend to treat them as such.

According to a few sporadic and unconfirmed reports from non-US sources Hoyt and staff are well but apparently under guard at Consulate.

Attempts by UN-CIVOPS and ICRC [International Committee of the Red Cross] to effect evacuation have so far been unsuccessful owing rebel refusal permit planes land Stan.

Department making every effort establish communication with our people Stan, ascertain their welfare, assure their correct treatment and arrange for their free movement.

You should not discuss this matter with host government or anyone else unless given specific instructions. However, any suggestions posts may have for making contact with Stanleyville Consulate would be welcome.

Chapter 8. Red Cross

1. Lending some credence to Olenga's remarks may have been what had happened some two weeks before this date to two American officers, Colonels Dodd and Rattan, and the vice consul from the American consulate in Bukavu, Lewis McFarlane. They were on a tour of ANC positions around the city when they were attacked by rebel forces. They fled and spent three days behind Simba lines before being rescued by friendly Congolese villagers. *New York Times,* 21–25 August 1964.

2. Information about the intercepted Olenga message appears in CONTEL 54, 5 August, 5:35 A.M. Hoyt Messages.

3. Hoyt and Grinwis Journal, 40–41.

4. Senn was a member of the International Committee of the Red Cross (ICRC), an all-Swiss organization. The ICRC should not be confused with the International League of the Red Cross (ILRC), an international organization.

5. The Red Cross plane returned to Bangui, the capital of the Central African Republic. U.S. embassy cables detail the debriefing of the ICRC team.

255

Bangui EMBTEL 147 to SECSTATE, 26 September: "ICRC plane arrived Bangui from Stanleyville at 1423Z Sept 26. Did not succeed in evacuating anyone. [Jean-Maurice] Rubli and [Cassius] Senn report they were permitted speak only to selected foreigners (mainly doctors) in Stan but were assured by Dr Barlovatz who sees American consular personnel regularly that Hoyt and staff safe and well. They are living in Sabena Guest House under surveillance after having spent five days in prison. We going into briefing session with Rubli and Senn now and shall report soonest. They have been in radio contact with Geneva and are awaiting instructions regarding further action. Gbenye agreeable to their returning Stan. For Geneva: Rubli and Senn request contents this message not repeat not be conveyed ICRC Geneva." Hostage Messages. Also, Bangui EMBTEL 151 to SECSTATE, 27 September: "In course of debriefing Rubli and Senn have made following points of special US interest. Feeling against Americans in Stanleyville running particularly high. Until conversation actually begun with ICRC mission, it was viewed with suspicion by rebels who suspected its operation as US 'spying' device. Gbenye and rebel government consider US 'aggressor' (Olenga reportedly going so far as to assert that state of war exists with US) because of central government's use of American made aircraft. Gbenye vowed that any US soldier falling in rebel hands would be caged and exhibited in Stanleyville so 'his people could see what Americans looked like'. With exception US staff, consular personnel move unmolested about standard carry out functions to extent local conditions permit. Rubli particularly mentioned unhindered and useful activities Belgian Consul and Franken in his Red Cross REP capacity. Consular officials excepting US have even attended recent reception given by Gbenye. Rubli stated Hoyt and group invited by Gbenye's personal secretary, accompanied by rebel officer, to send out Red Cross messages through ICRC mission. Secretary reported with some unhappiness that Hoyt prepared do so initially but after consultation with staff decided against it. In course one interview with Gbenye Rubli had dwelt on Hoyt's rights and immunities as consular official. Later Gbenye in short conversation just before mission's departure repeated back to him chapter and verse, saying he had instructed rebel staff and officials accordingly. Rubli remarked Gbenye 'good pupil' and felt this encouraging note with respect safety US staff. Gbenye had earlier stated that temporary imprisonment US staff after bombing Uvira had prevented summary execution by irate rebels. Rubli and Senn said they had neither seen nor heard of any ChiCom [Chinese communists], French, Belgian or other Communist presence in Stanleyville. 'No indication whatsoever' such influence there but admit possibility financial support. They feel Chinese not prepared throw in lot with rebels. Rubli emphasized he greatly feared for lives of 'all foreigners and suspects' in Stanleyville in event of any bombings or even overflights of

256

city. Any military action to take city would have to be so sudden and massive that key points could be secured quarter of hour, or run risk of general massacre, according Rubli. Franken told Senn that an American named Scholten died in prison at Aketi, date and cause of death unknown. Mission had no word concerning whereabouts and welfare of other Americans in area. However Dr. Barlovats [sic] informed them that he had ascertained during recent visit that no Europeans were being held in Stanleyville prison." Hostage Messages. The Department of State paid the ICRC $117,000 for its expenses in connection with the flight. See Fred E. Wagoner, *Dragon Rouge, The Rescue of Hostages in the Congo*, 89.

Chapter 9. Gbenye and Soumialot

1. The State Department had made it clear to the Red Cross mission that Grinwis was the priority candidate for evacuation. A cable drafted in the Congo Working Group and sent to the American embassy in Léopoldville, and repeated to the U.S. mission in Geneva and the American embassy in Bujumbura, confirms this. SECSTATE to Leopoldville 719, 20 September. Hostage Messages:

> *For Geneva:* 1. Request you ask ICRC officials that following unclassified message from Dept be discreetly delivered, if necessary verbally, to American Consul Hoyt Stanleyville by Rubli, Senn or whoever will go on plane:
>
> QUOTE. US Government is proud of courage, fortitude and patience you and your staff have shown in most trying circumstances. We have been deeply concerned re welfare of all of you since fall of Stanleyville, particularly since no direct contact.
>
> We have been in regular communication with your wife who reports your children and she are well and send their love. We have similarly been in continual contact with families of all other members of Consulate. They are also well and send their best.
>
> It is of course our hope that ICRC mission will succeed in effecting evacuation of 25 Americans Stanleyville including you and your staff. At the same time plane is to evacuate other foreign nationals. If only one American should be permitted to leave, Grinwis should come out. If only a few Americans allowed or able to evacuate at first you should endeavor arrange for departure Grinwis and women and children of missionaries and Loewen. Then missionaries themselves and Loewen. Next, remainder Consular personnel at your discretion in this order: Houle, Stauffer, Parks [sic] and yourself. Anyone sick should have priority. As holding responsibility for others, you will be last of Americans to depart (unless some missionaries do not want to leave) as we are sure you would wish. unquote.

257

2. Request you also advise ICRC officials that if all Americans cannot be evacuated at first we would greatly appreciate receiving news ASAP of American Consular personnel and other Americans, specifically:

a. Are US Consular personnel physically located in Consulate building?

b. Are US nationals in contact with Consulate?

c. Is Consulate permitted assist American community?

d. Are all Americans located in city? Where?

e. Are Americans well? Do they require medicines, food or other items? (If so appreciate ICRC assistance). How are they treated by rebels?

f. Ask Hoyt to provide list of all Americans Stanleyville.

g. Is Hoyt in touch with Consular colleagues?

h. State of rebel morale, including local supply beer, and thus whether city on verge anarchy which would greatly increase danger to foreigners.

3. ICRC should be made aware danger Gbenye and other rebel leaders may insist that as soon medical equipment and personnel off loaded Stanleyville, plane immediately transport them Nairobi. Would hope if such occurs, ICRC reps would insist on evacuation goodly number foreigners who wish leave before transporting rebels to Bujumbura, Entebbe or some other location en route Nairobi, as well as securing authorization for return of plane Stanleyville and evacuation remainder.

For Bujumbura: Re your 282, request you brief Senn on foregoing, particularly re American Consular official to leave first. RUSK

The message meant for me, of course, was never delivered. We were not aware of the information the State Department apparently had on the rebel leadership's wish to abandon Stanleyville. Mentioning three times the priority in getting Grinwis out is probably indicative of the CIA's concern over their clandestine officer.

2. According to a CIA memorandum on the Congo situation dated 27 August 1964, Gbenye's trip to Nairobi from Brazzaville was financed by the Belgian government in the hopes of achieving a negotiated settlement with the rebels. He stopped in Brussels and saw Foreign Minister Paul-Henri Spaak, who presumably talked to him about the foreigners in Stanleyville. Hostage Messages. I could find no record of Devlin's meeting with Gbenye. My former boss in the economic section at the embassy, Rob West, told me later he was wandering about East Africa at the time with $50,000 of private foundation money, looking for an opportunity to bribe a rebel official for our release.

3. Hoyt and Grinwis Journal, 46.

4. Translated from the original French version. Hoyt Collection.

5. According to the CIA report titled "The Congo Situation of 6 October 1964," Olenga's forces were "easily repelled" from Bukavu by government forces on 29 September. Hostage Messages.

258

Chapter 10. Stanleyville Central Prison

1. According to Thomas Powers's biography of Richard Helms, *The Man Who Kept the Secrets* (121–23), the CIA top leadership was concerned about the Americans kept hostage in Stanleyville. "One was the U.S. consul in Stanleyville, a Foreign Service officer named Michael Hoyt; the other four [*sic*] were a CIA team." Richard Helms was said to have thought mounting an operation was not practical and that the only thing to do was "wait." In the end, Powers said a group of "CIA Cubans" were sent with the mercenary forces to try to effect the rescue.

2. Olenga was in or near Paulis, several hundred miles northeast of Stanleyville, on 14 October. "This morning Dept became aware through ham operators in Congo of clear text rebel message from Colonel Opepe in Stan to Commander in Chief in Paulis (presumably General Olenga) stating American planes had bombed Bumba and requesting latter's permission kill all Americans who are in liberated zones." Secstate Circular 653, 15 October. Hostage Messages. The air raid was apparently undertaken by South African air forces without the approval of the United States. Secretary Rusk ordered a "stand-down" of all US aircraft operations which lasted seven days until Tshombé agreed to withdraw the South African aircraft. In addition, Godley was ordered to "take immediately all possible precautions to assure that no rpt no official American personnel fall into rebel hands even though this might necessitate evacuation Consulate Bukavu." Secstate 958 to Leopoldville, 15 October. Hostage Messages. Godley sent instructions (for the first time?) to the consulates in Bukavu and Elisabethville: "You will also take every precaution see that no U.S. personnel falls into rebel hands even though this might mean evacuation your posts." EMBTEL 1496, 16 October. Hostage Messages.

In addition, the embassies in Léopoldville and Bujumbura were instructed to deliver by any means possible the following message to me: "QTE You should deliver urgently following message to highest authority in Stanleyville. We have just learned that authorities in Leopoldville have established new air unit with South African pilots apparently for combat operations. USG has protested to Congo officials and in order dissociate itself completely from this unit has taken following steps. USG has ended all operations of US aircraft in Congo, all of which are non-combat planes. USG has demanded that Congolese authorities ground all aircraft supplied under US military aid program and is taking steps to verify that this is being done. Thus, we are taking prompt action to insure that all US Govt or US employed supplied aircraft are withdrawn from operations in Congo as rapidly as communications permit. We will continue efforts dissuade Congolese officials from use planes piloted by South Africans but cannot be responsible for their actions. You

259

should of course also make clear that we continue to expect Stanleyville authorities to take all necessary steps to protect Americans and other foreign nationals in areas under their control. Godley END QTE." Hostage Messages. We heard nothing of this in Stanleyville. The message was not delivered to me, and I cannot even imagine what the rebel leadership would have made of the obviously Western and sophisticated approach to a problem they could not even begin to understand.

Lewis Hoffacker in the State Department called my wife Jo at the time. She wrote in her book, *For the Love of Mike* (182–83), "'I wanted you to know this before the press gets hold of it,' he told me. 'We've intercepted a message from a Colonel Opepe in Stanleyville to rebel leaders. He's asking permission to kill the American hostages.'" Her reaction, she wrote, was to "come apart at the seams." The press also carried accounts of Opepe's message. *New York Times,* 15–16 October 1964.

Another action presumably precipitated by Opepe's message was full-scale preparations entitled "Planning for evacuation of U.S. personnel from Stanleyville." The mission was to "seize and secure Stanleyville, evacuate non-Congolese, and turn city over to friendly government." The force to do this would include two battalions of the 101st Airborne Division and ninety-six military aircraft. See White House Memorandum for Mr. Bundy, dated 15 October 1964. Hostage Messages. Thus military planning eventually led to the Dragon Rouge paradrop operation.

3. In this connection, it is interesting to read about Che Guevera's failure to engender true revolutionary fervor amongst the remnants of the Simba movement during 1965. See William Gálvez, *Che in Africa: Che Guevera's Congo Diary.*

4. We were not aware that the Sudanese consular people stayed in Stanleyville until late September.

5. The embassy in Léopoldville reported Paul's capture, and the press soon picked it up. EMBTEL Leopoldville 1630, 26 October: "Monitor of Stanleyville radio 25 October quotes Gbenye announcement that 'US Major Paul Carson' is at Stanleyville awaiting trial by military tribunal. Presumably both Gbenye and Radio Stan refer to US missionary Doctor Paul Carlson who was captured by rebels at Yakoma and last reported in Buta. Embassy strongly urges that ICRC instruct its Bujumbura Reps contact Gbenye in order clarify Carlson's status as missionary and doctor which precludes any possibility his active combat participation." Hostage Messages. In communication regarding Paul's situation, the words "mercenary" and "missionary" were frequently garbled.

6. Text contained in Bukavu CONTEL 262, 23 October. Hostage Messages. The press reported the consuls' message on 27 October, saying all were well

and all except the American consular staff were "able to pursue their normal occupations." *New York Times*, 27 October 1964. Hoyt Collection.

7. The State Department was aware of the general arrest order and hoped it would "impose a greater sense of urgency on other parties now that not just the American consular staff were taken hostage and imprisoned." Secstate 1082, 28 October. Hostage Messages.

8. Patrick's message is contained in Bujumbura EMBTEL 421, 30 October. Hostage Messages. It states that all Belgians and Americans under "house arrest" and that the cessation of all Belgian and American government participation in Congolese military operations is the "condition for liberation of its subjects."

9. In his book, *Dans Stanleyville*, Patrick Nothomb said he had been sent specifically to Stanleyville and had received a "blank check" directly from Foreign Minister Paul-Henri Spaak to do whatever his judgment told him to protect his citizens (93). In contrast, I had been given no specific guidance on anything when I was assigned to Stanleyville.

10. More than a month before the elections, officials in the White House and the State Department expressed concern that Jo might approach Goldwater with her story because she was a constituent of the senator. The suggestion was made that Jo be brought to Washington at government expense. See Telcon Brubeck/Ball memo dated 28 October 1964. Hostage Messages. Jo went to Washington on her own on 6 October and saw Secretary Dean Rusk. According to the memorandum detailing the conversation: "[The Secretary] assured Mrs. Hoyt of his own concern and the concern of the Department of State for the welfare of her husband. The Secretary also stated frankly that Mr. Hoyt and the others were in jeopardy and that he realized that we had no certain solution in sight for their difficulties. . . . The Secretary said that even though we hoped for an easy evacuation via the ICRC we have, nevertheless, examined other contingencies, the details of which it was best not to discuss. But he assured Mrs. Hoyt that the Department of State would use every means, overt and covert, to obtain the safe return of her husband. He said we did not wish to precipitate the situation because it risks physical harm to her husband and others. He said it might be necessary at a later date to choose a course of action which might involve risk. He promised, however, that before we did we would check with Mrs. Hoyt." Memcon dated 10/7/64 by Walker Diamanti. Hoyt Collection.

11. Mike Hoare, the South African mercenary commander, had told an embassy officer that his men had killed Olenga in Kindu. EMBTEL Leopoldville 1809, 9 November. Hostage Messages.

12. Stanleyville's paper, *Le Martyre*, reported what Gbenye said in the speech: "We will make fetishes with the hearts of the Belgians and Americans,

261

and we will dress in the skins of the Belgians and Americans." C.R.I.S.P., *Congo 1964: Political Documents of a Developing Nation,* 387.

Chapter 11. The Horror

1. We were unaware that news of the conviction and condemnation to death of Carlson had been conveyed to the outside world. The State Department instructed Godley to send a message to Gbenye that the U.S. government "holds the authorities in Stanleyville directly and personally responsible for the safety of Dr. Carlson and of all Americans" under their control. SEC-STATE 1278 to Leopoldville, 17 November. Hostage Messages. Gbenye replied on 18 November that the execution had been postponed "pending results of negotiations" with the Organization of African Unity. EMBTEL Bujumbura 485, 18 November. Hostage Messages.

2. I distinctly remember hearing Gbenye saying both "Monday" and "delay of four days" in French. A four-day delay would have meant the execution was to take place on Sunday, not Monday. It is also possible that Gbenye purposely meant to be vague.

3. The message was received by the embassy in Léopoldville that day and passed on to Washington. Hoyt Collection. Godley argued against any thought of a cease-fire and negotiations and used it to urge Operation Dragon Rouge to proceed. EMBTEL 2008 to SECSTATE, 20 November 1964, 7 P.M. (Hostage Messages):

> EXDIS [exclusive distribution]
>
> 1. Telegram just received from "Hoyt" (Ourtel 2004) makes it crystal clear as never before that rebels will not negotiate re Carlson, let alone other Americans not under death sentence, except on basis . . . cease fire and US decision withdraw all military aid to Tshombe government. . . .
>
> 2. Some of this is obviously bluff but shows that with little time for talking they are nevertheless asking negotiate on [garbled word] on basis of complete cessation of war in their favor. These are tough opening terms, probably meant to humiliate USG and Tshombe, for whom after all we have no right to negotiate re Congo's future. I assume there can be no question of entertaining terms [garbled word] Tshombe and [garbled word] could never agree to even consider cease fire on basis of giving rebels their victory or at least new lease on life in return for negotiations re lives of "whites." . . .
>
> 7. . . . We can't afford to play this game, for long range stakes for American prestige in Africa as well as fate our own people are at stake. Essential that no one must be given any reason believe we can or will force cease fire down Tshombe's throat or that we can or will in any way halt military advance on Stan.

By that time, planning and the pre-positioning of Belgian paratroopers flown in U.S. C-130 aircraft were well under way. The State Department had made it very clear that the rescue of the American consulate staff was the first priority. "Belgian assault forces will give priority attention rescuing five official Americans Stanleyville, who Belgians aware are in greater danger than other foreign nationals." SECSTATE 1262 to Leopoldville, 16 November. Hostage Messages.

4. No record of this message has been located in the archives. Hoyt recollection.

5. This was the first evidence I saw of arms other than those seized from the retreating ANC in rebel hands on the ground. The Communist Chinese delivered arms through Burundi (see CIA report TDCS 314/03345-64, reporting a Soviet source on this) and probably Soviet-origin material through the Sudan (see the "White Paper" on the Congo Rebellion ostensibly put out by the Congolese Press Service, 16). Hostage Messages.

6. Hoyt Messages.

7. The message was received in Léopoldville that day and transmitted to Washington with this comment from Godley: "Proper English and use of words 'prohibit SSB contact for now' leads us to believe this genuine message from Hoyt but obviously under duress. At least it proves conclusively he or some American official is alive." EMBTEL Leopoldville 2048, 22 November. Hostage Messages.

8. According to the CIA situation report on the Congo for 20 October, Kanza had visited Stanleyville the second week of October. Hostage Messages.

9. Jo Wasson Hoyt, *For the Love of Mike*, 178.

10. Hoyt Messages.

11. Tshombé requested that no Congolese be airlifted out of Stanleyville after the paradrop. EMBTEL Leopoldville 2059 to SECSTATE, 22 November. Hostage Messages.

12. Even now, thirty-six years later, I remember vividly the exhilaration and the horrors of that morning. Time had no meaning. All I could do was react. My mind was and still is incapable of absorbing and articulating all the traumatic details, thoughts, and emotions of those few moments. Suddenly it was all over. I had the rest of my life to ponder on the meaning of it all.

263

Chapter 12. Return

1. The press conference report appears in the *New York Times*, 24 November 1964. For some reason, the flag-eating quote in the *New York Times* was attributed to me.

2. Approximately fifteen years later, I met Scotland in the diplomatic reception room of the United Nations in New York. After he recognized me, he was most profuse in thanking me for saving his life.

3. EMBTEL 2141 to SECSTATE, 25 November. Hostage Messages.

4. According to a Belgian reporter in the city, Nendaka brought Aradjabu to Mobutu at the airport. Aradjabu claimed to have always been "loyal" to the central authorities. "Loyal," Mobutu was said to have burst out, "but it was you who delivered Stanleyville to Soumialot." Le Figaro, 27 November 1964, quoted in C.R.I.S.P., Congo 1964, 405.

5. EMBTEL 2137 to SECSTATE, 25 November. Hostage Messages.

6. Vandewalle later wrote to me that an early-morning linkup with the paradrop had not been definitely established. He said they were without effective communications with Léopoldville and were not aware that Operation Dragon Rouge had been decided upon for that morning. Hoyt Collection.

7. SECSTATE 1410 to Leopoldville, 24 November. Hostage Messages.

8. Thomas P. Odom, Dragon Operations: Hostage Rescues in the Congo, 14.

9. Jo Wasson Hoyt, For the Love of Mike, 209.

10. New York Times, 28 November 1964.

11. Odom, Dragon Operations, 179–80.

12. Both Patrick Nothomb and I hold Gbenye principally responsible for ordering the massacre of the hostages in Stanleyville and of the innocent missionaries held by the Simbas over the next year. See Nothomb, Dans Stanleyville, 327. In spring 1965, Gbenye made it clear to one of the British nurse hostages that they were hostages very likely about to die. "If we were called upon to die, well, there would be a martyr's crown for us." Margaret Hayes, Captive of the Simbas, 144.

13. The Stanleyville episode was not included in the State Department's "Terrorist Attacks on U.S. Official Personnel Abroad" (Department of State Bulletin, March 1981, 23–29) or "Hostage Incidents: Examples in Modern History" (Department of State Bulletin, April 1981, 34–37).

Bibliography

Abramson, Rudy. *Spanning the Century: The Life of W. Averell Harriman, 1896–1986.* New York: Morrow, 1992.

Attwood, William. *The Reds and the Blacks: A Personal Adventure.* New York: Harper, 1967.

_____. *The Twilight Struggle: Tales of the Cold War.* New York: Harper, 1987.

Bouscaren, Anthony. *Tshombé.* New York: Twin Circle, 1967.

Buhite, Russell D. *Lives at Risk: Hostages and Victims in American Foreign Policy.* Washington, D.C.: SR Books, 1995.

Carlson, Lois. *Monganga Paul: The Congo Ministry and Martyrdom of Paul Carlson, M.D.* New York: Harper, 1966.

Cohen, Warren I., and Nancy Bernkopf Tucker, eds. *Lyndon Johnson Confronts the World: American Foreign Policy 1963–1968.* New York: Cambridge University Press, 1994.

Conrad, Joseph. *Heart of Darkness.* London: Penguin, 1978.

C.R.I.S.P. (Centre de Recherche et d'Information Socio-Poltique of Brussels). *Congo 1964: Political Documents of a Developing Nation.* Princeton, N.J.: Princeton University Press, 1966.

Dabney, Joseph E. *HERK: Hero of the Skies.* Marietta, Ga.: Larlin, 1986.

Dowdy, Homer E. *Out of the Jaws of the Lion.* New York: Harper, 1965.

Forbath, Peter. *The River Congo: The Discovery, Exploration and Exploitation of the World's Most Dramatic River.* New York: Harper, 1977.

Gálvez, William. *Che in Africa: Che Guevara's Congo Diary.* Melbourne: Ocean Press, 1999.

Goonetilleke, D.C.R.A. *Heart of Darkness by Joseph Conrad.* Ontario: Broadview Literary Texts, 1995.

Hayes, Margaret. *Captive of the Simbas.* New York: Harper, 1966.

Hoare, Mike. *Mercenary.* New York: Bantam, 1979.

Hochschild, Adam. *King Leopold's Ghost.* Boston: Houghton Mifflin, 1998.

265

Bibliography

Hoyt, Jo Wasson. *For the Love of Mike*. New York: Random House, 1966.

Hoyt, Michael P. E., and David Grinwis. "A Journal of the Experiences of the Staff of the American Consulate in Stanleyville from 1 August through 24 November, 1964." Unpublished diary. Cataloged and available at Northwestern University Library, Evanston, Ill.

Jean-Aubry, G. *Joseph Conrad: Life and Letters*. Vol. 1. New York: Doubleday, 1927.

Kalb, Madeleine G. *The Congo Cables: The Cold War in Africa from Eisenhower to Kennedy*. New York: Macmillan, 1982.

Kelly, Sean. *America's Tyrant: The CIA and Mobutu of Zaire*. Washington, D.C.: American University Press.

Kestergat, Jean. *Du Congo de Lumumba au Zaire de Mobutu*. Brussels: Paul Legrain, 1986.

Kraus, Max W. *They All Come to Geneva and Other Tales of a Public Diplomat*. Cabin John, Md.: Seven Locks, 1988.

Law, Virginia. *Appointment Congo*. Chicago: McNally, 1966.

Lewis, David Levering. *The Race to Fashoda: European Colonialism and African Resistance in the Scramble for Africa*. New York: Weidenfeld & Nicolson, 1987.

"Messages from Consul [Michael P. E.] Hoyt, American Consulate, Stanleyville, the Congo, July 14 to November 25, 1964 [and other related messages]." Collection of unpublished messages obtained through the Freedom of Information Act. Compiled by Michael P. E. Hoyt. Cataloged and available at Northwestern University Library, Evanston, Ill.

"Messages from Consul [Michael P. E.] Hoyt, American Consulate, Stanleyville, the Congo, July 14 to November 25, 1964 [and other related messages]." Collection of copies of unpublished informal messages retained by Consul Hoyt. Compiled by Michael P. E. Hoyt. Cataloged and available at Northwestern University Library, Evanston, Ill.

"Messages Relating to American Consul [Michael P. E.] Hoyt and his Staff Held Hostage in Stanleyville, The Congo, August 4 to November 24, 1964." Vols. 1 and 2. Collection of unpublished original messages obtained through the Freedom of Information Act and copies of supplemental messages from the Lyndon B. Johnson Library at the University of Texas in Austin. Cataloged and available at Northwestern University Library, Evanston, Ill.

Naipaul, V. S. *A Bend in the River*. New York: Vintage, 1980.

Northrup, David. *Beyond the Bend in the River*. Athens: Center for International Studies, Ohio University, 1988.

Nothomb, Patrick. *Dans Stanleyville*. Paris: Duculot, 1993.

Bibliography

Odom, Thomas P. *Dragon Operations: Hostage Rescues in the Congo, 1964–1965*. Ft. Leavenworth, Ks.: Combat Studies Institute, Leavenworth Papers No. 14, 1988.

Pons, Valdo. *Stanleyville: An African Urban Community under Belgian Administration*. New York: Oxford University, 1964.

Powers, Thomas. *The Man Who Kept the Secrets: Richard Helms & the CIA*. New York: Knopf, 1979.

Press Service. *The Congo Rebellion*. Democratic Republic of the Congo, Léopoldville, 1964.

Reed, David. *111 Days in Stanleyville*. New York: Harper, 1965.

Remilleux, Jean-Louis. *Mobutu, Dignity for Africa*. Brussels: Albin Michel, 1989.

Roosevelt, Archie. *For Lust of Knowing, Memoirs of an Intelligence Officer*. Boston: Little, Brown, 1988.

Rusk, Dean, and Richard Rusk. *As I Saw It*. New York: Norton, 1990.

Schoenbaum, Thomas J. *Waging Peace & War: Dean Rusk in the Truman, Kennedy & Johnson Years*. New York: Simon and Schuster, 1988.

U.S. Department of State. "Five Who Survived Stanleyville" and "The Department and the Congo Rescue." *Department of State Newsletter*. No. 44, December 1964.

Vanderwalle, Colonel E. R. *L'Ommengang: Odyssée et Reconquête de Stanleyville 1964*. Brussels: Collection Témoinage Africain, 1970.

Wagoner, Fred A. *Dragon Rouge: The Rescue of Hostages in the Congo*. Washington, D.C.: National Defense University, Research Directorate, 1980.

Weissman, Stephen R. *American Foreign Policy in the Congo, 1960–1964*. Ithaca, N.Y.: Cornell University Press, 1974.

Index

269

Index

Index

evacuation of consulate, xvi–xvii,
23–24, 27–28, 35–37, 39, 44, 46,
48–49, 127, 247n. 30, 251n. 8,
257–58n. 1; procedures of, 36–37,
41–42

Faeles, Michel, 33, 70, 82, 268, 225
Fédération des Entreprises Congolaises (FEC)
("chamber of commerce"), 70, 79,
95, 139
Force Publique, 2, 72
Ford, Alan, 229
For the Love of Mike, 260n. 3
Franken (Red Cross representative and
Dutch consul), 68–69, 80, 108,
256–57n. 5
Fredericks, Wayne, 231

Garrison, Lloyd, 222
Gbagbeu, Dominique, 128–29
Gbenye, Christophe, xvi, 10, 15, 71–72,
135–36, 175–81, 188–89,
195–201, 210, 236–37, 241,
243–44, 256n. 5, 260n. 5; arrives
at Stanleyville, 150; author meets
with, 159–60; held responsible for
hostages, 264n. 12; and Monteagle
Stearns, xxi; and speech at
demonstration, 195–98; and
responsibility for massacre,
262n. 2
gendarmerie, 8, 29, 82, 228, 245n. 2
Gerlache, Joseph, 80, 149–50
Gizenga, Antoine, 15, 24, 29, 85, 114,
153, 176, 232
Godley, George McMurtrie "Mac," 4,
35, 37–38, 60, 73, 199, 207,
210–11, 221–24, 227, 259–60n. 2
Goldwater, Barry, 185
Grinwis, David, xxiii, 9–11, 30–39,
46–52, 54, 56–57, 59–60, 66–68,
71–76, 87–90, 93–99, 104,
119–20, 128–30, 140, 143–44,
148, 158–59, 170, 184, 192–98,
201, 205–6, 212–16, 218–20, 222,
226, 229, 231, 234, 237, 257n. 1;
on communist influences, 107;
discusses communications,
164–65; identifies agent, 101–3;
identified as CIA, xxiv; and journal
entries, 126–27, 133; nixes Red
Cross form, 154–55; and priority
for evacuation, 257–58n. 1; and

reports on rebels, 20–24; retrieves
CIA money, 42; safety of, 218; on
Scotland, 221; at USUN, 236; value
of, 10; and views on Clingerman,
11; and views on Kinghis, 83
Guevara, Ernesto "Che," 260n. 3
Gullion, Edmund, 4

Hagis, Dr. (Greek consul), 74, 80,
112–13, 191, 252n. 12
Hammarskjöld, Dag, xii
Harriman, W. Averell, 233–36
Haut-Congo Province, 11
Heart of Darkness, xiv, xxiii, 8
Helms, Richard, 259n. 1
Hoare, Mike, xviii, xix, 228, 259
Hoffacker, Lewis, 233, 259
hostage-taking, xi, 84, 107, 113,
118–20, 131, 136, 138, 182–84,
218, 222, 226, 241; of Belgians
and Americans, 181–82; and incidents of Americans, 264n. 13;
rebels realize value of, 107, 183,
198; suggestion that U.S. take
counter-hostages, 254n. 3
Hôtel des Chutes, 19, 181–83, 187, 208
Houle, Ernie, 9–10, 37, 41–43, 46,
49–52, 57, 60, 66, 68, 85–86, 88,
90, 95, 99–100, 113, 119–20, 125,
132–33, 140, 144–45, 170,
192–98, 225, 229, 231, 249nn. 1,
2, 252n. 11
Houphouët-Boigny, Félix, xxi
Hoyt, Evans W., 4, 6, 17, 28, 31, 33–34,
38, 40–41, 71, 77, 80, 181, 192,
205
Hoyt, Jo Wasson, 4, 6, 10, 19, 29, 31,
33–34, 38–41, 53, 70–71, 75–77,
89, 99, 192, 204, 209, 223–24,
229–32, 235, 260n. 2, 261n. 10
Hoyt, Michael P. E.: and Carlson,
177–79; birthday of, 190; and
claustrophobic panic, 195; and
Davis, 121; and debriefing, 232–33;
decides to stay, 38, 44; on evacuation, 34–35, 46; holds Gbenye
responsible, 264n. 12; and massacre, 214–17; meets Gbenye, 199;
military service of, 37; negotiates
for cease-fire, 207–11; and Olenga,
80–81, 90–91; and Operation Flagpole, 67, 249n. 2, 250–51nn. 6–7;
and press conferences, 234–35,

271

Index

Index

About the Author

During his twenty-five-year career in the Foreign Service, Michael P. E. Hoyt served in Pakistan, Switzerland, and Africa and headed four diplomatic and consular posts. He received the U.S. Department of State's highest honor, the Secretary's Award, for his courage during the 1964 hostage situation in Stanleyville. His assignments in Washington, D.C., included being desk officer for Southern Rhodesia, Zambia, and Malawi and then for UN specialized agencies dealing with transportation. His last assignment was counselor of the U.S. Mission to the United Nations in Geneva, to promote human rights.

Mr. Hoyt received his Bachelor of Philosophy and B.A. in history from the University of Chicago. He earned his M.A. in modern European history at the University of Illinois at Urbana and did further graduate studies in economic and African studies at Northwestern University. He served four years in the U.S. Air Force as an air traffic controller during the Korean conflict. Mr. Hoyt has been consulting, writing, and lecturing on international affairs and teaching college-level African history courses in New Mexico since his retirement from the U.S. Foreign Service in 1980. He currently resides in Santa Fe, New Mexico.

The Naval Institute Press is the book-publishing arm of the U.S. Naval Institute, a private, nonprofit, membership society for sea service professionals and others who share an interest in naval and maritime affairs. Established in 1873 at the U.S. Naval Academy in Annapolis, Maryland, where its offices remain today, the Naval Institute has members worldwide.

Members of the Naval Institute support the education programs of the society and receive the influential monthly magazine *Proceedings* and discounts on fine nautical prints and on ship and aircraft photos. They also have access to the transcripts of the Institute's Oral History Program and get discounted admission to any of the Institute-sponsored seminars offered around the country.

The Naval Institute also publishes *Naval History* magazine. This colorful bimonthly is filled with entertaining and thought-provoking articles, first-person reminiscences, and dramatic art and photography. Members receive a discount on *Naval History* subscriptions.

The Naval Institute's book-publishing program, begun in 1898 with basic guides to naval practices, has broadened its scope in recent years to include books of more general interest. Now the Naval Institute Press publishes about one hundred titles each year, ranging from how-to books on boating and navigation to battle histories, biographies, ship and aircraft guides, and novels. Institute members receive discounts of 20 to 50 percent on the Press's more than eight hundred books in print.

Full-time students are eligible for special half-price membership rates. Life memberships are also available.

For a free catalog describing Naval Institute Press books currently available, and for further information about subscribing to *Naval History* magazine or about joining the U.S. Naval Institute, please write to:

Membership Department
U.S. Naval Institute
291 Wood Road
Annapolis, MD 21402-5034
Telephone: (800) 233-8764
Fax: (410) 269-7940
Web address: www.usni.org